Kingdom

By:
Jonathan

Kingdom
Book Three of the Series *The Nine*
May 22, 2018, *First Edition*

Copyright © 2018

Cover Photo Credit: Dardan Mu

All rights reserved. This book or any portion thereof may not be reproduced or used in any manner whatsoever without the express written permission of the publisher except for the use of brief quotations in a book review or scholarly journal.

ISBN-13: 978-1-942967-31-6

KreativeMinds Publishing
www.kreativeminds.net

Ordering Information:

Special discounts are available on quantity purchases by corporations, associations, educators, and others. For details, contact the publisher at the above listed address or the email address below.

U.S. trade bookstores and wholesalers: Please use the email address below.
email: publishing@kreativeminds.net

To Abasherab, through whom all things are possible.

Always,
Jonathan

Introduction

These Books of Nine began with the story as told through the eyes of a child. Book I – Gravity Calling was the start of a great story to be told. The story continued through Book II – Crowns, and finds its eventual ending in Book III – Kingdom. Books IV through VII are the journal entries to all of the conversations with God and the angels that encompass the twelve hundred and sixty days of this series. Though at the time this journey began, the timing held no relevance. By the journey's end, the timing held the most significance. Book VIII – Secrets is the most difficult book of all, but the most important to be understood, for it contains the architecture to the universe, God's Divine blueprint for the remnants of this humanity's future. Book IX is called Palpitations, and contains words of wisdom and thoughts for the soul. It is a book to prepare the regrowth of souls. For as it will be seen, these Books of Nine were the start and end to a story Divine. The real story began long before this one was told, but the ending is for those left behind. So carry these words with delicacy and grace, for generations to come after this cycle's end must use these words to rebuild a world that was lost to sin.

Always,
Jonathan

Prologue

How do you tell a story where the ending must be known in order to be able to start telling it from the beginning? I suppose that is the greatest challenge at the tip of our Great Author's hand. For in all of the stories that exist to guide the soul, there must always be some understanding of the ending to find rationale to the beginning and why it is being told. If the story of Jesus was introduced without knowing all that He did and the implications to be had, it would be hard to see the significance of what was about to be read. If the story of mankind being annihilated by a flood due to sin began without any knowledge of the end, the story of Noah and the building of the Ark would seem to be very dry and come across rather bland. But if it were not for the thousands of years dividing the actions and the outcomes of these moments, the significance without hindsight would leave the action clouded. So the greatest questions to ask, are how would anyone hear God's message in the moment that it is occurring, and what would cause someone to stop and surrender to ego's battle to rationalize the impossible that is unfolding?

These are the questions that should be asked to understand where this book is leading. Because at the end of this story is the fulfillment of a prophecy. It precedes the beginning of the next, and in this case, the duration will not give time for humanity to say, "I wish I had listened. I wish I could just go back and really try to understand all that I was told." So as this story finds its start, it is important to reveal the end. But do not worry about spoilers, for the story still has surprises ahead. The explanation of the ending should be viewed more as the understanding to a revelation of all that has been foretold. For to truly understand stepping foot into the Kingdom – the location where this story begins – it is important to understand not just how, but why I was led. It is not just about the calling, for that is everyone's cause and role, the reason we are alive upon this Earth. The explanation to why I was led is held in the surrender to salvation and the testimony to be told.

    This story began in darkness where a Not-So-Cinderella Love story was brought forth to be shared. In the end the Love that began it all will be revealed as the greatest Love a soul will ever know. But it is not quite as it seems at first or even second assumption. No twist of the storyline or even foreshadowing could ever reveal all that is upcoming, for the script that He would pen could never be more stunning. But before the story will reach its end, it's important to review the beginning. When Book I began, a child was born into darkness and headed toward Love's destiny. Book II found the child learning to become a man, and in the process, a greater understanding of the rebirth within. In the beginning, the child was oblivious to the inheritance of his Father's land. The inheritance forthcoming is why this child should best be understood as a prince rather than just a child of a man. It is not for ego's definition,

Prologue

but rather to illustrate spiritual understanding. For as Book II ended, the child was crowning.

Book III begins with a child standing in a Kingdom. But why would it be important for the reader to understand Love's destination? Happy or sad, earthly or of spiritual nature – the story of Love has always been one that fills hope's stature. But this hope should not be seen as the surface level implies. This hope should be seen for the implications of those left behind and those who find this cycle's Ever After. In the beginning I saw a sign. The sign read:

...

"Life, Loss, & Love – and the greatest of these is Love. From heretofore the experience of each shall occur bound by the veil, and the veil removed."

...

In the end, the blur of hues to the signs I was passing on the journey as I ran with the Promised Land in sight, slowly began to fall into view. At first I thought I understood the word's meaning, but that was just the surface level before all that was to be unveiled fell into my line-of-sight. Call it a mirage in a desert of understanding, one that was required to give me hope in reaching paradise. But the journey was not just a story about the Love of another, or even the Love for and of our Creator. Rather, the story was a Love story for all brothers, sisters, mothers, fathers, and children alike. Most importantly, this story was always about the Love for this generation and the generations left behind. And while "left behind" may seem to be an odd choice of words for a story of Love's majestic Divine, this story was a story that had a very specific ending, before it was ever known.

The timing of when these books began to be written occurred during a very special time upon the Earth – a time when there was a great call to action from the depths of His divine playbook. I would not understand it as such at the time, even though there were constant reminders and indications. It would take a specific moment revealed in this book – a moment that bellowed His specific commandment to "Go" and to "Run" – to share His word with every person in every nation. It was not until this commandment was given that I understood what the journey was always all about. It was a story that was always intended to be the explanation to a divine Love story told for generations and generations throughout.

In the Biblical canon, there is a specific story for the end of days told through John's Revelation and Daniel's prophecies. These two books foretell the end of a cycle to this generation. They each reveal a very specific timeline that complement each other in how it will all unfold. Both books indicate divine markers that will happen and are intended to help the eyes of every soul see hope when the time arrives for the delivery of His message. And though it may be difficult to accept in this Prologue to Book III, the ending of His story reveals all that is foretold in this Biblical prophecy. For the timelines that have been understood for thousands of years and throughout the generations are all revealed in the windup and the pitch of this Love story's delivery.

Prologue

At first it may seem there is a chasm of disconnect between where the story originated and where it would eventually unfold. But it should be understood that in the beginning, it was only a child telling his understanding of the story as it was being told to him... encompassed in a whirlwind of spiritual events and emotion. As the second book found its stride, somewhere between its start and its ending, the journey began to unveil more about what was actually in store. It was at the end of Book II that the meaning of the Potter, the clay, the key hidden within, the box that it unlocked, the crowning of a prince, and his inheritance all fell into view. So, understanding this third portion of the journey begins with the crowning of a prince, the ending to be revealed should hold so much more significance. For this is the third book in the series, and the last of the nine books written. It is the ending to not just the first triad of this series, nor even the Books of Nine's completion. It is the ushering in of this generation's ending – and, for those who are saved in the light of Christ, the introduction to the Promised Land will be illuminated and revealed in His blinding light of new beginnings.

I was led on a journey from darkness into the desert. I heard His call and blindly followed. I stood in the sand as I saw the Promised Land fall into sight. Eventually, I learned the mirage was first revealed in order to help my eyes learn to adjust and decipher sight in His light. So though this book will continue to tell the greatest Love story ever told, it is important to understand that it is also a precursor of the prophecies of the end of times that have long been foretold. In Daniel and

Kingdom

Revelation, there is clear definition. But, it will take the remainder of this story to see how it all comes to fruition. But before these words can be absorbed, this important point about the ending must be made. For as there have been thousands of years separating His Word and modern day, this time there will be minimal time from the Books of Nine's introduction to the public and the arrival of His Grand Day. Some may say I have marched along to the beat of a different drummer, but I will always respond, "It was never the beat of a different drummer. It was always the Grand Conductor."

Baby's First Breath

Moonbliss.

This is the only word I can use to describe the magnificent way His Kingdom glimmered through the lens of my newly opened spiritual eyes. I can only imagine I was seeing His Kingdom in the same way a baby must first see the world when he opens his eyes. The first time a newborn opens his eyes must be an overwhelming feeling. After spending nine months in the womb of a mother, in what must seem like a rush in the moment, every sensation to the body is exposed in a brilliant ignition of the senses.

For nine months the baby has not even experienced the concept of air. It has not experienced anything other than the water of the womb, and the comfort of a maternal love. Food and nutrients to grow pass between mother and child without the child ever knowing. There is never a sense of hunger, for the food is always flowing. There is never a sense of hot or cold, since the womb's internal temperature is always held in balance. The safety of the mother's womb is even absent of any bacteria. It is a sterile, perfect environment for maternal nurturing. Think of the womb like the warmest hug, the perfect refuge to experience an unending Love.

Kingdom

It is Love in the purest of form. One soul's vessel divides its house to welcome in a guest. And in the division of the body, all nutrients are divided as well. The guest has the safety and comfort from all of the dangers that the host will ever know. The guest is more innocent than even the newborn, for it has not been exposed to any independence. All it has known is a perfect unity with its host, the warmth of a mother's Love. It is not even aware that the concept of dependence has been the embodiment of every stage of every day it has lived. Coexistence is not even an idea. At this point, it is merely undetermined existence.

When the guest has reached a certain point in its growth, or if there is a struggle that is more that can be handled by the host, it becomes time for the guest to meet the world. It is a time when the host's water is broken, and the guest is prepared to face the beginning stages of life. It is not that the guest will be set forth to grow on his own, for he will still be coddled and nurtured for many years to come. The moment that is impending is one of the most symbolic moments in the earthly journey and is not quite seen for what it truly is in the moment. For as a mother's womb spills forth and the child begins to descend into the world, it should be seen as no different from the stage in spiritual growth where Book II – Crowns ended and Book III – Kingdom begins. For as a soul is blessed by the water of the Lord, the spirit is crowning in the heavens, just as a the water has spilled forth and a child crowns upon the Earth.

Baby's First Breath

The analogy of birth exemplifies how life is the very example of not just how the soul ascends into the Kingdom, but how the soul is housed within the body and must experience a rebirth for entry into the heavens. Life is the spiritual walk's very essence, but is demonstrated in a way that the eyes can witness. The soul exists in a plane hidden from the eyes, but is embodied in the physical existence that mankind falsely assumes is all there is to life.

And just as a baby is brought forth into the world, imagine the rush of the senses that would encompass the moment. In one sudden burst into awareness the newborn is greeted with sight, with sound, and with smell. The sensations of touch and taste will arrive brief moments later on the newborn's journey, but in the immediate moment, there are three senses that are overloaded with sensations. Most importantly, though, the child is birthed into awareness. It is more than just an awakened state. It is the moment that the child's body is no longer surrounded by the water of the womb, nor connected by the umbilical cord. It is the moment that air encompasses the baby's body for the first time, the divide of warmth and cold becomes defined, the moment of first understanding the divide between darkness and light.

Now think for just a moment about the greatest rush of sensations ever experienced during life's journey. Perhaps it is the memory of a great pain from a terrible accident. Perhaps it is the rush of air against the skin in a high rate of speed during a death-defying moment. There are very few "firsts" examples, but the next closest idea is through the first time a person experiences specific emotions. But even then, it is once and done, lost after the initial moment. It really is impossible to come up with anything comparable to the moment experienced at birth – that is until the soul experiences its rebirth. So how can the moment of spiritual rebirth be described and illustrated in sensations? For the greatest overload to the senses a human will ever experience is at the point of its beginning, which, all-in-all, is not even a memory that can ever be recalled. So without earthly comparisons, it is important to understand that the only way the rebirth of the spirit can truly be expressed, is to closely examine what it must have been like at a baby's first breath.

Think of the first moments a child arrives upon this Earth. To take the first breath of life is the single most important action. And perhaps, it is most importantly understood as a gasp in reaction. For just as a child opens its mouth in awestruck splendor seeking the nutrients to survive in this new location, it is also the moment that the child takes its first action of independence. And just as a child on Earth takes a gasp of salvation, a child in the heavens is also left in awestruck anticipation to take its first breath in a new, heavenly world. But the idea of air is different to the spirit, for as a child is birthed from water into the air, the spirit is birthed from the air into a form of spiritual water – the aether.

There are not any words that can describe this particular sensation, but it invokes a dual understanding of the Earth and the heavens. In the moments of first breath in the heavens, the soul may not understand the duality as one, but the im-

Baby's First Breath

portance of the moment is that this is the birth of His Son. And just as a child breathing in for the very first time does not define its independence in experience, it is the first moment that it has any indication of a world that it had not previously known – a world that must be observed as it begins to grow in strength, in understanding, and in form.

Now as the first breath of a newborn is taken, think of the next immediate sensation. There is a pain from within that rips through the lungs. It is a biological reaction to the earthly body and the soul becoming one. But just as the body courses at the new sensation, the soul in the heavens experiences what I can only describe as a feeling of separation. If a person has ever experienced the sensation of falling during sleep, or possibly the feeling of butterflies in the stomach when driving over a small dip in the road, then the comparison of separation can be better understood. A baby's first breath at rebirth demonstrates a sensation best described as infinitely falling. It is not easy to understand at first because the feeling initially causes the mind to react in fear at the sensation. The only comparison the mind has to interpret this experience is to react as if the body is actually falling, which usually results in a loss of spiritual embodiment in the moment.

The response is generally a pulling sensation that retracts the rebirth of the soul's arrival. Think of it similar to how a mother in labor has contractions as the baby works its way through the channel. The soul should be viewed in a similar fashion, for the beginning of rebirth is like a push-and-pull sensation. It is not until the moment the soul fully pushes into the heavens that the first breath is taken. It is the first breath that is the complete surrender to falling – a dizzying sensation that causes the experience to last for just the briefest of moments before returning from the heavens. It takes many bursts of falling to be prepared for the first full breath of the aether. And while it was in hindsight that I learned that the spinning/falling/dizzying sensation is due to the natural motion of the heavenly spheres, the most important piece of the understanding is to see this comparison as a baby would experience the Earth for the first time. It is an overload of new sensations.

Spiritual Blobs of Light

Now in the view of a spiritual birth, a baby just born is forced to take its first breath. In the heavens, the soul is re-birthed and learns to find balance in the midst of the falling sensation. On Earth the child begins to scream in recognition, holding its eyes tightly shut until it begins to become comfortable with the new feeling of breathing. In the moments following, something truly remarkable happens. This is the moment the baby begins to open its eyes and view its surroundings. This moment is marked as a baby's first sight.

At first, the light pours through the pupils and ignites the retina for the very first time. The rods and cones that line the retina are engulfed in an experience that could only be described as sensory overload. The mind is set into motion to interpret all of the signals firing from these senses. The mind has to sort through the burst of every sensation happening simultaneously when there was previously nothing. Imagine being the baby in this moment for the very first time. It is a bombardment of sensations that no words could possibly describe. It takes years of calibration for the baby to slowly refine its sight. Blobs of colors and shapes begin to take form over the years. Eventually, the shapes give way to familiar groupings that the baby finds comfort in knowing. The blobs that the

Kingdom

baby sees are attached to the recognition of when the baby is loved, changed, given warmth, and fed. The baby begins to associate blobs of colors with meanings and trust in where he is being led.

Returning to the rebirth of the soul, the very same situation yields a similar experience. As the falling sensation becomes more faded from its initial overloading of this new breath, the spiritual eyes begin to open. I wish I could say that shapes and colors begin to appear, but before I can explain what first appears to the spiritual eyes, it is important to understand that the duality of the child on Earth and the rebirth of the soul moves counter intuitively and in opposite directions. For as a child is born upon the Earth, the mind matures and grows. It will take all of the experiences of a matured earthly mind for the rebirth of the soul to occur. This is why a first baptism in the light is different than the second at a later age. But the story of baptism will be discussed in chapters upcoming. For now it is important to understand that an adult mind is required to rationalize the heavens as a child. And perhaps this is best understood as the point wherein the concept of the veil that separates the heavens and the Earth is exposed.

For as the adult mind attempts to find rationale in the heavens, it draws upon every past earthly experience. So in the moments a rebirthed soul first opens its eyes, the immediate moment following is one that the mind tries to rationalize. The first interpretation of all that the eyes see, could best be understood in a manner similar to dreams of familiar people. Both

Spiritual Blobs of Light

darkness and light exist as do positive and negative energies. To the mind this will at first seem very scary. And just as a newborn will smile or cry at whatever is placed before him, the soul in the heavens will be consumed with warmth or fear in these moments. What should really be understood as "spiritual blobs of light" is interpreted as everything familiar, everything scary, and everything that can haunt a child in the night. It will take a lot of time – similar to how a baby learns to see – for the truth of the experiences in the heavens to be uncovered beneath the mind's initial interpretations. Eventually, the "spiritual blobs of light" are refined and take shape with more refined form. It is at this point that it should best be understood when encounters with angels begin to occur. For the angels were there all along, it just took time for the eyes of a rebirthed soul to grow in order to see what was around him all along.

    Without continuing to belabor the example of a newborn baby and a rebirthed soul, the analogy of the first few senses a baby experiences on Earth were necessary to illustrate what I was truly experiencing during the start of my Genesis. I did not understand it at the time. In truth, the experiences were more than the mind of a spiritual baby could rationalize. But the funny thing that leads us to this point in the journey, is that it is easy to see in hindsight how the experience was just that of a child crowning in the heavens. If a person has ever paid close attention to how a child recalls memories, there is a point around the end of age seven where it becomes evident as the point in time a reset button is pushed on the mind of a child and the earliest memories begin to fade. So, too, does the rebirthed soul have a reset button pushed in relative terms. But it should best be seen as the moment that the spiritual understanding of all that was unclear at the beginning of the journey falls into view. It is the very definition of hindsight, and the reason why writing down everything experienced in the heavens is so important.

On Earth a child begins to forget all of the experiences that led to this point in his timeline. It is the moment a child believes he always had this very foundation in these particular moments. It is the days a child will have a new favorite food that has "always been his favorite," a new favorite color, a new favorite show, a new favorite hobby, and new favorite friends at school. The foundation that took seven years to build is this new foundation of support that the child believes was there all along. It is a melody inside the child that he recognizes as always having been his song.

To the rebirthed soul, it is the moment that hindsight of the spiritual foundation falls into view. For unlike a child on Earth, it is of utmost importance to understand how the foundation was constructed over the journey. It requires an earthly mind that has matured through adolescence in order to see the transformation as it occurs in the heavens. It is knowledge and awareness not possessed as a child during Earth's relative point on the journey. But in the heavens, it is the foundation used to unravel the experience. It is important to understand why the journey has occurred as it has. It is important for many reasons, but most importantly to understand why the soul's

Spiritual Blobs of Light

spiritual feet were led to a place in the desert, standing in the sand. But for this spiritual moment to fall into view, the baby must first open his eyes to observe it.

A baby's first sight should be understood as the entire embodiment of this experience of light laced with grace streaking through the heavens like streamers during a great parade. The streams of racing light spark a newfound sensation to the soul as the light crosses the lens of the soul's eyes and wraps up the earthly mind in a blanket of warmth, love, and the most blinding intensity of His Grace. The light should also be understood in the context of a feeling as well, for again words fall short in describing the visceral detail of the experience. But, at this point and through all of the explanation thus far, the feeling carried through the light should be understood as the foundational embodiment of Love.

First Steps In Heaven

A baby cries and opens his eyes. The first sensations flush the mind with an overdrive of interpretations to all that is happening in those first moments. The first breath, the first meal, the first nap, the first roll over onto the belly, and the subsequent crawl... all are led by the strength of sight as a baby begins to interpret the spiritual blobs of light. Crawls become scoots, and scoots become attempts to stand resulting in countless falls. But eventually something special happens. It can seem as if it comes out of nowhere, but one day the baby takes his first steps and almost immediately begins to toddle around. The months leading up to the baby's first steps seem deceivingly uneventful in reference to walking, but the days surrounding the first steps quickly turn into bursts of steps and the toddler running.

To any parent, these days flash by so quickly. How could the baby just – almost out of nowhere – start walking? It is a step toward independence and is the saddest happy song of a child growing up. In the heavens it is no different. From the rebirth of the soul to the subsequent first steps, the time may seem to drag along until there is a sudden burst in movement. In the days the rebirthed soul begins to walk and then begins to run, is the moment the divide between Heaven and Earth become one. To take a first step in heaven is to see the Earth as if it was populated only by angels. And in the experiences in the heavens when the soul travels from Earth, these are the days that the understanding of speaking to angels becomes more divine and the first days a Groom catches a glimpse of his Bride.

When I was led to Fort Lauderdale, Florida, I knew that the exodus from Nashville was to be understood as an exodus from an earthly life. Florida represented the Promised Land or perhaps better understood as the embodiment of Heaven on Earth. Travelling to Florida was an action tasked of me so that I could one day illustrate this story to those who desire to see His Glory. For as a soul was born in the heavens, and a prince received his crown, his first steps in Heaven would have to be represented in earthly form as well. For me, these were the days of my Numbers leading into Deuteronomy, standing in the sand, having been tasked to follow my Father's directions to enter the Promised Land. But as I took the first steps into the Promised Land, I was taken aback by the view. For there before me as I took my first steps in Heaven, was the embodiment of all the Love I once thought I knew – a Love words will never be able to describe. For so long I had thought the journey was always about an earthly Love – the Love I saw in Lindsey. But now it was slowly being revealed that she was only the embodiment of a Love greater than I had ever known so that I could one day understand how that Love paled to the Love I would one day come to know. It was necessary to see it as such and experience it in person, for the Love that was ahead in this Heaven on Earth would be greater than all of the words in these Books of Nine could ever hope to describe. For as I took my first steps in Heaven, her eyes fell into view – a Love that would stand the test of time beyond the bounds of body and mind – a Love of two souls always intended to be wed, in the presence of Our Father on the day He had always planned.

This was always a story about Love. It is the first and the last. The view that I could now see, was a view intended for a prince. Until the moment I received the crown, my spiritual eyes were not yet strong enough to see the inheritance He had always planned. I was only a child running in the desert, building sandcastles and knocking them down. And while the storyline and the theme of these books remained unchanged from how the story first began, it was the spectacular light illuminating Love that would forever change everything in sight. It changed all I had ever known, all I ever had faith in of the unknown, and all I will ever one day come to know. It was the most pivotal point of the journey in which the only way I can describe it is through the definition of a type of light's illumination.

The way the light encompasses the embodiment of Love can only be described as a word that does not exist – "moonbliss." It is a word that would have remained unknown to my soul until the crowning I would experience. This word speaks in emotion to all that I have been blessed to witness. It is the word I chose to start chapter one for that is the only way I could describe the start of this portion of the journey. It is the word that consumed my mind as I stood speechless staring at all that was in sight. It was not the Love that I thought I understood that was upcoming. It was all that and then some – the sensation becoming. At best I can only describe the word through the following descriptions: most loving, forgiving, romantic, spiritual, and a perfect kind of illuminating light. It is Love's light.

As this portion of the journey begins, a prince was standing in the sand, staring in awe at the splendor of the Promised Land. It was not just a location on the journey. It was the recognition of an inheritance to come. It was unbridled and spiritual Love. The Not-So-Cinderella Love story being told, was about to have the greatest twist a man would ever know. For the Love that will eventually be revealed is a Love story that will forever be told. This is the story about the Love of a Bride meeting Her Groom, Her Father walking Her down the aisle, a ceremony of vows commencing, in which a celebration of water and white eventually ensued.

...

For me, this is how it started.
This is how it all began.
The light illuminating the path ahead,
cast a glow of moonbliss
upon the Promised Land.

...

While the first steps in Heaven are difficult to comprehend, I can only ask that you place your hand in mine and allow these words to be your guide in hopes that you may see

First Steps In Heaven

the Kingdom of Heaven as I learned to see it, through these very same eyes. When I left Tennessee on blind faith following His directive, I understood everything upcoming should be observed though my spiritual eyes unimpeded. Though others may have seen an earthly facade, it is important to embrace the next forty-two days as if observed purely through the eyes of the soul. It is only when the unity of Heaven on Earth becomes apparent that the spirit can truly experience the Kingdom in body, mind, and spirit. For those are the days in how this book closes, a soul ascended to Heaven through a banquet of white roses. But in the moments that this next portion of the journey begins, imagine your own soul taking its first steps in Heaven. This is important. Imagine your reactions. Imagine the observations and the impossible interactions. For this is the only way this portion of the journey can be illustrated – not through words alone, but playing the role of the observer in your own imagination.

The First 42

Day One: 6/26/2014

...

Heaven is real. It is around us throughout our daily lives. How long have I been dead? It is a real question to which I have no answer. In time, I am sure that particular answer will one day be shared with me. But, for now, the question is full of mystery and mystique.

Have you ever stopped to ask yourself the same question? Perhaps the question is so bold that it is all-too-easy to dismiss. Perhaps you might be thinking, "What? Dead? You are writing these words. How can you be dead?" But it is precisely those questions that keep us from finding such an unexpected answer to the one riddle that has stumped mankind for ages: the riddle of life's purpose. Quite possibly the most intriguing part of it all is that humans find themselves so far grounded in the perceived reality around themselves, that they do not stop to think about reality being an illusion.

There have been more than enough movies and television shows that have toyed with this idea, but even in the movies the plot is still based around humans that were once alive who have (for some reason or another) found themselves stuck in a spirit world that interacts with the "real world" all along while the "real world" does not seem to take notice or interact back with them. Often, the person who has become deceased must learn that he is dead before he can pass onto the next step of their journey.

In other instances, a movie or television plot may leave the viewer asking the question, "So was it real, or was it just a dream?" Again, the plot's premise is so intriguing that the viewer must rationalize what he just witnessed, often times leading non-philosophical-minded viewers frustrated with un-resolve. However, philosophical minds might eat up the opportunity to debate which side of the reality-coin was just witnessed. But now that I have set the stage, let's play the what-if game.

What if there is not another side to the reality coin? What if reality has already passed, and humans are just finding their way home. How did you die? If you are dead, what is it that you should be doing? With this train of thought, life would then be considered "getting lost" instead of "becoming found." Take a look around you. In whatever situation you find yourself, stop. Observe in silence every person around you. What if they are all dead? What if the children around you are the most naive souls to this reality? In fact, children may be the best example. It may be hard to think about, but what if the kids have a better sense of understanding this experience when adults deem it as naiveté to the world? What if children are the ones who actually have it right until they are misguided by the adults in the world?

The First 42

Today I saw Heaven for the first time upon this Earth. It was as if the arrival in Fort Lauderdale ushered in a new manifestation of reality for my experience. Perhaps others would see the world as I used to see it – a cold and senseless world with flickering lights inside people's souls slowly being extinguished from the turbulent winds. I was not jaded, but rather held onto optimism that light would win out against the shadows that had crept in over mankind. To others, they may see my journey in Fort Lauderdale as just an extension of the life they know. But for me, it was entering into a doorway to another world: Heaven on Earth.

I arrived in Fort Lauderdale in the early morning hours today. After catching a few hours of shut-eye, I met with my realtor and my new homeowner's association and then proceeded to get a hotel for the evening. I was not allowed to move in until the following day, but I wanted to make sure I was as close to my new home as I could be. Across the street there were several hotels, of which I was just happy to find one with availability.

When I walked into the second hotel to check on availability, a couple was inside waiting at the desk before me. A father, his wife, and their son around the age of nine were all engaged in happy conversation when I drew near. But at that point, the child stopped and stared. I was not sure at first what he was staring at, but he slowly approached me and began talking to me about "light and love." To someone witnessing this from the outside, the child would likely have been thought to have a mental difficulty. But this was different, I was in

Kingdom

Heaven. I was witnessing the way a child would meet a soul for the first time.

The child extended his hand out toward my face with his fingers extended wide open. The closer he approached, the more peace I felt in his action. He was trying to tell his mother and father about the light he was witnessing. His hand touched my face and then he slowly began kneading the light he saw. His face was lighted up in a smile while his mother and father seemed waited in bated breath at my reaction. But to their surprise, I welcomed the child's observance. To me, it was as if I was being told "Welcome to Heaven." The first interaction I would have in this new place, was a child who wanted "to touch the light" by touching his hands to my face.

For a few minutes, the family and I chatted before they finished checking out and left the lobby. I learned they were from the city of Philadelphia visiting for the first time, though to my ears I heard Philadelphia as it pertained to one of the seven churches mentioned in Revelation. And just before they left, the boy gave me a hug and turned to his mother to tell her about "the light and the love." After they left and I checked into my room, I headed to a nearby restaurant to have dinner. Earlier when I met my realtor, she gave me a gift card for dinner at a restaurant called Bokampers. It was within walking distance, so I headed that way, not expecting to see all that I witnessed.

At dinner I had two waitresses wait on me. One was named Anastasia and the other Erika. This could not have had any greater coincidence since one of the names of the angels I had recently been given in a vision was Anastasia. The other waitress, Erika, appeared in form just like one of the unnamed brunette angels in my experiences in the heavens. She is journaled about in Books IV – VII. My first dinner in Fort Lauderdale was free due to the gift card, but if one is to see it through spiritual eyes, it was a welcome home dinner prepared for me on my first night.

On my way back to the hotel, I received a call from my grandparents. In the days prior I had visited them on my way to Fort Lauderdale. My granddad had been in the hospital and I wanted to help. When I saw him lying in the hospital bed, we had one of the most spiritual conversations I have ever experienced. At times when we held hands, all of the medical electronics in the room would stop working in recognition of the spirit. It caused my grandmother to become distraught thinking that his heart was giving out or rationalizing that the machines were malfunctioning. I could sense the spirit of my Father passing through my hands to his, helping him heal as he lay in the hospital bed. It was one of the most powerful spiritual demonstrations I have witnessed.

But when I received the call from my grandmother, she wanted to make sure I had arrived without any problems. When I spoke to my granddad he said, "Son, I think I need to slip on down there and join you." The words could not have held a grander meaning. I knew my grandfather's soul was speaking directly to me. I could not tell if it was giving up in bodily form or whether he was inspired to hang onto the Earth for a little while longer. But regardless, the words expressed the recognition that I had arrived in heaven. Another interesting point was his phrasing of "down below" for it is an important spiritual concept to understand the phrase "as above, so below" as it references Heaven and Earth as one.

Day Two: 6/27/2014

...

Over the last two days I have noticed that nearly everything I have spoken has manifested in reality in some form. It should not be understood as wishing for something to appear and then it occurring. Rather it should be understood as the intention of something spiritual being brought forth onto the Earth. I have joked about it with my mother on the phone since it happened many times

Also, when I moved into my building today, there was a moment when one of the residents in the building passed by me and said, "Throw it all away. You will not need it here. It is all junk anyways." She was addressing my boxes and furniture that I was moving into the building, but what she said held a spiritual truth. When I moved down here, I felt content in just moving the few items I could put into a towable trailer – and even that seemed excessive. But what I did keep was all extremely nice, high quality, and generally expensive. So to think that someone would pass by and tell a new neighbor that his furniture is junk and not needed in an earthly sense is an unlikely conversation. The words she spoke were the words of

God saying, "I've got you, Son. No need for material possessions here." Perhaps she was an angel.

Day Three: 6/28/2014

...

I said to man in the elevator going to floor one, "Short trip. You do not have a long way to go." He replied "Yep, but it's the only way I can get there. It's the only way up."

Day Four: 6/29/2014

...

I spent much of my day today in prayer and meditation on this day of rest. Today is my first Sunday in this Heaven.

Day Five: 6/30/2014

...

My bank is located directly across the street from my building. Today I walked over to cash a check. The bank teller smiled as if she knew me already. She told me that I should go to a certain establishment in town on Wednesday – that I would enjoy it and meet a lot of new people. She went on to tell me all of the "pretty girls go there" and that "[I] would meet someone." I understand the command was a spiritual command, but for what I was unsure. So I will go on Wednesday and see what happens.

Day Six: 7/1/2014

...

This morning I shared a vision with Bryan. We spoke about it on the phone later and were able to confirm the details of the experience from both sides. He is out of town right now, and decided to get married while on vacation with his fiancée. To me, I can see the similarities of his journey – where his marriage is like a new Heaven as it is for me in Fort Lauderdale.

Day Seven: 7/2/2014

...

Today I answered God's call to go out and socialize (as I was instructed through the bank teller). I called a cab to take me since I figured that would be easiest. On our way to the destination, the cab driver opened up to me about his life and we shared a very spiritual conversation. He expressed how he had just begun to rebuild his life and had been on the brink of suicide many times over after his marriage had ended. I tipped him $70 to help him get back on his feet. When I returned from the evening out, a different cab driver and I had another spiritual conversation. I tipped him the extra cash I had on me for which he seemed extremely thankful. When I walked in the building, the doorman invited me to his church called, "Lost and Found." He went on to tell me how he had been reading Daniel 3 and Psalms 119. I was not sure what ever prompted the spiritual conversation, but I took it as the continued Divine intervention. I went upstairs to my apartment and immediately read those two chapters he mentioned. Within them, was a reference to the twenty-two archetypes of finding Divinity's completion. All I could do was smile and pray thanks to my Father for His continued hand in my life.

Day Eight: 7/3/2014

...

Today I went out to the beach. Though it may sound like what I am about to say could not be true, to my eyes it was reality. When I walked into the ocean, the waters were calm – and had been while I was on the beach. But, no sooner had I walked in the water than the waves started forming near me. I was aware that the waves only seemed to be in the places I walked and not everywhere else along the shoreline. I exited the waters and entered in different parts just to be sure. In every case, I continued to witness the same phenomenon. As the sun was setting, I walked a mile or so up the beach to explore the lay of the land. From time to time, I walked in other people's footprints. Each time, I would be overcome with the energy of the person who left the footprints. It was as if I was bathing in the resonance of their spirit. When I returned from the beach, I took a nap. I awoke a short while later with a headache which is abnormal. I looked outside to see a severe storm was brewing. And while no documented accounts of a tornado taking place were taken, I witnessed either a tornado or a waterspout hit the courtyard by my condo. It was so severe it knocked the power out and tossed all of the chairs into the walls of the courtyard. I understood the water spout/tornado to be the embodiment of God speaking to me. Maybe he was angry, or maybe he was just getting my attention. Maybe it was to make me get out of the condo for a while. Perhaps there is someone I should speak to.

Day Nine: 7/4/2014

...

I walked down the street today where I was stopped by a kid who thought he recognized me. He said, "Happy 4th, Sir." I replied, "You too." He became excited I spoke to him and began telling his mother about me. She was standing there all along next to him. She was beautiful and just smiled at me.

Later in the evening I walked a couple of miles in the direction of where the fireworks were supposed to be shot off for the 4th of July celebration. I had no idea where they would be shot off, so I just wandered aimlessly with no specific intention for the night. As dusk set, I stopped and decided I would just wait. I shared in a conversation with another couple waiting next to me, who continued to tell me they wished their son was like me. We never got into any specifics, nor did I say anything to prompt that reaction or conversation. It was just a casual conversation they started with me as we were waiting for the fireworks to begin. And while it should not have been a surprise, when the fireworks were shot off, we were squarely in line. I had no expectation I was anywhere near where the fireworks would be shot off, but I was standing not even 1° off center from their location. It was the best place I could have been standing.

Day Ten: 7/5/2014

...

Today I was sitting in my car at a red light when a large white feather landed on my hood. It fluttered there for a minute or two as I sought to understand the meaning. I smiled, recognizing the meaning. I said the word "anointed" aloud as the feather immediately tumbled away. It caused me to smile uncontrollably and say in a prayer aloud, "Father, I understand."

I decided to go have dinner at the Hard Rock casino, which was across town. Throughout the week I have been in Fort Lauderdale people continue to ask me if I gamble or if I have been to the casinos. It seemed like there might be a purpose to going, so I chose to follow the lead. When I arrived at the casino, I found a restaurant for dinner. When I sat down, the waitress at the table next to me spilled her drinks all over her clients lap. If it were not for the continual spiritual conversation I have been engaged in since I arrived, I would have thought it was just an unfortunate coincidence for the waitress and client. But in the context of the moment, I sensed my arrival caused a spiritual ripple to occur as I sat down.

After dinner, I went to the casino. I had the idea I would spend a little time playing blackjack or roulette. But the way things continue to play out, this trip would be another lesson for me – one that I had to experience. After returning home, I immediately wrote the following passage. I wanted to leave it here in this journal entry in its entirety:

...

Gambling. What makes the concept of wagering on a game of any kind so bad in the eyes of others? Many people will tell you that gambling is an unhealthy addiction...a gateway to numerous other uncontrollable urges. Others may say that gambling is a fool's game and a way to potentially create a large hole to climb out of – where, at times, it can lead a man to desperate measures in order to seemingly solve the financial troubles that were created. Finally, some may say that gambling is "a sin" because it is forbidden within their religious affirmation. But nowhere in any religious, theological, or philosophical text is there an adequate description for why gambling is thought to be immoral. Indeed, every example I gave above is only because of the "potential" to lead a man astray.

However, the events that unfolded this evening must surely have been intended for me to learn how God provides for each and every one of us, and through which an understanding of our thankfulness should be demonstrated. Up unto this point, the last nine days here in Fort Lauderdale have been a metaphorical sandbox for this next phase of my spiritual journey. Every day there have been new lessons. Every night, new tests have been placed in my communion with God. Fort Lauderdale is a mecca of every potential to serve as a learning experience for me and I have noticed that God has used this location to reach out to me in ways that Nashville no longer could. If this location is best seen as the Fourier of Heaven, there must certainly be new knowledge to unearth.

Tonight, I was led to Hard Rock Casino. At first blush, it would seem that human desires to have a night out on the town may have superseded God's spiritual plans for me. But, this was not a typical night out, nor was it of my choosing. I have no desire to drink, but the gambling aspect of my life was something that I needed help in understanding. In the years following my divorce, I took two separate trips to Vegas and one trip to Tunica, Mississippi – each time losing a tremendous amount of money (but not so much that it affected my finances). It was clear then that gambling was a hurdle for me, so I never went back or tempted fate. So tonight I went with no intentions of gambling, but rather to observe whatever it was that I was supposed to see.

The evening began with me arriving at the hotel and casino and walking around to find a place to eat. I found a restaurant and sat down in an empty seat only to be subsequently asked to leave the place where I sat down to order because "someone was sitting there." I knew it was not reserved, and clearly no one was sitting there, but the waiter insisted that I must leave by pointing at the still folded napkin and silverware resting on the tabletop (as if to indicate it was someone's silverware). I looked around and realized there was no difference in any of the other tables and the table I was at, so I took it as a sign and left the restaurant. I went to another restaurant where, upon opening the menu, I suddenly had a strange craving for pancakes. I ordered the pancakes listed on the menu only to be told that they do not serve pancakes for dinner, even though they were clearly listed on the dinner menu I was reading. I eventually ordered a Belgian waffle, assured it was really large and would fill my appetite. But, when the waffle arrived, it was disappointing in size and I finished it in less than a minute or two. Disappointed in the strange way my dinner had played out, and the brevity of my dining experience, I understood that my lesson was to observe the casino – so, that I did.

    I walked around the casino for a while and eventually decided to register for a casino card. Casinos typically give out free plays on the cards, so I figured there would be no harm in playing for free. I walked over to the concierge desk and waited in line to register. When I reached the desk, it was easy for me to see that the man who would help me was purposed into my life for a reason. The man was older than me by a few years, but suffered from a major neurological disorder. I could not quite figure out what he was suffering from, but he lacked motor control and his conversation was disjointed. When he asked for my license he became enamored with my birthdate. He then went on to tell me how much older I look than what was on my license. This was a first for me. In all of my years, I have always appeared younger than my age. However, this man helping me thought I was much older. That would not have been too wild, except he then went on to tell me he was six years older than me and that I look much older than he does. It was in this moment, I recognized that the man was observing spiritual age and not physical age. It took me a bit to wrap my mind around the conversation, but once I did, I understood why God had purposed him into my life.

If Fort Lauderdale is to be seen as Heaven, and some of the people here are "just visiting," as opposed to the others who are chosen residents of Heaven, this man was speaking spiritually to me in a way "as he was visiting" that I would speak to angels when I travel to the heavens. He – likely unknowingly to him – was speaking the honest truth about what he saw, perhaps without recognition of even where he was or who he was speaking to – perhaps struggling to hold onto harmony in this new world for him. It would be akin to me traveling to the heavens, but not having the experience register strongly enough for me to separate heaven from Earth, therefore having strange conversations with the angels, whom I would have "thought" were other humans on Earth until I gained full harmony in the moment.

It was an interesting experience – one that still resonates strongly within me. But the experience did not stop there. As he attempted to scan my driver's license to auto-populate their system, he had trouble getting it to scan. This would again be a testament of how Heaven and Earth bleed into one another and how the realms do not always work in harmony with each other. Eventually, he was successful getting it to scan, but then looked at his screen with a confused look. He said, "Well, it does not look like this new technology is going to work for you. Funny how that works." I laughed, entertained at the circum-

Kingdom

stances. He then went on to say, "Yeah, it says your name is Sex."

I paused. This was again another spiritual interaction with me for multiple reasons. I knew that in an earthly sense, the scanner had just taken the word on my license where it indicates gender "M" or "F" and plugged it into my first name. I looked at him and said, "Well, that will not work. That's definitely not me." He replied back more quickly than he had spoken with me thus far, "Really? Most people would say, 'Great! That is me.' I guess you are different." His words, perhaps unknowingly to him, were heavy on my soul. I knew that one of the main challenges I struggle with on Earth has to do with sex. To just put it out there, I wish I could have it all of the time (as I would guess most guys would agree). However, when there is an opportunity, I rarely have ever taken advantage of it because I know that it is morally not what I should do. It is a constant battle of desire versus morality. Within the bounds of marriage, it is another animal, but not outside. Over the last two years, I have managed to keep myself out of that predicament. But even during that time, I have even struggled with the concept of self-gratification.

I know it may seem that this is off topic from the casino, but it really is not. This is how God works. He speaks to people in the ways He knows they will hear. In my case, a prayer I said last evening asked for help in understanding if self-gratification was bad in lieu of waiting for the right girl. This is the hardest question I have recently needed help with. Over a year ago, Bryan and I made a vow to remove pornography from each of our lives in recognition of the message that God was telling us. That was, previously, the hardest challenge I had ever experienced, but I have held strong. It was clearly an addiction that I did not recognize as such. But, now I am debating on whether celibacy is the only real way to take the next steps along my spiritual journey. And, while I am debating that thought, here I am standing in a casino being told my name is "Sex" by a man who is having a much more spiritual conversation with me than he likely realizes…or perhaps he was an angel in disguise all along.

So, as I let the conversation marinate, he eventually completed my registration and went on about how there was a $100 guarantee with the card, but that I would have to use my own money. It seemed apparent that I had been given the green light to gamble $100. I went to the ATM to withdraw some cash, but it would not physically allow me to type in my pin. It would only accept three of the four numbers. It was as if the pin pad decided to quit working for me. Maybe this was a yellow light for me, but I continued on undeterred. At this point, I took note of the potential of my actions being missteps, but moved on to another ATM. This time, I was able to make the withdrawal, but I had to visit the casino cashier to pick up the cash – another caution flag in my actions.

When I found the cashier, I had a nice conversation with her as she struggled to find my transaction. This was warning number three for me, but I did not want to hear it. I was excited to be in the casino and gamble. After she called her manager over for help, she got everything worked out and told me to come back when I had won $4000. I hoped that could be a divine sign, but the other challenges in withdrawing $100 spoke otherwise to me. I knew that her words were a false comfort for why I was led to be in the casino in the first place. She told me to play blackjack and to avoid playing it all on a $100 hand. I decided to take her advice. I walked around until I found a blackjack table where the energy felt right. The hand minimum was $50. I assumed I would have at least two plays and then be on my way home. On the very first hand, I hit blackjack. I doubled up my $50 bet and received half of that bet as a bonus for the blackjack. This is when I should have stopped. Honestly, that was my sign and I knew it, but I wanted to tempt fate and see if I was about to go on a crazy winning streak to $4000. This was my sandbox experiment. As it turned out, I lost every subsequent hand where I was dealt dreaded twelves and fourteens.

After I lost, I was frustrated with myself. In the scheme of things, this had no financial impact to me whatsoever. But, I was disappointed that I did not see how God gave me an out as soon as I sat down. I thought about it and decided I would withdraw $200 more and that would be it, regardless of what happened. As much as I have lost gambling in my life, I have been up that much and more each time. It all is relative to when you walk away – any gambler will tell you that. This time, I took the $200 and went to the high stakes table. I found a blackjack game where I would be the only player and decided to play two hands simultaneously. On the very first deal, I hit blackjack on one hand, and beat the dealer on the other.

The First 42

One hand was doubled up, and then bonused half of the bet for hitting blackjack. The other hand was doubled up. It was at this moment that I should have gotten up again. I took the winnings off the table and left the two initial bets. I now had won $150 total on top of my $300. I told the dealer to "hold on and let me breathe" while waving my hand at her to let her know to wait. Whether it was clear or not, my intent was to pause and think about whether I wanted to get up. Instead, the dealer flopped down the next hand. It was too late. Fate had stepped in. I ended up having to double down on one of the hands and ended up losing. Dejected at having to play a hand I did not want to, I took my remaining $50 and found a different table to play one hand. I lost that one as well.

Now the point of this escapade should not be "when I should have walked away" or even how much money I lost. Again, in the scheme of things, the $300 I lost was not damaging and was more like petty cash for whatever I wanted to do with it. But, I was extremely disappointed in myself for losing. I do not like losing. However, I made a vow that $300 would be it for me, so I went home. As I drove away, I thought about the events of the night and the gambling…and this is finally where the purpose of the evening shined through.

For me, the $300 was the tuition price in this next lesson from God. He has provided me the means to be in Fort Lauderdale. He has provided me the ability to reside in this landscape for His lessons. And, He led me to the casino for a reason that I did not then know. But now I got it. Even if I missed all of the other messages in the evening, the most important message He had for me was in the law of doubling. God has provided everything for me. I do not create my financial circumstances. Rather, I hear His call and honor His directive. Therefore, first and foremost, the money that He has provided for me is a gift that should not be squandered. In fact, any attempt by me to personally create wealth will never come to be. God will provide as He sees fit for me, in the way that He knows will be best suited for me. When money is viewed this way, it is easy to see that gambling is throwing away and risking what He has provided. But even as this may be, the possessions that God has offered into your life is blessed – meaning that He can and will still do great things with them, if you understand how He works. In this case it was the law of doubling.

As heaven is founded on the Equidistant Bouquet and the law of doubling/halving, so too is how He provides. In my case this evening at Hard Rock Casino, I used money He blessed me with and sat down at a table to see if it could multiply. The best part is it actually did. In fact, not only did the first hand double my earnings, but there was an additional half bonus for hitting blackjack. A $50 bet became $100 which became $125 after the bonus. But just as quickly as He demonstrated how his blessings can and will multiply, He also demonstrated how quickly and painfully he can take it all away. A blessing grows quickly, and grows immediately. But, desire to make it continue to grow and place it all at risk will cause Him to take it all away.

The First 42

This was demonstrated a second time with the two $100 hands I played after going back to the ATM. As I have mentioned ad nauseam, God's voice is confirmed in two's to me. This has been the case for quite some time, in examples such as seeing two birds to listening for a repeated message. It is essentially God repeating Himself to me in order for me to hear. In this case, I laid down two hands at $100 a piece. I immediately doubled up each hand, and on one of the two hands (half of the hands I played), I received a half of the bet as a bonus for hitting blackjack. On the very first play at the new table, God doubled and halved my earnings to take me back to a net positive for the evening. In fact, this one play put me at having netted exactly 50% of what I wagered on the entire evening. Two major winnings on first-hand plays. The first time, had I walked away, would have been a $75 profit. This time, had I walked away, would have been a $150 profit...exactly double what the initial profit would have been. But I have to think that the dealer flopping down cards when I asked her to hold on was more than just bad luck. I have to believe it was God demonstrating that He can and will take it all away when He needs to make a point. He used the $300 as the cost of tuition for this lesson.

For me, I am not sure I would have seen everything as I have written it had I kept winning, or even decided to walk away before the dealer laid down that next hand causing me to double down and lose it all. I have to believe that God wanted me to understand that gambling is taking what He has provided me and placing it at risk. To Him, this could be seen as

Kingdom

spiteful. For all that He has provided and will provide should not be the subject of human mockery. Some may say this is conjecture at best. Some may say I am really reaching for meaning in the events of the evening. But, the point is that once the conversation has begun with God, it is fluid and ever-present. He is in everything and everyone I see. Everything – and I mean every single thing and person around me – serves as a vessel for Him to communicate to each of us. It is up to us to learn how to hear His voice.

As I have said before, we are all children learning His alphabet, learning to hear His words, His voice, and finally learning how to have a conversation with Him through all things around us. For me, this is what happens on a daily basis. And while the events of the day may not adequately describe the gravity of the conversation I had today, His words did not fall on deaf ears. For today, the events that unfolded were the period to the end of a sentence that God has been forming with me over the last several weeks. Today, this period will begin the formalized next steps for my journey. And while it will be tough, and I absolutely do not look forward to the struggles that could ensue, as of today, July 5, 2014 – in the most simplest terms – I will no longer subject human risk to anything that God has provided for me. In prayer, I humbly offer to Thee:

...

The First 42

Lord, God, my Almighty,

I ask for Your forgiveness of my sins and in my naiveté to Your intentions. Everything around me is beautiful and perfect. It is as You have created it, a perfect paradise for me. This is truly Heaven in the version You intend for me to experience at this point of my journey. But with this great gift comes great responsibility for furthering my pursuit of training as a King. And in that, I offer the following unbreakable seals, that shall only be broken by You. The first seal is of my celibacy. Not only shall I remain celibate, but I shall also refrain from any personal sexual desires. Lord, You know my heart. You know my soul. You know my bodily urges. This is the hardest thing I have ever tasked myself with, and I know that You understand that. You know how much I want to Love and find the one whom I will one day Love. So, until You see fit to break this seal by placing the girl you intend for me into my life, and even then, only after You and I have communed in disambiguation of Your intention to break the seal, this seal shall remain unbroken.

The second seal is that I shall not gamble. Gambling demonstrates a disrespect for all of the wonder You have placed into my life, so I shall not place it ever at risk. I know that You shall provide for me in the ways that You see fit, and I shall be gracious for anything parted to me. Even a friendly wager subjects Your gifts to risk, and this is not a way that I wish You to see me act. Therefore, I have placed a seal over my desire to gamble.

The third seal is that I shall not drink beer or liquor. While I have left the door open for wine, it is only because I am unsure of Your intentions for it on Earth. It has become easier to understand that sexual pleasure has a purpose, as it is meant for a man and woman to experience

Kingdom

in Love — but, any other use of it is a perversion of Your intention. It is also now apparent to me that gambling demonstrates a disrespect to the gifts you have placed into my life. Money is purposed into my life by You and can serve as a vehicle for multiplying wealth, but not in a way that places Your blessings as a slave to my ego. However, the greater picture of gambling is that by placing money into something that is not a vehicle for You, it demonstrates a callus attitude toward Your wonder. This concept even transcends into buying beer, liquor, and anything that does not serve a purpose for life, Love, and happiness.

I recognize spiritually that both liquor and beer are filled with a negative aura that permeates the mind upon ingestion. It damages the body — the only temple that I have to commune with You. I have not tested my body with wine in the last year as I did not want to sway my understanding of liquor and beer. With beer and liquor, I have only tested the waters twice in the last seven months. But each of those two times should be seen in the same way You respond to me in twos. For each of those times offered no benefit to my body — only detriment. My body took more than a week to fully recover to a noticeable harmony with my spirit even though I did not over-consume, and even then it took closer to a month before I could feel Your spirit permeating throughout my body in full. So by ingesting even the tiniest amount of beer or liquor, I am essentially saying that I am okay with not communing with You for at least a week — and this is not okay.

So these are the three seals that I have placed upon my body in demonstration of gratitude and growth for the gifts You have bestowed into my life. I ask for Your understanding and care in helping keep me comforted in times of strife — especially with respect to the removal of all sexual pleasures. You know my heart. You know my soul. You know how badly I want to Love, and most importantly, how I long to be Loved. I am indebted to the mercy You have shown me, and I pray that I may find the strength to not let a minute pass where I am pulled in a current away from You. For You are the Light, the Wonder, my Ever-after. I ask these things in Your Holy Name.

Amen.

Day Eleven: 7/6/2014

…

I woke up this morning and immediately put money I had put aside into my bank account to offset the use of the money my Father purposed into my life for Fort Lauderdale. Though the amount of money was negligible overall, I wanted to make sure there was a clear delineation between the money I understood had been purposed into my life from His hand versus money I had earned prior. After I went to the bank I checked my email, where I had seven unread emails – a number of recognition in the action I had taken in demonstration of the forgiveness I sought.

Later in the evening, I went to a Thai restaurant to pick up dinner. When I entered, an older man had just picked up his food and turned to head out the door. After he left, he walked back inside and stared at me with a certain recognition. He said, "Do I know you from somewhere? Are you from New York?" I said, "No sir" and just smiled. He kept staring at me strangely and said, "Well you have a double in New York then." I wished him well, and he went on his way. This is not the first time I have had people recognize me upon my arrival, though there would not be a reason. In the context of the journey, I know it is the angels welcoming me into this Heaven on Earth in a way that is distorted through the human vessel.

Before bed I prayed about the archangels that have been appearing in my travels to the heavens. At one point I thought I sensed the presence of at least one of the archangels in my bedroom with me. At this point, I asked if it was Uriel, to which there was a knock that occurred twice on the upper portion of the wall above me. The unit above me is vacant, so I know there was no possibility of chance when I heard the knocking. This was a first for me and sounds almost like something out of a séance , but it is what it is and it occurred as I have stated..

Day Twelve: 7/7/2014

...

I spoke with Bryan for the first time in a couple of weeks today. When we began to speak, my soul welled up in spiritual recognition of my brother. I could tell he was overwhelmed with school and work again. Even so, it was still good to hear his voice. This was the first time he had time to chat since the days before being wed to Mindi a week or so ago. The conversation was good. He was excited to share with me an experience he had in the heavens the previous evening. It was his first experience in months. His experience echoed the concepts I have been coming to understand about heaven on Earth and how it relates to Fort Lauderdale for me. While he was caught up in the details, I was caught somewhere in the clouds of multi-dimensional and existential thought.

We chatted about it for a while even though I was fearful he would think I had lost my mind. To even begin to tell someone that the world around us does not exist in the same dimension for everyone, and that transitions between the dimensional levels is seamless (like opening a door in a dream), is enough to leave a person exposed as a crazy-person. I had just reason to worry about his response, but I thought I needed to share it with him so that he could find his doorway. It is no coincidence that my pilgrimage to Fort Lauderdale occurred the same week that he took a surprise vacation with Mindi to the mountains for a week. It is no coincidence that they decided to get married months ahead of their planned date and begin a new life together. His marriage is his door, and I wanted him to understand he was no longer living on the same plane he was in the weeks prior. But alas, to explain that concept is near-impossible.

As I write this, I know it sounds crazy and that I am on the verge of an existential crisis, but the truth is that writing is the only medium – the only common thread between all of the souls rooted to Earth. Books can contain the knowledge each person needs to learn and understand existence, but the very fact that books are written by someone viewed as existing on their same plane of existence can cause most people to dismiss the idea before it has time to resonate in the mind. This is the hardest concept I have tried to explain, and I was fearful that

Kingdom

Bryan really did not understand it, though he said he could wrap his mind around it.

    Near the end of the conversation, I wanted to further substantiate all of the events I have experienced in Fort Lauderdale and how it truly is a place that God prepared for me for this next phase of my spiritual journey. I began to read to him the notes I took from my grandest experience in the heavens in recent months – the experience where God appeared to me and explained I was learning in the way He wanted me to learn "for me." Even my shorthand notes were long and detailed before I journaled the experiences, but I thought that was the best place to start. Often I like to share the experiences with Bryan through the notes I took immediately upon returning to my body. Then, as the conversation progresses, there is potential to share further extrapolations or share the formalized thoughts that I arrived at during journaling the experience from my notes. In this case, I thought it would be best to help Bryan understand the gravity of everything I was attempting to explain to him through the justification of God appearing to me. I figured that since our experiences in the heavens are taken in full faith as truth as we discuss them with each other, I needed to drive home my point by bringing out the hammer.

    I began reading Bryan the notes from the experience with God. The notes began with me meeting "my other mother" in heaven and beginning to spar with her. As I began to read the words, I suddenly became overwhelmed with the feeling that the words were not intended for Bryan. I desperately wanted

The First 42

to share them with him, but with every word that crossed my lips I felt like I was breaking a bond that God had shared specifically with me. Suddenly, my phone vibrated with what I assumed was a text message. I took note that it could be a spiritual warning about sharing something I should keep to myself, but it takes two confirmations for me to be sure that God is speaking to me. No sooner was I halfway through the next sentence, when some other piece of technology started beeping in my condo. I assumed it was my iPad, though I always keep it on silent, and it was three rooms away. Regardless, it was enough that I stopped mid-sentence and said, "Bryan, I cannot. I want to tell you about this experience so badly but everything in my house started beeping at me, and I know that I am not supposed to. I do not want you to think I am withholding this from you – you know I want to tell you. But I cannot right now. The rest of the experience was apparently intended just for me at this point."

I felt like a crazy person. How could I speak to my spiritual brother and, mid-sentence, just quit speaking? He had to have thought I lost my mind, but he replied with an attempt at being understanding. He said, "It is okay. I understand. When you can tell me, I would love to hear it." I replied by saying, "That's just it. I do not know when – or even if – I will be able to tell you. All I know is that everything around me is telling me to stop." It was like warning flares being sent up into the sky as danger was fast approaching. After I re-affirmed to him that I would likely not ever be able to tell him, I heard a single beep from wherever the original source of the noise in my house originated from. It was the mark of confirmation that I was doing the right thing. It was a seven and seven moment of the grandest kind, but in a more advanced conversation than just seeing the number seven around me. This was purely aural and the recognition of the spirit inside of me.

As Bryan and I wrapped up the conversation, I could not help but feel proud that I heard God's voice, yet still somehow dejected that I had to be given direction due to heading astray. Perhaps that is just part of the learning process for me. For how can a person know his boundaries without first testing them? I suppose I am caught somewhere between blindness and a higher set of standards for myself in the blind. And in that, my Father's grooming of me will undoubtedly continue to shine brightly enough to bezel away the sharp corners of my rigid, earthly mind. Bryan and I said our goodbyes, and I moved onward to working on the project that was purposed into my life so that I may continue to reside, learn and grow in this place of Heaven.

Day Thirteen: 7/8/2014

...

Every day has been filled with something beautiful. Whether it is just the simple words of a passer-by on the street or a collision of the greatest spiritual sorts through the world around me, everyday has held a unique spiritual lesson. I have never viewed my life in such a way as to expect that everyday the Lord would teach me something new. Possibly, in a hopeful sense, I would have talked about it. But, to experience it is surreal…I suppose "not of this world" would be an apt description.

This morning began with me awakening early to a violent thunderstorm. My alarm began blaring at 7:00 a.m. this morning in an effort to get myself into a routine now that I am settled in here in Fort Lauderdale. But, my body has been so heavy in sleep the last few days that it was difficult for me to awaken. I did look outside to see the sun rising when my alarm sounded. It was overcast, but day was breaking. I hit the snooze button in typical fashion, and before the next seven minutes of my snooze timer had expired a violent thunderstorm shook the building. Maybe I am just not used to the thunderstorms in this part of the country. But, all I can say is that the pops of lightning and the way the thunder was rattling the entire building was different than I have ever experienced in Nashville. My mind immediately recalled the tornado that struck the building a few days prior. I then, recognized the thunder. It was the spirit of God.

In the events that followed, I can only assume they were prepared specifically for me for my journey. I rolled over onto my back and looked up at my ceiling and told God, "I hear you. I'm getting up. This must be when you want me to get started today." I sat up and turned off the snooze alarm that was about to go off again. And just like that, the thunder stopped. The lightning quit. The rain stopped its downpour. Moments later, blue skies appeared. I'm sure for anyone reading this there will be an air of skepticism about everything I am saying. And honestly, if I were on the other side of this story – reading it instead of experiencing it and writing it – then I would scratch my head as well. So I can only ask that you keep an open mind because this is truly the reality of my existence. Only in thinking about the world as a fluid, multidimensional existence, can the context of this book be understood.

I started my day by getting up and writing. I knew that I had extremely strong and lucid experiences in the wee hours of the morning, but a false awakening caused me to think I had written down the experience. In fact, I awoke to having taken no notes at all – and that was frustrating to me. But I felt extremely compelled to write today and to begin getting into a routine of writing first thing in the morning.

I sat down at my laptop and began plugging away at my Day 12 experiences. Up until today, I have tried to let the events of each day marinate while I have attempted to understand God's intentions with my experiences. I have taken notes and, in some cases, formally written the day's events. But, I still had not been quite sure of the form this writing will eventually take. I knew that each experience has been part of a greater story. This initial recognition did not take very long at all for me to understand how these experiences would become the underlying content to Kingdom. I just was not sure how the experiences would need to be expressed. But, I can now see that they should be expressed in the same way as they happen to me, fluid like the world in which we live, though this recognition did not come until I was nearly finished with my Day 12 writing. At the end of the entry, I began to extrapolate on my thoughts as to why God wanted to halt me from sharing my experience with Bryan. I had just written about understanding God's signs to me through the beeping of the different devices in my house. I then typed the following sentence:

"Did the warnings appear because the experience did not need to be put into voiced words?"

Just as I placed the question mark at the end of that sentence, I was interrupted by what sounded like a phone ringing in my bedroom. I immediately recognized that God was grabbing my attention. I did not need two signs. I just needed the one sign, like the single beeping confirmation I had when I stopped sharing my experience with Bryan. But just as quickly as I recognized His voice, I was overcome with a startling recognition that the sound I heard was neither my ringtone, nor would it have been coming from my phone since I had my phone with me. I was baffled, dumbfounded at what could be ringing in my room. And almost as quickly as the ringing began, the ringing abruptly stopped. The shortened ring would be akin to having someone call your phone and immediately hang up, where only a partial ring had an opportunity to ring out.

My mind raced in that fraction of second. Every thought blazed through my mind even before the partial ring abruptly ended. I looked down next to my laptop to make sure I had my phone with me. I did. This was not "just" God grabbing my attention. He added an exclamation point to His thought. And perhaps that is the best way to think of the confirmation I was having. If my question to Him is to be seen as, "Did the warnings appear because the experience did not need to be put into voiced words?" He simply responded "!". It was as grand as the smiley face I received as an answer to my prayer with Him earlier this year. That was the moment when, during my prayer, I said, "Perhaps faith is experiencing the earthly experiences just like I experience the heavenly experiences – to no longer see a divide but to see them as different perspectives of the same experience" to which He replied simply with a smile.

My mind raced in recognition of His voice. Just to make sure I was not completely losing my mind, I walked into my bedroom to hunt down the source of the sound. I discovered it had originated from my iPad – a missed FaceTime call that showed as "cancelled." I was even more puzzled by this because I was positive that my phone did not ring, and I have never talked to anyone on FaceTime on my iPad (though it would share the same settings as my phone). I walked back into the other room to double check my phone. I confirmed that I had not missed a call on it. However a person may choose to rationalize this scenario, the point is that God communicated with me in the way that He knew I would understand. In the entire time I have been in Fort Lauderdale, I have only received a handful of text messages or calls – and those were expectedly from my daughter. Changing my number and telling hardly anyone the new number was part of the process of moving down here so that the unexpected FaceTime call could only be His voice.

The First 42

I digested all of the thoughts in those moments. Why would God not want this experience put into words? I now understood that I was not to speak of the experience, but my mind raced in an attempt to understand His intention. Could it be that the way He appeared to me was in a way that only I should be privy to? But if so, how are others supposed to know about it? Maybe no one is supposed to know about it. Maybe it was just meant for me. Perhaps it could be seen as placing a giant target over my head for the man in rose-colored glasses to see. And while it is no-words-can-describe-humbling-feeling to think that God could very well have been serious in His words to me during that vision, I've tried to not allow my ego to take hold of the words by trying to think of His intent in the words as glorified "atta-boys" while I am being trained "in the way of a king." But maybe, and most importantly, it was because Bryan did not need to hear those words at that time. We are each on separate paths heading to the same destination. He had just had his first vision in months, and it was a lot for him to soak in. And, as much as I tried to help disambiguate it for him, his mind seemed to be firmly rooted in the concrete cause-and-effects on Earth rather than the existential, archetypal meaning. Maybe our roads have diverged. That saddens me, but strengthens me – as it should strengthen him. To know that God is the center of everything; to recognize that existence is not rooted in a firm reality, but rather in our own unique realities (that co-mingle with other realities) through which He intends for us to see, is a paradigm shift from the concrete belief that our existence is on one linear plane.

Kingdom

After I finished typing the sentence that God chose to respond in exclamation of my recognition of His intention, I tried to continue writing about Day 12. But, alas, I was continually interrupted. I woke up early and began writing for reasons unknown to me, but those reasons would continue to unfold. As I tried to finish my thoughts about the potential interpretations of whether I should continue sharing the experience with Bryan, I was set on a new course to help me see that the only answer was the one in which God gave His mark of exclamation. At that moment, I received a text from my landlord's realtor who said he would drop by in an hour. Unsure of why he would be dropping by, I gave him a call. As it turned out, he had an appointment to show my apartment (it is for sale) to a potential buyer. I mentioned that I would get it ready to show, but asked why there was such short notice. My lease terms say that I would have at least 24 hours notice, but I did not want to press the issue. Obviously God had me up-and-at-it this morning for a purpose. I recognized that this was likely a piece of it.

I showered and straightened up anything that seemed out of place. I thought that maybe God wanted me to get out of the house and go write at Starbucks (somewhere to keep me focused on writing). I gathered my laptop and headed to the elevator. To my surprise, the elevators were not working...all three of them. The service elevator did not respond to my button presses and the high-speed elevator button lit up to my button press, but the elevator continued to bypass my floor. It was inexplicable. Perhaps the service elevator was being

The First 42

worked on or having challenges. But why would the main set of elevators continually not respond to my button press? They were clearly moving up and down to other floors and returning to the ground floor. I stood there puzzled momentarily and said aloud, "Okay, God. It seems to be your intention for me to stay, so I will."

In the past, anytime I have had a realtor show a place I have lived in, the expectation was that I would not be present. And, on the flip side as a buyer, I expected the tenant to be absent if I were to view a place. I wondered if staying would sour the relationship with my landlord or his realtor. But really – it did not matter. I was clearly instructed to stay, so I did.

To my surprise, the realtor rang the doorbell when he arrived at my place. I honestly expected him to just walk right in. He was clearly expecting to see me and help show the place. I was introduced to Carlo and Patrick and made sure to introduce myself. Carlo made a comment about how he liked my wine collection (which was interesting in and of itself because I have not drunk wine in over a year and am unsure if I will again). Maybe it was the spirit speaking through him, letting me know that wine was okay. Regardless, we chatted for a few minutes. It was obvious that something was bothering Jay, the landlord's realtor. In the end, I shook his hand and said it was good to see him again. Unexpectedly, Jay just randomly decided to open up about a stroke he had last week and everything else that was burdening him. Until then, he had been very silent throughout the showing. I let him know I was

Kingdom

here for him if he needed anything before everyone parted ways.

After they left, I knew the significance of me staying was to help Jay. Most importantly it was to shake Jay's hand. I could feel the spirit pass through me to him when we shook hands, and I know that God touched his soul in that moment. I am still unsure of how all of this works, but it seems likely too audacious to say, "You are healed now" even though my gut tells me that was the purpose of all of it. God needed a strong vessel to help touch an ailing soul. I suppose I just need to just watch it all unfold because, after all, I am still learning. But in understanding that the spirit is in me, then it stands to reason that the spirit touches others through me. And if that is the case, it stands to reason that anything is possible through touch.

Perhaps there were other aspects to the visit that were outside of the encounter with Jay. Perhaps there could have been a spiritual "staking of territory" to anyone interested in viewing the place. Perhaps my presence would help sell the place for my landlord (or help filter the right buyer for the place). Perhaps, if God intends for me to stay in this place, the buyer will need to see my soul in person. I am sure there are many dimensions as to why I was to be there today, but this I know for sure: it was another spiritual training day for me on this Day 13. I am not sure why I am in this specific location outside of it serving as a slice of heaven prepared for me for this time in Fort Lauderdale. But, maybe, that is part of the bigger story to unfold.

Day Fourteen: 7/9/2014

...

My fourteenth day in this Heaven falls on one of the most special days of the year. Today is July 9, 2014. Numerically, July is represented by the number 7, the day is the ninth, and the year reduce-sums to 7. So that makes today 7+9+7 which reduce sums to the number 7. Anyway, I wanted to make note of that because today being the 14th day is a multiple of the number 7. I know that some people keep away from anything pertaining to numerology, but despite each person's belief, I wanted to at least make note of the way my days here aligned to one of the most divine days of the year.

Other than the significance of today's numeric meaning, the most important event began on the tail-end of my prayer from last night. I have been praying for guidance on a particular area of growth in my life. After I took a shower and got ready to leave the house, I picked up my phone before heading out the door. As I reached for my phone, I was praying aloud to God asking Him to help me know if I was following the right lead. As I looked at my phone, it vibrated to let me know I had unopened emails. There were seven.

Day Fifteen: 7/10/2014

...

Today I drove back to Nashville from Fort Lauderdale. I had an appointment with a client and wanted to have my car, so I thought it would be a good opportunity to have some quiet time in prayer while driving. On the drive I attempted to sit in silence for the first three hours. That turned out to be much harder than I expected. The purpose was to just listen to my thoughts without the distractions of music or singing along to the radio. Even in times like these, I find myself praying aloud, so it was a greater challenge than I expected.

On the drive, I noticed a bright red billboard on the side of the road. The only thing upon the billboard was a large number seven. At this point, music started playing on the radio, though it clearly indicated the word "stop" was its setting. Just then a lightning strike occurred less than a hundred yards to my left. It was reminiscent to the lightning strikes I experienced on my initial drive down to Fort Lauderdale. During that drive, lightning struck either side of the road just ahead of me. At the time I thought it seemed like passing through the uprights of a field goal made of lightning, but I could not have foreseen the meaning of it then. I now understood that just as I entered through a doorway, I had to exit through one as well. Just after the lightning strike, the music stopped playing. Everything went back to silence as I noticed a red Focus in front of me. This was another symbolic gesture of signs, telling me to "focus" though I still was unclear of the color red's meaning at that time.

When I arrived in Nashville, I had trouble finding a hotel that was inexpensive and available. When I entered the one I knew I was intended to be in, the owner gave me a discount "due to his own journey through Nashville." I understand discounts happen at hotels, but this one was different. Not only was it the greatest discount that was possible, but his reasoning made no earthly sense. It was only a spiritual conversation taking place. From one soul to another, he saw me passing through and offered me a place to stay.

Day Sixteen: 7/11/2014

...

Twice in Nashville, my radio flashed the word "stop" as I passed billboards that said the same thing. I have to believe it is a sign to understand I need to leave behind everything I once knew. It was as if I was being flagged by God and reminded I had a new home – that place was Fort Lauderdale, home to angels and His Love. I also took this as a sign to pull over and pray for a while.

I went to a coffee shop before the meeting with my client. I saw a mother (who worked at the coffee shop_ sitting down with her two older children. I overheard them talk about the daughter's car being broken down which caused the mother to be stressed out. It was clear she was unsure about how to pay for whatever problems had happened with the car. I walked over to her and offered to help resolve the problem. She was grateful and told me where to drive to help her children. When I arrived, I saw the car had overheated, but as it turned out, it was just a bad seal on the radiator cap. I told her daughter and her boyfriend how to fix it, and they left for the auto store to pick up the part. I returned to the coffee shop and let

Kingdom

the mother know the problem was just a radiator cap and that she had nothing to worry or stress about.

After my client meeting, I grabbed some lunch. I decided to blindly pay for a happy couple's meal and a woman who seemed sad and alone. It is something I enjoy doing without fanfare or acclaim. I always ask to remain anonymous and then slip out the door. This time, after I returned to my car, when I went to back up all I could see was a car with a Florida tag directly behind me. Being that I was in Tennessee, it was just another way of God's affirmation of the destination.

When I pulled up to my stopping destination, I sat in the car to watch the moon for a few minutes. At this time, I received a phone call from the CEO of a non-profit company which I serve on the board. After we exchanged hellos, she said, "Well, I'm calling to see if you can save the day and be my superman." I know that she was just being playful with her word choice for the problem she was about to share with me, but it was still a nice touch of God speaking through her. It was a moment of spiritual recognition that the words spoken embodied more than what others heard. I gladly volunteered to help her out, and eventually wrapped up the conversation.

After hanging up, I stared up at the stars and watched the moon fall out of view as the clouds rolled in for a storm that was incoming. As I watched the moon fade out of sight, the last three words of the song on the radio garnered my attention. At this point I was not listening to the radio as much as staring at the moon while in deep thought. But I suppose as the moon faded from view, my senses reacted like a movie fading out saying "The End." The last three words was the soundtrack to the night ending. Those words were, "Cowboys and Angels" from the Dustin Lynch song by the same name. While this song is much more spiritual in nature than the surface level understanding of the lyrics indicate, most people will miss the greater message. But in this moment, it held a greater message. It was as if God dotted His "i's" and crossed his "t's" to the story that was unfolding for me. As I watched the moon fade from view on my last night in Nashville, it was as if God was identifying the Cowboy as Nashville and the Angels as Fort Lauderdale. All I could do was tear up and smile.

Day Seventeen: 7/12/2014

...

I spoke with a man named Mitch today. As we spoke, the name "Peggy White" filled my head. It was an unusual feeling. I honestly have no idea who "Peggy White" is, but I have to imagine in the context of everything being viewed through a child's spiritual eyes that I was being imparted about this man's life... similar to how spiritual conversations take place in the heavens.

Day Eighteen: 7/13/2014

...

Today I was returning to Florida after picking up my daughter. Since I had to be in Nashville earlier in the week, I decided to drive instead of fly. And while it makes for a long drive back, it made for a great opportunity to talk to my daughter. Though I do try to show her how God is working through everyone and everything, it is always amazing to hear her perspective on things she sees. Today was no different. At one point in the conversation, my daughter was prompted to say, "What if this place (Earth) is really a place where all of the spirits have gone once they have died and we are all figuring it out?" And while I am sure some readers may assume this was prompted through our conversation, I had not shared with her anything remotely in the ballpark of this thought. Even though it mirrors the opening salvo to these first days of journals from arriving in Fort Lauderdale, this was a thought she arrived at on her own. Perhaps it was God speaking directly through her to add confirmation to all I have been experiencing. Either way, it was an amazing thing to hear.

Along the journey back to Florida, we stopped at a gas station to fill up on gas. While I was pumping gas, a man walked up to me and began talking to me about my Jeep. He pointed over at his Jeep across the way and told me how his girlfriend had been complaining about her Grand Cherokee. It was a strange conversation to have occurred, but one I must again take note of. The man did not want anything at all. He just wanted confirmation that the Jeep was a good vehicle. After he left, I thought about the conversation and what it could have meant. I determined he must have been talking about the "vessel" with which I move and how others may not always like the vessel that works for you. These types of conversations have been non-stop since I made the pilgrimage to South Florida, so I have to believe there is always more to these interactions than how it appears on the surface.

Day Nineteen: 7/14/2014

...

Today I took my daughter swimming in our condominium pool. As we swam, a lady came up to us and began a conversation. In the midst of the conversation, she told me to check out "The Eden Project" after telling me all about England. If I had ever doubted spiritual conversations through bodily vessels, this was the type of moment that removes all doubt.

Day Twenty: 7/17/2014

...

My daughter began talking to me about her desire to learn more about religion today. She does not go to church often with her mother so I began to understand that it would be up to me in our abbreviated time together to share with her all I can about God.

Day Twenty-One: 7/16/2014

...

This morning my daughter and I went to the surf shop to pick up a boogie-board for her. When we arrived, we looked around and picked up a couple of towels and mats for the beach. I told Georgia that I really needed to find my beach

Kingdom

bag so that we could carry everything to the beach. We even looked at the beach bags in the store but could not find one that I liked. We were eventually ready to leave and went to the cashier to check out. After the lady rang us up, the cashier said, "And today, you will receive a free beach bag from us." She then handed us a beach bag from behind the counter and we went on our way.

On our way back to the condominium, my daughter and I began talking about the palm trees as I pointed out the coconuts. Just after the conversation about coconuts began, we rounded a corner to see a man cutting down coconuts from a tree. When he saw us walking by, he cut one down and opened it up for us so my daughter could try one for the first time. She was really excited about the new experience, and I was grateful to the man. As she tried sipping the milk, a woman showed up and talked to us. She told us how she had moved from Belgium and had been in Fort Lauderdale for 16 years. The conversation would have seemed out of place, but the number sixteen is a special number for many reasons... partly because $1+6 = 7$. It was another reminder of Heaven on Earth.

Later in the day, we went to a Mexican restaurant for dinner. The waitress asked for my order and when I said, "chicken fajitas" she said, "Oh no, no. You can have chicken fajitas anywhere. You should have the [an indistinguishable word]." She went on to say how good it was and that it was a special Mayan recipe that no one else has in town. She emphasized that I would experience food I could not get anywhere else. I took her advice and ordered that specific meal. It was not even on the menu. It was amazing, and I continued raving about it to the waitress. Afterwards, she asked how I found out about the restaurant, and when I told her Yelp, she said, "Really? That is great. If you can, please leave some feedback, your good words will come back to you and give you something in return." I knew she was talking about the way karma works and how Fort Lauderdale is such a special place for souls.

Day Twenty-Two: 7/17/2014

...

Today the fish in the ocean surrounded my feet everywhere I walked. I could again make the oceans move from calm to small waves but never a big wave. Though it seems like I may be making this up, I assure the reader that this is the reality I have been allowed to witness. And how appropriate that it would occur on this twenty-second day in the Promised Land. For there are twenty-two archetypes in the progression of the soul, and today would represent the completion of the circle and ascension to a new chapter. By witnessing the fish and the oceans move in recognition of the spirit within, it is akin to seeing hints of the miracles of Jesus, Moses, and Abraham. Now I am not attempting to place my journey on a similar level, but rather demonstrate the signs that I have been allowed to witness. It should be seen that the signs are illustrations to greater understanding, not as a definition to a person or an identity – and I want to emphasize that point specifically.

Day Twenty-Three: 7/18/2014

...

This morning I awoke from an experience of battling Cerberus in the heavens. And while I will not belabor the details in this entry about my daily walk through Fort Lauderdale, it should be noted that on this twenty-third day – the first number after the completion of the twenty-two archetypes, I fought a battle against the animal that guards the gates of Hell as foretold in Revelation. And while it seemed like every bit of the battle was real, it leaves two questions in my mind: 1) Is everything that is foretold in the Bible actually experienced in real-time in a parallel spiritual world that is unseen to earthly eyes? If so, it would seem we are in the midst of the final parts of Revelation. 2) What if a single person's journey has always been the intention in understanding the Bible? Meaning, what if the End of Days is completely relative to each person on his journey where he can learn to experience everything as I have and as others have before me? While I do not think this is necessarily the answer, it might have to be experienced by a person and written about in such a way on a micro level for the macro to come to pass. Anyway, that is just a thought...

Day Twenty-Four: 7/19/2014

...

Tonight, Georgia and I had another meal at the Mexican restaurant we visited before. As it was last time, they had me order something not on the menu. Earlier in the day, Georgia heard me tell my cousin Bryan on the phone a little about Cerberus. She had asked several times throughout the day what I was talking about, but I had told her I would tell her at dinner. So after spending some time talking to Georgia after we had our food, I told her that I did not want to say too much in the restaurant but would tell her more at home. Just after I said this, a number seven appeared on my plate written in food. Georgia saw it happen too. That led to us talking about the number seven and what it means in the way God communicates to me. It was a wonderful conversation – one that she seemed to understand.

When we returned home, I shared with her a little more about the experience in the heavens in carefully guarded words. I know she understands, but I want to hold her hand to understand all I have been allowed to see. After I tucked her in and she said her prayers, I went to my bedroom to pray and go to bed. I placed my Bible on my bed in case I decided to do some reading, but the first call to action was to pray about the events of the day. As I prayed, I felt God's presence fill the room. I talked about how I wanted to understand more about the meaning of everything that seems to be happening. It was at this point I was forced to open my eyes. I watched my Bible open up to Daniel chapter twelve all on its own. Now perhaps the fan that was on in my room could have blown open the pages, or maybe the air conditioner kicked in with a sudden burst of air. But in either case it would not explain how a textured cover was opened and five hundred pages were turned. There is not a wind inside a house strong enough to reproduce what I witnessed. And, just to note, I also attempted to roll over on my bed and force my Bible to fall open, but to no avail. So though this was one more experience to add to the books, I spent the rest of the night trying to read Daniel chapter twelve and study its every word. Something in that chapter was important enough for God to open up my Bible in inexplicable fashion and have the pages stop on that particular chapter.

Day Twenty-Five: 7/20/2014

...

This morning I shared with Georgia about what happened to me with my Bible last night. Then I proceeded to share with her all I had learned in Daniel chapter twelve. I explained how that entire chapter is linked to Revelation and the story of Cerberus that I shared with her. I explained that Daniel was a man spoken to by God, and commanded to write down every word he was told and was blessed for being a servant to God. So all in all, there were many lessons to understand, but most importantly for our conversation, Georgia found peace in understanding the End of Days where she had unrest the previous evening.

Later this evening, Georgia called her mother for her nightly conversation. As I was making French toast for dinner her mother said she had just made French toast for herself. While it seems like an unimportant event to include, the relevance is that I had never made French toast before, and on the day I did, so did my daughter's mother. We each apparently had the same craving…or perhaps Georgia had the craving and both her mother and I sensed it though we are in different states. It is something to think about at least…

Day Twenty-Six: 7/21/2014
…

I met a lady named Melinda outside today. She talked to me about how the world needed my mind and understanding of the spiritual nature of sound. She talked about using these concepts in yoga and helping people become more acutely focused with their soul. It should be noted that I had not met the lady I spoke with before, nor have I ever talked to anyone about yoga. Whether or not she could have heard about me from someone else should be viewed as irrelevant. For through my spiritual eyes, I had to experience the moment as it was spoken to me – which resonated with everything I had learned thus far on the journey. Honestly, there was no other context that could set the stage for the conversation we had. She waved at me in passing, introduced herself, and then shared those words.

Day Twenty-Seven: 7/22/2014

...

Today Georgia and I were talking about how we did not have any good recent pictures of us together. Though we spend a lot of time together, I do not usually break out a camera. And, if I do, it is usually just a picture of her since I am taking the picture. But in typical form, what I spoke came into existence.

Georgia and I went to the mall today to pick up a few items for the house. While we were there, a lady at a kiosk jumped out in front of us and began taking pictures. She took several pictures of Georgia and me and showed us their picture packages for sale. I know it is her job to try to entice customers, but to me it was something more. This was the first time anything with a photographer like this had ever happened to me in a mall, but it was in direct response to our conversation from before. I understood my Father heard our conversation and offered His hand in helping us have a new picture together. Georgia even commented on how we were just talking about needing pictures of us and how this happening was meant for us that day. So I bought several pictures and hung them on my refrigerator when we returned home.

Later in the evening, Georgia and I walked to Dunkin Donuts for a coffee and hot chocolate. When we walked in, there was only one couple sitting at a table. Before we even walked near to them, I heard the couple speak aloud, "Where is Fort Lauderdale from here?" They were a well-to-do couple and dressed very nicely. I would have assumed they would have had access to maps on their phones, but instead they were just speaking into the empty room. Even the cashiers were not anywhere around – possibly in the back restocking or cleaning up.

    I walked up to them since no one was around and said, "You are here." They were entirely confused at my words. They began talking in a very spiritual conversation explaining how they "had arrived near Boynton, but wanted to move to Fort Lauderdale but do not know how." Nothing in there words held any earthly sense. It was completely spiritual conversation of angels on Earth seeking the Promised Land. The truth is they were already there, but the doorway they entered through was not the same one I did. As we spoke, I learned the man worked from home. He had to get a pen to write down what I said. It was odd because they had their phones on the table but said the phones were acting weird in the building. I looked at my phone and sure enough it was not functioning correctly. I assumed their spiritual manifestation was causing electromagnetic problems. The man asked about a realtor and about the buildings in the area. It was as if he could not see the buildings right behind him. After he took notes, Georgia and I ordered our drinks and found a table to sit at outside. Though I did not explain to her what we had just witnessed, she saw on her own the spiritual conversation taking place. She told me all that she saw, but was still trying to piece together the oddities that could only be explained by understanding they were angels that appeared upon the Earth.

After we returned to the apartment, Georgia and I walked out to the beach to stare up at the stars and just have a father-daughter moment. As we sat there, a man approached with a tall walking stick. It was nothing that is normally seen in modern times. The walking stick was more like a staff that came up to his head in height. The man had long, straight brown hair like an Indian. I could not get a good look at his nationality, but I could tell his skin was either darker or well tanned. When he walked by us, he said hello and told us about the turtles hatching on the beach. As it turned out, he volunteered in helping the turtles hatch. He introduced himself as "Michael" and then seemingly out of nowhere told me I should become vegan. He then talked about his belief in animals and souls. At this point, I realized this was another divine encounter. The conversation was full of spiritual meaning to ponder. At one point in the conversation I said the word "we" in reference to humans versus angels. It was then that he gave me a look of recognition and an almost disapproving look of identifying myself as a human rather than a soul. We spoke just a little longer before we parted ways, having realized I spoke with another angel.

Georgia and I continued to sit on the beach and look up at the stars. I used a constellation map to see what constellations were above. Directly above us was the constellation Hercules – which is interesting because earlier in the day we had watched the trailer for Hercules which revealed the seven-headed beast. It was the first time either Georgia or I had seen the trailer but it seemed quite relevant given the experience with Cerberus and now seeing the constellation Hercules overhead.

Day Twenty-Eight: 7/23/2014

...

Today my daughter was deep in thought throughout the day. Usually when she has these moments, I know something interesting will eventually be said. So while I was patient, I was eager to hear her thoughts. When she finally arrived at her philosophical idea she said, "Dad, what if the sun is like God and all of the planets are where angels live, even though we cannot see them?" It echoed similarities to the day she described Love through the idea of gravity and the orbits of the planets being like angels holding hands. But this new thought was even more interesting. Through her own conclusions, she was questioning the spiritual dimensions that so many in the modern world dismiss without scientific proof. We spoke for a while about it as I helped her explore her thoughts.

Later in the day, we went to Home Depot and Lowe's to look for patio furniture for my new place. The stores are located a couple of miles west of me, and it seems like some sort of spiritual boundary for my experience. And while that may not make much sense in this writing, by that I mean everyone seemed soul-less inside. It was almost as if the souls of everyone inside were in some zombie-like state while the souls near my building are all angels and filled with grace.

The murphy bed I ordered arrived today as well. And though I was not having any challenges moving most of the parts from the pallet, the one time I struggled, a man appeared out of no where to help. Without words, he walked up and gave me a hand, and once I had everything under control, he went on his way. I have never seen him again.

Day Twenty-Nine: 7/24/2014

...

Negative energies seemed to be all around today. In what seemed to be a continuation from Home Depot the day prior, everything seemed out of balance today. It began with me realizing that I needed to purchase a different type of drill bit than I purchased yesterday. On the way out the door of my apartment, I realized that the keys that I had made (two additional sets for my new place) did not work in my door. I decided to take everything back. When we arrived at Home Depot, the returns cashier did not want to let me return anything. Apparently the box of screws I purchased had 7 screws instead of 8 inside and she thought I had taken one. Eventually she let me return everything, but it was not without tension.

Since the store is technically not in Fort Lauderdale, I have to believe that the energies on the cusp of this Promised Land for me must be negative. It is the proverbial souls standing at the gate. I felt saddened for the area. When I arrived the first night in Fort Lauderdale I stayed in a hotel right beside the Home Depot which I knew felt very negative. I could not sleep that first night. There were shady people in and out of the hotel all night long. The next morning, when I left to meet my realtor, it took nearly 30 minutes to drive a couple of miles...again resonance from the negative location of the hotel. So today's lesson was in learning boundaries. Anything further West is a no-go for me. Even my daughter noticed how everything kept occurring in a bizarre fashion.

Day Thirty: 7/25/2014

...

We saw a large manta ray while snorkeling today. At first the shadow of the massive, majestic creature was startling in the ocean, and of course we began to get out of the water. Unsure of what type of animal was swimming by, Georgia and I quickly got out of the water. In hindsight, I wish I had snorkeled alongside of it.

This evening Georgia and I went out to the beach to see if we could see any sea turtles hatch. Even though there are hundreds of nests on the beach, it is still rare to catch them hatching. This was further emphasized by the guides I have met upon the beach at night. They check on the sea turtle nests and document if they have hatched. Some of the guides had never even seen the sea turtles hatch even though they had been serving in their position for quite a while. But even against the odds, tonight would be the first time Georgia saw "life" happen. We managed to walk out and right when we arrived at a nest that we knew could be hatching over the coming days, a guide appeared. To me, she was an angel, but to others she was just a guide. This person informed us that the nest we came to see had "dropped" but was not sure how long we would have to wait. I asked the girl how long she thought it might be before it hatched, and right then they began hatching. Georgia was even able to name a turtle.

Day Thirty-One: 7/26/2014

...

Today my daughter and I spent a great amount of time on the beach and in the ocean. I again noticed that the fish seemed attracted to my presence. I know it may not sound believable, but there are undeniable events that happen with me in the water. I am learning to form waves through intention, and I am now seeing the attraction of fish to the spirit within. I like to think of all that is happening as spiritual conversation with the spirit flowing through me... where I am only an observer to all that my Father is doing. To be honest, the whole situation in Fort Lauderdale has been the most amazing – if not unbelievable – experience. It is why I am writing down all of the events from each day – because when each event is observed for the one event, it is easy to dismiss. But, the sum total of all that has occurred is the unmistakable support to understanding the truth in the journey.

The First 42

Day Thirty-Two: 7/27/2014

...

Georgia and I have been spending the last several days figuring out my patio furniture situation. To me, my patio is the place where I plan to write the remainder of my books – outside, with the sun and sounds of the waves crashing to the shore, the sun glistening off of the pool below my condo. That type of setting helped me complete my first book on my trip to Haiti, and I know that the patio of new place in Fort Lauderdale is intended to serve in the same capacity for me. Over the last couple of days, Georgia and I have been picking out the ideal furniture for the patio, and we had already picked up the first two "must-haves." Those must-haves consisted of a modern-looking rocker and a bistro table with two chairs. Each of those items was placed at the ends of my patio, so that left us with room for some type of couch, love-seat, or chairs for lounging. We had seen a set of chairs that formed into a sofa a few days prior on sale at Lowe's, but when I searched online, none were available anywhere near my area. After a couple of days of searching, I eventually found a store that had two chairs in stock, but they did not have the third. As it happened, that store was the store closest to me. All of the surrounding stores (up to 30 miles away) were out of stock. Even though the store only had two chairs and we initially thought we would need three, we decided to go check them out anyway.

Kingdom

Before we arrived, we stopped at a restaurant. While we were eating, a couple came in and sat a table a few booths away. I did not even notice when they came in, but somewhere in the midst of their conversation, either the lady's speaking grew louder, or I became more aware of their conversation. The phrase that caught my attention was, "You cannot say things like that. Other people may take it the wrong way, even though I know what you meant. You have a higher standard to maintain. What was it that the spirit said to you anyway?"

It was as if my mind heard the last sentence and then replayed the preceding seconds of their conversation for me to hear the context. As I listened, I noticed that the lady was talking about both of them as "souls" and they were interacting with "spirits." I glanced over at them but quickly looked away so as not to cause them to take notice that I heard their conversation. I was immediately filled with a sense that the lady was an angel in human form and that the man was being guided by her. She continued to ask him about "which spirit" he was talking to and what each scenario was where the conversations took place. Their conversation went on for a few minutes before I could no longer hear them. There were no other people between us and only one or two customers inside of the entire restaurant. It was as if I was allowed to hear a certain portion of their conversation to help me understand that I was not alone on my journey in Fort Lauderdale. It was quite a warming sensation, and I knew that this trip I was taking to look for furniture was a blessed trip.

The First 42

When we arrived at Lowe's, we discovered that even the display unit we had seen a few days prior had been sold. We walked around and eventually found the two chairs located on a shelf. As we stood in the store, I went ahead and "ordered them online with a ship to store option" so I could use an online coupon I had. We did not plan to leave the store...it was just a way to save some money since the coupon was not valid "in store." We walked over to customer service to pick up the order. A man, who had clearly had a long day, helped us with the order. When he saw the pick-up description for the items, he immediately said, "We do not have any more of that item. We sold all that we had – even the display units. They were used and on the floor for display for at least six months" I mentioned that I found two on a shelf and he seemed surprised. We walked over to the shelf so that he could see what I thought I saw.

To his surprise, I was correct. He seemed utterly shocked. He went on about how everyone keeps asking for those items, and they have continually searched the store and through all of their inventory. As recently as the day prior, he was confident they had none in stock. He went on to say how the two items must have been returned earlier that day, or arrived on a truck this morning before his shift began. We all just laughed about it saying how it must be my lucky day even though I understood the subtext in how this situation was prepared for me by God to help me finish out my patio so that I may be able to pray and write in an inspiring environment. I did not want to spend a lot of money, but my patio needed to have a certain "feel" and "resonance" to it when I walked outside to write or to pray. And while it may seem strange to say that God provided me a luxury, this luxury should be seen as the fabric supporting my being. I did not spend a lot. In fact, most of the items I bought happened to be on clearance even though I would have picked out these exact same items regardless of the discount. I have to think that, again, everything was divinely timed to the rhythm of my journey to Fort Lauderdale. As it turned out, only two of the chairs would fit into my Jeep when we loaded them up – so I would have had to make an additional trip if I was to have purchased three chairs.

After loading up the chairs, Georgia and I debated whether I should get the small end table that was part of the set. I knew that it would look better than just the two chairs alone, but I was still trying to be price-conscious. However, if the set was on clearance, I thought it was probably best to get the matching table before it was out-of-stock permanently. We walked back inside and over to where there was a display of the end table. As Georgia and I were talking about it, the man from customer service walked over to us and looked a little confused as to why we were still there after he had already helped us pick up the chairs. I did not have to say anything before he said, "You should get the table too. After all, those chairs were meant for you, and you have to have the table if you purchased the chairs. I think it is on sale as well."

There was no sale sticker, so this was music to my ears. He checked on the price and realized it was not on sale anymore as the manufacturer placed the table back as "current stock" rather than "non-stock clearance." The man looked puzzled and then said, "Well, this tells me they are not discontinuing your chairs at all, but just updating the model for the next year. You got a really good deal then. A few weeks ago, this table was discounted 30%" He looked at me and said, "Well you have to have the table anyway. You already have the chairs." I knew that these words were words of guidance placed into my life. I knew he was not working on commission and he really did not have any reason to help me out at all. So I heeded the words. I said jokingly, "So you think I can get it at the clearance price then?" fully expecting him to tell me no. The man smiled and said, "I cannot sell it to you that low since it is current stock, but I can discount it for you. He offered to basically split the difference in the older clearance price from several weeks ago and the current price, which I immediately accepted. Overall, I was able to fully furnish my patio with furniture that exceeded my highest expectations under my budget. These items helped shape the final form that my "prayer and writing-inspiration oasis" would take, and is where I am writing these words.

Day Thirty-Three: 7/28/2014

...

Today's theme consisted in the recognition of "the 10%." It seemed as if everywhere Georgia and I went we were offered 10% discounts. At one store where we were picking up odds-and-ends items, we were given an additional 10% coupon that could be used today. There were billboards with "10% savings" written in bold print. Overall, I do not know why it was a day wherein I needed to notice "10%," but I wanted to make sure I took note on this thirty-third day in Fort Lauderdale.

Day Thirty-Four: 7/29/2014

...

In typical fashion, as I have looked into buying something new in Fort Lauderdale, I was met with an inexplicable discount. Over the past few days I have been looking at paddle boards for a way to stay healthy as I live down here. The board I found that I wanted, turned out to be more expensive than I wished to spend. When I awoke this morning, I pulled out my phone to check my email. On the main screen was the webpage that I was on the previous evening. The page refreshed when I unlocked my phone. That is when I saw that the board I wanted went on sale that day for season closeout, putting it in the range I wanted to spend. At this point, I smiled. I knew God was looking out for me. I went ahead and checked my emails. I had seven.

After my daughter and I got ready, we went to spend the afternoon on the beach. We snorkeled for a while. There were so many fish in the sea today. Schools of fish surrounded us after I showed her how I was attracting the fish to me. From the days prior, I understood that the fish were responding in

The First 42

kind to my spirit – similar to Biblical accounts of Jesus drawing fish near. It was unexplainable to anyone around. All I had to do was enter into the water and the fish would chase after me. They did not chase after anyone else around. When we were snorkeling, I could see that the fish were swimming from great distances to be near me. When I showed Georgia, she was fascinated at how they swam to me and followed me where ever I went. They never left my presence while I was in the water. Just to make sure I was not losing my mind, I would enter back into the water where no fish were present and watch the fish in the distance with my goggles. Inexplicably, they swam to my presence every time. The experience allowed for a great opportunity to share the Biblical stories with my daughter once we returned from the beach.

When my daughter and I went to dinner, we stopped by two different art galleries and found a painting called "The Garden" by an artist named Paul. It spoke so much to me that I knew I would buy it if the pricing worked out. I asked the artist to hold it for me, and that I would return to buy it after I took my daughter back home over the coming days.

Walking back from dinner, a large man sitting on bench started speaking to me as my daughter and I walked past him. He asked if I could spare a dollar, which I showed him how I did not have any cash on me. He then asked if I could help him with food and began talking about how "God would bless me." This was distinctly different than "God bless you." He had strange eyes... he appeared blind, yet he saw me. I offered to pick him up Subway for him, which was across the street.

Kingdom

My daughter was with me so she got to witness this series of events. We picked him up dinner and took it back to him. After we headed back home, I told Georgia about how I felt led to use 10% of all of my earnings to help others – without a second thought. This was the understanding I had gained from events from the day prior. We discussed if the man was an angel, or if it was possibly a test by God for me. In that moment, I told my daughter that I wanted God to know how I wanted to use the money he had graced me with in a giving way. With that, we walked to the ATM and withdrew $100 (10% of my recent purchases I have made for my apartment). I told Georgia that we should pray for guidance so we did.

    I asked God that if it was intended for me to provide him the money, for the man to still be on the bench. I asked God to see my heart. Immediately as I said that, a bright bolt of lightning lit up the sky just behind where the man was sitting (a few blocks away) and a loud roll of thunder occurred. I discussed with Georgia the significance of the thunder as God's voice and how it could have been the angel returning to heaven. I then went on to describe to her how God speaks, and I closed with something along the lines of, "and God sees my heart and knows that I heard His voice in the thunder. If nothing else, He knows I am trying to listen for His commands." Just then, the thunder rang out again, but rolled along for some time. These were the only bellowings of thunder during our whole outing. I told Georgia that it was the second sign – the confirmation that our effort was just. When we made it within sight of the bench, the man was no longer there, and two others were in his place. We never walked back over, but I knew that God saw my effort.

Day Thirty-Five: 7/30/2014

...

Today I flew my daughter back to Atlanta to be with her mother and then took a return flight back to Fort Lauderdale. When I arrived home, I had a great conversation with my cousin, who had been receiving more messages from God. This time, the subject matter revolved around Wormwood. We discussed the possibility that we were truly in the End of Days as all of the messages were leading us to suspect. It is not a concept we accepted initially. It took nearly three years of divine communication, with the emphasis on the most recent. As we determined it could very well be nearing the End of Days, Bryan led me to read Joshua and Amos. Each book follows an important book in the Bible, and he was led to read these by an angel. Bryan expressed how our roles in "becoming leaders" were the part of the journey we were on. He then went on to tell me his "plate" added to his spiritual weight bar was having to learn how to find quiet time for meditation after being newly married. Near the end of the conversation we tied the seals of Revelation with the numbers five and seven, which ended up bringing us back to where we are standing today. Though I will not go into much detail in this entry regarding this topic, the recent experiences are captured in the journal

Kingdom

entries in Books IV – VII will support the content of this particular conversation.

Day Thirty-Six: 7/31/2014

...

Tonight after walking back from a coffee shop, I met a man named Ivan. He approached me and asked for a cigarette. I told him I did not smoke and began to carry on my way when he began apologizing for his actions and proceeded to talk about his day. The man was in a dark place, one he knew he was in. But his awareness could not stop him from drinking, and for this he kept apologizing to me. Whatever the reason we crossed paths, I knew he needed someone to listen – so that is what I did. I listened to him talk for about forty-five minutes there on the sidewalk. I learned how his dad was a preacher and that his daughter's name was Ivy. As he told me that his daughter was about to come into town to visit him for a week, he wept uncontrollably at the shame he felt for his given state. He told me how he had not been drunk in six months until tonight. He was extremely apologetic but thankful for the forgiveness I offered. I learned that he was a musician and we talked about God. He warned me about the wars upcoming – the wars that were a sign of the End. Eventually he closed out our conversation with a quote, "Let God be true and every man be a liar." With that, we parted ways for the evening.

Day Thirty-Seven: 8/1/2014

...

This morning I awoke to seven emails just after praying about the lack of a woman in my life. I got up and began my day. After I got ready, I headed to my doctor's appointment about my hair. I had been concerned about losing it prematurely and wanted to explore options (if any). However, I suddenly began to feel like I had made a bad decision in scheduling a consultation. Just as quickly as that thought entered into my head, I heard a vibration on my phone as I was getting ready to walk out the door. I had an alert that I had just received seven emails. If nothing else, I knew the consultation was just.

Later in the day, the security guard at my building became curious about where my daughter was. I explained I had to fly her back to her mother. He seemed saddened for me. He asked about my marriage, which I then had to explain we were divorced. That is when he told me that I needed to find another girl and not to let myself get down on my past marriage. He then told me to go to the "Living Room" to meet a very nice girl that I could date. This was interesting as it was another answer to my prayers the past two days regarding my celibacy and desire for love. I know meeting a girl at the Living Room does not constitute God lifting the seal on me (by no stretch of the imagination). But, what it does answer is that God is looking out for my heart, helping guide me to where I may eventually meet someone I will date.

I also encountered a lady in the elevator of my building today who looked saddened. I asked her how her day was, and she broke down and told me that it was pretty bad. She then told me about how she had lost a lot of money at Isle Casino and pointed to the name on a bag she was holding. I tried to offer words of advice – mostly in the way of light humor about how that is the purpose of the casinos…that they will always take your money. It was more of a conversation with myself about my gambling seal being just, but I used the opportunity to speak to her for both of us.

Day Thirty-Eight: 8/2/2014

...

Today I decided to take action on the words I was told yesterday on going to the "Living Room." Before I planned to go, I decided to go have dinner. I was not quite sure where I was going, but I felt compelled to drive. I went down the elevator, got into my Jeep, and began to head out of the parking garage. As I reached the exit to turn out, the security guard who told me about the Living Room the day prior came out to speak with me. I told him I was going to go tonight, but his facial expressions reacted negatively to my decision. He mumbled something about it not always being the right time to go and then went back inside the security office. I was a little confused by it all since yesterday he was exuberant about it.

I decided to drive across the street over to a restaurant I frequent regularly. It was near an art gallery where I have been eyeing a particular painting for my apartment. I went in to eat and was welcomed by staff I had not seen since the first few days I arrived there. Everyone continued to walk up and talk with me even though the place was more crowded than I had ever seen it. The reception was surprising, but warming. I had dinner and walked over to the local art gallery owned by an artist named Paul. The painting I have been eyeing is called "The Garden" and is an abstract impressionist painting of so many spiritual symbols in one. Mostly, the silhouette of a girl is first noticed, but then the colors of creation, angelic wings, a caterpillar turning into a butterfly, a snake, temptation, lust, and the waters of creation are all shouting out at the viewer. To some, they may not even be able to see the woman's torso. But to me, it speaks wonders.

When I walked in, Paul was excited to see me. He asked about my daughter (who was with me the first time I saw the painting) and showed me all of the new stuff he was painting. He was proud to tell me about it. We discussed the painting and determined a price, and I told him I would come back with cash for him the next day he was open (since he was about to close). He originally had stated he did not plan to open the store until Tuesday, but after our conversation, he told me to return Sunday at 7:00. I knew immediately that was a divine sign that God had blessed the purchase as right for me and right for Paul. I left, content with the decision. I planned to get back home and pray about whether it was God's will for me to go out to the Living Room tonight. And, while that may seem like a decision that I could make quite easily, everything in Fort Lauderdale has been ongoing dialogue with my Creator. I want to make sure that I am following all that he intends for me to do, and not making any missteps along the way.

When I got back to my place, I called Bryan. We had a great conversation about everything from the days prior. The conversation was fantastic, and eventually he said things that (unbeknownst to him and out of context for the conversation) helped me realize that I would never be able to "find" the girl God intends for me, but rather that he would place her into my life. After our conversation ended around 9:30 p.m., I prayed to God and let Him know that I understood that I understood my role was not to "find" but rather to "wait" for Him to place her into my life. I let Him know that instead of going out and trying to meet others tonight, I would just go get a coffee and take time to meditate and pray on the beach.

I left my apartment, walked downstairs and through the front door. I did not even iron my shirt before I walked downstairs (since I was just running next door for a coffee and heading to the beach after). To my surprise, I was met by the same security guard that I spoke to in the garage earlier. My building has somewhere around six or seven security staff working at any given time, so it is rare to see the same one frequently, or, much less in a different location. But, he had apparently changed shifts to the front desk instead of the garage. As our paths crossed, he stopped me, and told me not to go to the Living Room. He asked if I had ever been to Blue Martini (which I had) and then proceeded to tell me not to go there either. He did not know that I was planning to just go get coffee. He talked to me for a while about where I would meet people in the town. I was careful not to lead him to any answers, or ask him any questions. Instead, my goal was just to see what was on his mind and, when he ran out of things to say, go about my way. Anything else and I would inject my intention and color any words placed through him by God.

As the conversation came to a close, I asked what time Dunkin Donuts closed since it was getting late. He looked at me strangely and then said, "No. No, no, no. You cannot go to Dunkin Donuts. You must go somewhere. I know I told you Living Room and Blue Martini, but not tonight. Tonight you need to walk across the street to just see people around this area." He told me to stick my head in Dive Bar and then go to Chase (a place I knew nothing about). Since I no longer drink beer or liquor, all of the locations he suggested seemed like poor choices for me. I have left it open that I may have a glass of wine, but that is still in a "to be determined" stage for me. Other than the potential for wine (though it has been nearly a year since my last glass), I no longer ingest anything that could negatively affect my mind/body/spirit balance. If I cannot regulate the harmony my body has, then they have no place in my life, and that is why I made those seals before God.

Regardless, we eventually parted ways. He wanted to make sure that, at a minimum, I would "stick my head in each bar for just a minute." I walked out of the building dejected. Right after I had come to terms with not seeking out the girl for me, I have this conversation which I cannot deny is part of an ongoing spiritual dialogue. I knew there must be purpose, so I decided to abide by his words. All along the walk to the first bar, I prayed aloud reaffirming to God that my actions are only because I think I am following His directives. I walked into Dive Bar and was met with the stench of cigarette smoke. I was repulsed by it, but decided to walk around and see why I was there. There was a man on stage talking to the crowd about all of the prizes they were giving away for the evening. I listened as he wrapped up his announcement by saying, "So make sure you get your raffle ticket, this is your last chance." Just then, a man walked in front of me and handed me a raffle ticket. At this point I saw the lesson unfolding.

    I waited for about fifteen minutes while everyone took a break from the festivities while music played through the speakers. Eventually the man walked back on stage. He was funny, but it was clear that he ascribed to the "everyone must get drunk all of the time" philosophy. He rattled through the first few gift cards and then got to the cash prize. At this point it was only for $20, but I knew from the start that I was about to win whatever the cash prize was. It was going to be a vehicle for me and a confirmation from God on his desire for me tonight. When the announcer tried to get the audience's attention for the cash giveaway, most people seemed disinterested. In fact, they were so disinterested that he made some pretty distasteful remarks about how the bums and beggars on Broward Boulevard would love to have this $20 for cigarettes. He continued making distasteful jokes about the poor and what $20 meant to them while everyone there did not care about the $20. With every word I knew that my number was about to be called. And it was. I walked up, accepted the $20 and left the bar.

So, to this point, I walked across the street and into the first bar where I was basically given $20 to start the night. Earlier, when I was talking to the security guard, he told me Chase usually had a $10 cover. Since I never have cash on me, I did not plan to go, even though that was the directive I heard. Now I had been provided the vehicle to go there. I walked the long walk to Chase and entered. It was a great looking establishment – very modern and upscale. I realized as I was standing inside that I was not charged a cover for entering. And the more I thought about it, the stranger it was. When I tried to give my ID to the security guards out front, they just waved me in like they knew me. So, I decided that there must be something for me to see. I sat at the bar, ordered a water and a glass of wine and waited. I slow-sipped my glass of wine. After about forty-five minutes I was only half way through my glass of wine but was bored and unsure what the purpose was. I was more closely monitoring how slowly I drank the wine than I was paying attention to the other ten people in there. So, I decided to leave. I paid cash and left.

I walked back to my apartment, the beach, and went outside to pray. Here I asked God for clarity on the events, though the only answer I seemed to find was that God wanted me to experience everything he has prepared with Love for me. It is a paradise prepared for me to be happy and live for generations to come. But, during my prayer, I wanted God to know that my desire is not to just be "good enough" but to

Kingdom

continue to be "trained in the way of a king" even if I may never succeed at one day rising to that occasion. I want to have given my all to Him, and that I feared my missteps more than I trusted my decisions to enjoy His blessings. It is an incredibly hard place to find myself, and one that I no doubt have to learn to accept. I suppose it is part of "learning to be" which is the only defined purpose I have been told directly, though more will one day unfold.

Day Thirty-Nine: 8/3/2014

...

Today I spent a lot of time praying while in the shower. When I stepped in the shower, the skies were overcast (as can be part of a typical day in South Florida). After I washed, I sat along a bench in the shower and opened up to God. I prayed for forgiveness, strength, and guidance. I further clarified my prayer on the beach from the night prior. I acknowledged that I felt like I was no longer "ruled by" anything on Earth. I know my finances are in His hands and have felt confident that He will provide for me in whatever way He intends. Libations no longer control my desire to have a good time, though it is not like they controlled me in a way that anyone on Earth would be able to see. Instead, at one time in my life a few years ago, it just seemed that if I was watching a sporting event, then I should have a beer. It is kind of like having a cup of coffee for a morning routine. If I went out with friends to a restaurant – even if I had no intentions of drinking – I would still accept a drink that was purchased for me. But now, I feel content having conquered the ability to say no. But, even more importantly, as I told God, the seals of abstinence from liquor and beer were created by me because I recognized they negatively affected my ability to maintain my mind-body-soul balance and ability to commune in the heavens. And – anything that has a negative impact on that aspect of my life has no reason being in my life in the first place. This is why I believe the Bible says a drunkard will never enter the kingdom of heaven. While the literal interpretation is part of the meaning, we are all tasked with seeing Heaven and Earth as one and walking on Earth as if we are walking in the Heavens. Any intoxicating substance causes a person to lose harmony with the world around him. On a more granular level, liquor and beer affect the ability to commune in the heavens during meditation and cause the body several days of rebalancing, which is something I am not willing to risk in my walk with God.

So as I prayed, I mentioned the seals on liquor and beer. I continued by speaking about the seal on gambling and how I did not wish to subject His provisions to me to chance, as I thought that would be viewed as disrespectful to His generosity. I then went on to pray about my most difficult seal – the seal of abstinence from sexual pleasure. This is the seal that I have asked my Lord to break for me only when He deems appropriate. And, at least in my thoughts, I imagine that seal will not be broken until I am married to the one of His choosing. There is also the possibility that this seal will never be broken by my God and the possibility that I will remain single the rest of my days on Earth. But while the other seals seem almost like a passing thought, everyday I awaken and realize how strongly my body desires to be with another. The days grow long when my body reminds me it has been ignored. I usually just try to find something else to do in its place, but I have held strong to my seal and I will do so for all of my days.

I have to think this is why the statue of David depicts him with an extremely small part of the male anatomy. Art historians will tell you that he was depicted in a way that was seen as "ideal" in the day. But, I would further that by adding that the definition of "ideal" is to be understood as "of spiritual purity." The statue is intended to be part of a series of statues of prophets from the Bible. And when one is to think of prophets, one must think about their states of mind. The only way to achieve a closer relationship with God is to be able to overcome anything that rules the body. Mostly this means what the body desires – drink, food, wealth, fame, but also sexual pleasure. While God created us to procreate on this Earth, the understanding has been abused, and mankind has fallen slave to its desire as its master. Nearly everyone fights this battle, but few choose to rise above it. In truth, it is the hardest thing for me to rise above. It is the one aspect of my life that I can say I have been not just a slave to, but an overjoyed, exuberant servant to all of my life (though, as contradictory as it sounds, with only a few times of acting upon the desire). And while it is true that mankind is intended to experience the joys of this aspect of our lives, we are not to be ruled by it – meaning we should be able to abstain from all pleasures and let the heart

The First 42

learn to seek love and not lust in another. But this is too great of a task for many. In truth, I once felt sorrow for those who chose this path. And while abstinence is one accomplishment (and one that is easy to me), abstinence from all sexual pleasure is quite a task to overcome. This is where my prayer led, and is much of what I spoke about to God.

After I got out of the shower, the sky erupted into a violent storm. It was reminiscent of the storm that heralded the water spout or tornado after I moved in. The winds were voracious. I could not even open my patio door. And while most would think this was just a passing storm, I knew that God was getting my attention to let me know He was there. He was using the storm to pass as a way to let me know of his presence around me. And with that I felt content.

Day Forty: 8/4/2014

...

Today I walked outside for my evening prayer time on the beach. Most of the day it rained. Even when it appeared sunny, a storm would roll quickly through. Before lunch, I went out to paddle board. The sun was out, and it looked like the storm had passed. I was not on my paddle board long before the storm came through, and I had to return to shore. For a moment I was nervous I would not make it back for the storm appeared out of nowhere, and the winds and rain started whirling the ocean around. After I made it to shore, I went back to my apartment where I showered and dressed before heading to lunch. I checked a few emails and waited for the sun to come back out. I walked down the road, stopped and had lunch, and then went to pick up groceries. As soon as I entered the store, the rain started pouring down. And while I took my time in the store, there would be no escaping the fact that I would have to walk back in the rain. I eventually returned to my place where I might as well have taken a shower in my clothes. I was that wet.

Now I say all of that to help set the stage. Today was a day geared for me to work and reflect on a great lesson which I did not know had occurred. Throughout the day I received phone calls from various people I had met here. The first call was from the clinic that I visited this previous Friday regarding hair treatments. They were doing a routine follow-up to see when I wanted to schedule my appointment. In truth I had not decided if I even wanted the procedure, so I told them that I would let them know in the coming weeks.

I later received a call from the attorney who wanted to talk to me about helping me resolve my wrongful collections case with American Express. We chatted for a bit, and he asked me to send him some more information. The call ended, and I thought nothing more of it.

Eventually, it came the time of the evening when I walk out to the beach for my nightly prayer. The storms had subsided, though I knew the beach would be wet. So I took a mat to set upon on the sand. When I made it to the gate that led to the beach, I noticed that none of the key-fob locks were working on the door to exit the complex. Not one of the doors I

The First 42

could use to regain entry into the building was working. Baffled, I returned inside and walked down to the front desk to let them know of the issue.

When I reached the front desk, the security guard let me know they were working on the issue but then went on to tell me about how lightning had struck the building last night. I knew that I heard a giant crack of lightning last night while I was working which caused the internet to go out, but I did not know that it struck our building. This was the moment that I was about to see how all of the events of the day were part of a larger lesson for me to understand.

The previous evening I was looking at a couple of pieces of furniture to order for my place. I placed all of the items in my shopping cart and saw that the total was "$666.84." Immediately, the six-six-six part of the number startled me. I usually have messages in numbers coming in confirmations and not in alerts of wrong decisions. So, I puzzled over the possibility of the meaning. Truthfully, the only number that would have given me pause was this number. Anything else would not have caused me to have a second thought on placing my order.

So, as I puzzled, I stopped to think about the possibilities of what other furniture may be good to have instead of this particular chair. I almost laughed to myself as I thought about a feng shui tantra chair I had remembered hearing about a year or so before. Perhaps it can be seen that this was not a thought orchestrated by me, but by the same energy as the $666 total from my previous order – not for the chair itself, but the lesson that was to be explored. Unhindered, I thought to myself that maybe I should take a look at it to see if it would fit. No one would know what its purpose would be since it is has a modern, artistic appearance.

I sought out the website and saw the chair. They had a sales/promo video, so I began to watch it. To my surprise, the video showed a couple demonstrating the use of the chair. It was artistic, tasteful, and truthfully meant to illustrate how the chair could improve intimacy. I did not think of the images as "porn," though I did question myself how it would be viewed in God's eyes according to my vow to him I made over a year ago to rid my life of anything pornographic. I hate that I even have to type that, but everything I say is in an effort to present the most unfiltered understanding of the journey I have taken. As that thought came to my mind, I stopped the video and decided to just check out the prices. I had seen enough to understand how it would be beneficial to a couple. However, I think the novelty of the idea was weighing in my mind more than the reality of whether I should get it. I noted the price, and then decided to complete my writing for the day.

I must have worked on my writing for about an hour and a half. Almost immediately when I started writing, I heard a giant crack of lightning strike outside. I thought to myself, "It would be cool if I could find the place on the beach tomorrow it might have struck and find the sand glass creation the lightning would have made." I did not think much else until I finished my writing and went to look at the furniture items in my shopping cart one more time to ponder more whether they

The First 42

were the right items for that particular space in my apartment. It was then I noticed the internet was out.

So all of those details lead me to my prayer today. While I was praying to God, I rambled on about some of the challenges I was seeking to understand. One of the challenges was regarding hair restoration. In the end, I came to understand through prayer that anything that leaves a scar upon the body is to be seen as a learning experience or an accident. Anything that would leave an intentional scar would be basically creating an intentional, brazen learning experience for me on the lesson that he wanted me to understand. I came to realize in those moments that the events of the last couple of days have all been part of a greater learning experience about my understanding of mortality and his intention for me. My frustration and desires about finding whomever I am meant to be with have been exacerbated by my fear of losing my hair and therefore being found unattractive. This fear, as I came to realize during my prayer, is not actually the fear of not being seen as youthful and attractive, but rather it is the fear of losing part of my earthly identity. I have always found identity in my hair. If nothing else was remembered throughout my life, my hairstyles have always caused others to take notice and compliment – though never out of boldness or brashness. They were just something always complimented. So it should be seen that my hair has always been my strength.

And while I fully believe that we are each tasked with keeping our bodies as beautiful as possible, as I talked to God, I began to realize that subjecting myself to chemicals that change the roles of the endocrine system in my body and/or undergo a procedure that would make me appear younger was only my ego holding on to one of the remaining parts of my mortal life. For if a person were only to identify me by my hair, he would not truly see me or see my essence. I can maintain my body, my physique, my form and take care of the vessel that I am. In doing so, I am helping maintain God's creation in the way He intended it to be. There is a natural order to things. For me to choose to interject my ego's desires by augmenting the vessel I have been given for this journey could be seen as saying, "God, this is not good enough. I want to fix that which you created." And, I cannot find any reason why that would ever be an appropriate answer. Can I work out? Yes. Can I maintain a physique that is as ideal as possible? Yes. Can I ingest only that which helps my body, mind, and spirit maintain its natural chemical and harmonic balance? Yes. Those three things should be seen as how we are to maintain God's beautiful. That is what we should see in another's physical form. Makeup and accenting features are fine. They help enhance that which has been given. But physically altering His intention in a vessel for me is something I cannot allow myself to do. I would be making a decision that would physically place a scar upon my body so that I may entertain ego's desires.

As all of this realization hit me, I then saw how petty my thoughts were in all of my talk about finding a girl for me. In truth, all happens in His time. But this time, I wanted it to be on my time so that I could beat the clock of losing any remain-

/ The First 42

ing youth in the eyes of another's ego. So as I pondered the lesson, I prayed for forgiveness for my petty prayers in the preceding days. I knew that it had all been a great lesson that He knew I would see. He knew I would hesitate upon making a quick decision on hair restoration, which would cause me to reflect upon it all and understand the lesson. Every night I pray for about an hour in fluid dialogue with my Father. It is through this dialogue that clarity is gained on all that He wants me to see and where greater questions are raised.

If I had correctly rationalized that God wants me to enjoy all that He has provided for me in this Promised Land, then it would stand to reason that He would want me to be happy where I may have doubts. He led me to the specific doctor, the specific clinic, and continued to give me signs that I was following His intentions along the way. I just could not come to understand during my prayer why God would walk me into a situation where my gut instinct continued to give me pause whether it was the right action. As I thought about it, the idea that God wanted me to have hair restoration became more and more absurd. I cannot help but think that if I had the procedure believing that it was His intention for me to be happy since He has provided me the means to help this come to be while also providing the place and doctor for the procedure, that it would still be a blessed action. However, the action would still come with a scar...a scar that would serve as something to reflect upon my decision the rest of my mortal days. The surgeon was undoubtedly the one that God knew would be perfect for me, but the lesson was even more important –

whether I understood it before or after I made a decision on the surgery.

As I prayed I came to the most basic of rhetorical questions: If God truly wants me to have the confidence that a full head of hair would provide for the remainder of my days on Earth, why overcomplicate it with money, doctors, scarring, healing, and time? The short answer is, "He would not unless there was a lesson to one day be learned." Perhaps the greater lesson could be learned before – which is that whomever and whenever God intends for me to cross paths with my other half, she will see me for me. She will see the light. She will not see receding hairlines or someone trying to hold on to youth. She will see me in form, physique, and the care I take to maintain the vessel I have been given. Every one of us is beautiful in this specific, but unique way. Many just do not realize it.

As these revelations struck a chord with my soul, I knew that if God desired, He could just touch my head and I would have hair as long as I live. But the outcome should be as He intends, and I have to trust in His decision – not in one controlled by my ego. As these thoughts raced in my mind and through the words of my dialogue, the lightning strike suddenly came into view. During my entire time in Fort Lauderdale over these forty days, something special has occurred each and every day. There is no possibility in my mind that my actions of viewing the tantra-chair video and the lightning strike on my very building only moments apart were anything other than divine conversation. In the rush of the seconds this thought began to cross my mind, I knew that anything that

The First 42

causes the body to react in desire is considered pornography. It is not a word for sexually-explicit videos. Instead, it is a concept to describe anything that causes the mind and/or body to become a slave to a thought. I realized anything that pulled me in as a slave to a service (other than the service to my Father) is something that is not needed in my life. The lightning strike was a warning strike to grab my attention in that moment – to see the larger lesson I was placed to learn.

My mind continued racing, and I realized that even dating sites (an idea that I have been toying with recently as well) were again just ego's attempt at trying to bend God's rules to fit my ego's timeline. The constant barrage of emails they send you about "who viewed your profile" and "who your new match is" are ways to make a person become a slave to its service. The service is not bad or wrong. I just know now that it is not meant for me with where I am on my journey right now. As further evidence to this whole chain of thought, when I sat down to write this entry after my prayer, I had an email from a dating site letting me know about a new match for me. I did not even have a profile setup. I had only created an account a few days prior, but it did not stop the emails from occurring. Their emails are vague enough that a person must visit the site if curiosity gets the best of him. For a moment, I thought, what if God divinely placed an answer before me? What is she is "the one" that was shown to me yesterday in my travels to the heavens? I clicked on the link only to have it come up as a solid white webpage. I clicked the link again making sure that the web browser loaded the site correctly. It again, showed up white. I tried just going to the site directly, but it showed up as a white web page as well. My employment has been in the field of technology all of my life, so rest assured I did everything I could do to attempt to resolve the issue – but no resolution was to be found.

Obviously there was symbolism in the white webpage rather than a "page not found" occurrence. But most importantly, it reminded me that I was again, being a slave to the service. I quit trying to check the site and decided to write this entry. And after I finished, I went back and deleted my account. Perhaps it was "her." Perhaps not. Perhaps the greater lesson was to be learned first, before I was to ever take action. Perhaps it was just one final test of my faith to help me see all that He has provided for me and to serve as an answer to my prayer this evening. When the time is right in my life (this one or the next), the Not-So-Cinderella story will come to be. This I know. For as I was told my purpose in Fort Lauderdale was "to be." I have fought through the three battles, and placed three seals upon my soul. For I now know that I am learning to be, so that He may.

Day Forty-One: 8/5/2014

...

Though at first I thought these entries would end after the first forty days, today I was led to ensure it lasted through Day 42. Sitting on the beach around sunset, I felt the spirit fill me. A couple walked past me. The lady carried a pink bag on her shoulder. I closed my eyes as they approached from the distance. My eyes were closed when they reached me, but the two souls illuminated my vision when they walked by. It was after this moment my Father shared with me that these entries should capture two more days. They are to include this couple, the light they illuminated, and the pink bag upon her shoulder and whatever tomorrow may bring. I do not know why these entries should continue through Day 42, but I will oblige as I always do.

Day Forty-Two: 8/6/2014

...

Today I talked to Bryan about the seven visions I had recently on Day 40. In the conversation, I realized the progression – how Satan appeared in #6. As Bryan and I spoke, the phone changed into a strange underwater sound as Bryan was about to interpret the last sentence of the seventh vision. Another stamp – a seven and seven moment. Feeling resolved in understanding God's message in the visions and Bryan's interpretation, I went outside to the beach. The elevator was on floor 7 when I pressed the button. It came down to take me to my destination. After praying for about an hour on the beach, I came back in. The elevators were on floors 8 and 16 (a number that is important for many reasons, and also sums to seven), letting me know the next level was breached for me. The elevator on floor 8 came down to take me up. It should also be noted that I have been reading the Divine

Kingdom

Comedy by Dante and that I stopped on the section in Dante's inferno entitled the 8th ring of Hell. I will start that section tomorrow.

Final Entry as Instructed by God
Day Forty-Two: 8/4/2014

...

There is a pier located where the road meets the sand on Commercial Drive – the northernmost road that runs horizontally (West to East) along Fort Lauderdale's edge. This is the beginning of the Galt Mile – a mile long stretch of beach that runs south of the pier. Along that strip of ocean you will find me in the Place of the Sun in an apartment unit number that sums to seven This is where God has led me to begin this part of the journey, and the land that God has prepared for those who hear His call. I will be waiting in the sand when all that has been said comes to pass. It is when the End begins and the journey becomes manifest for those to see.

On top of Sand Mountain, my Father will be waiting for those who have been chosen to come to Him in that part of the land. It is located north of Gadsden, Alabama and South of Chattanooga, Tennessee. It can be reached along the interstate and then climbing a road that winds by a great valley. The mountaintop springs forth lakes of fresh water from beneath the Earth. The mountaintop is a sand that is the highest quality in all of the area. This is a blessed land for those days.

Mama and Daddy

When this journey began I did not quite understand all that my Father was telling me. It was not for lack of trying, but rather just how my soul was developing. Think of the example of a baby once again. Once a baby is brought forth into the world, it is consumed by all of the external stimulation overloading his senses. Eventually, as the baby grows and understands how to navigate the sea of external stimulation, the discernment of the spoken language becomes the next task at hand. In the beginning, one of the greatest accomplishments during a baby's growth is when the words "mama" and "daddy" are first uttered.

The moment a child manages to articulate this most primitive thought, parents erupt in happiness and pride. The happiness in the parents is reflected in the child. The happiness the parents express is a form of emotional support for this important stage of growth. It is a form of confirmation to the child that progress is being made in communication. In the mind of the child, the sensations of hunger, warmth, and Love are already defined. The ability to express any of these most basic ideas are still bound by the formation of words to the mother and father., who first need some form of labeling for the child to find comfort in attempted communication.

Kingdom

Prior to ever speaking a word, a baby can understand how the melodies of the different sounds rolling off of his parent's lips carry different meanings. Inflections, articulation, and the delivery are also understood in the most basic terms as well. The primary barrier to communication is in the divide between the ideas racing through the mind and how to articulate this swirl of sensations to the others that already exist in this foreign world. The child is the guest – the visitor. The parents are the residents in this new sphere. It is a difficult idea to think about as an adult because communication is one of the most fundamental aspects of survival and existence. Words are the basis to the fluidity of thought, though thought is the actual basis of existence.

So think of the divide a child must learn to conquer. It is difficult for even the wisest adult to think without words and to feel without definition. But this very idea is how first words in the heavens must be understood and illustrated. In Gravity Calling, I began discussing the concept of the origin of language. It was an important concept to explain in order to describe the spiritual playground my soul found itself standing upon as the journey began. And while each aspect of the explanations offered in Gravity Calling should be viewed as the foundational pillars to the spiritual language, as this book is written, it is best to refine the explanation of spiritual words and language through the form of octaves to a musician.

In music there is a concept of an "octave." It is a note exactly eight steps above another. In the simplest terms as the octaves move upward, it is the same sound played, but with

Mama and Daddy

twice the information. To the ear, it is heard as a higher pitch than the previous one. But in terms of math, it should best be understood as a sound that has exactly twice the amount of vibration. On a piano keyboard, the notes are labeled by the letters A through G. At every eighth letter, the sequence starts to repeat. So, it can be seen that for every eighth note, it would be called by the same letter. Without any musical knowledge prior, it should be easily understood that the notes of the same letter sound higher every eighth division.

In popular culture, some may have previously heard the phrase "higher vibratory levels" used in conversation. It is typically brought up in esoteric discourses between spiritualists and philosophers regarding angels and "higher planes of existence." But bear with me for just a minute for I will not lose you through this definition – even though in academic terms, there really is no difference in the way I am illustrating it. But perhaps the explanation through the experiences I have witnessed will offer a much easier road to comprehension to a generally difficult-to-understand subject. For while I found myself standing in the sand receiving a crown, I learned that there was so much more depth in understanding in all that I had observed. It was not as if everything prior was misinterpreted or had new meaning. It was that everything I thought leading up to this point was just a fraction of the understanding to where His Voice was leading.

And though there is much more to be learned in the way my Father's words took form and were intended to be interpreted, for now let us allow the story to resume from the point

Kingdom

of the crowning. At the end of Book II, a child was receiving his crown. It was a coming of age ceremony on Earth as it was in the heavens, filled with a spiritual chorus of unmistakable sound. The level of understanding was not wrong at first sight. But just as a child has a reset button pushed and memories become the foundation of the next part of his journey through earthly life, this was a moment the spiritual reset button had been pushed that revealed a hindsight of understanding. Though every word and definition my Father spoke to me led me through my Genesis, Exodus, Leviticus, and Numbers and to this place – I found myself standing in the sand. This was the moment that the meaning of it all began to be revealed.

The hindsight to everything I had experienced during the first two years of the journey slowly began to reveal how all I thought remained ahead was just a portion of the view. I knew it was still bound by Love, though at this point my journals became a myriad of clues. I had to return to all that I had written to understand where it was leading. But even in the newfound understanding of the clues left behind, I still did not have definition in the ending. The Promised Land still existed before me – that was unmistakably true. But the mirage of how it first appeared was giving way to something new.

During the time that transpired from the ending of Gravity Calling to my exodus from Tennessee, my Father spent this time continuing to help me learn to hear and to speak. The conversations we shared transitioned from the most basic prayers and expressions to fluid and intimate conversations. During these days my spiritual words grew exponentially in

Mama and Daddy

capacity of expression. It was also a time I learned to hear my Father's words with greater definition. At the end of Gravity Calling, the conversations had become more fluid, but it would take months of time passing to gain the hindsight needed to better understand the depths of the words in His messages. From His first words until now, there had to be a dramatic revelation in understanding. It was a revelation that has unveiled layer after layer of His intention. And perhaps "intention" is the greatest concept to understand in spiritual conversation, because it removes the mind from egoic interpretation. In this, the truest meaning of all can be found for spiritual intention reveals the story He was telling all along. It is the story my mind found too irrational at the time of interpretation, for I was just a rebirthed baby experiencing every new spiritual sensation.

Wrapping Presents

The divide had been bridged, an arc had ignited in light. Over the duration of Book I and Book II, my Father led me on a journey to this place where I found myself standing in the sand. It was a divine marker on His timeline akin to Deuteronomy. As my Father and I had journeyed forth to the Promised Land, I ran blissfully and blindly along while holding His hand. At some point along the way, I realized He had let go as He began to let me run on my own. He was still there to catch me if I were to stumble and fall, but He was helping me learn to grow. The place I was led was a place where the Promised Land fell into sight. Initially I ran blindly in Love, thinking it was always about Lindsey. For that is the mirage He intended for me to see. It was how I had to see it for my mind to have any rationale in those moments. The passion inside of me was unfolding at a rate blinding to the senses. The experience of this newfound Love racing inside of me was everything I could handle, but stretched me to the brink of insanity.

It was a Love, even as I wrote about it in Book I, I understood to be not of an earthly origination – but one of a Spiritual foundation. My previous marriage to Stacey was every ounce of the embodiment to all that I could ever have known in earthly terms of Love. But this portion of the journey was different. The heartbreak left behind in the wake of our separation marred my senses from recalling the bliss I had once experienced with her. And in moving forward in the direction toward Lindsey, it was a time that the Lord spilled forth all that was embodied in the way He wanted me to see it. This was his presentation of a perfect Love – the way it should be on Earth, as it is in the heavens above. It was never about Lindsey, but about helping me find Love's true destination.

It was not that this aspect was missing in my marriage – and I want to be extremely clear about this point for many reasons, but most importantly to illustrate the special Love that will always be held in my heart for Stacey. For as my timeline progressed, there had to be a new interest placed into my life to help me see. It was not just the embodiment of song I found in Lindsey's soul, or even the words written to her beautiful melody. It was the hope, the potential, and the promise of what was to come. It was everything that remained unopened, a present wrapped up in white lace and blue, that God would deliver to me to be opened in front of everyone.

At the end of Gravity Calling, Lindsey was delivered a package that included the first book completed. It was a package that I had wrapped up for her with every bit of care I could put into it. I have always believed that presentation is one of the most important aspects to the completion of any project. I have applied this mentality throughout every task I have ever sought to complete. To spend time on the polish and presentation separates the exceptional from the meek – it is the

Wrapping Presents

soulful embodiment of Love performed through earthly expression. So, when it came time for Lindsey to receive the book, I was led to package it in a hand-crafted box wrapped up in blue tissue and white lace. The inside was filled with a handmade satin pillow top for the book to rest. It was honestly one of the most breathtaking packages I have ever seen – and would be the case even if it was not crafted by these hands. But the craziest thing about the package is that I can see it was never intended for Lindsey, but rather for me to understand the symbolism in how my Father led me to complete the task I had been given.

Perhaps this is one of the most amazing aspects of the journey for me to experience. For in every task that my Father has asked me to perform, there has always been a message greater than I could understand in the moment. It is a form of blind faith that hindsight will one day allow me to see all He intended. Even before the last three years of the journey began, if I had ever placed blind faith in following my Father's plan, I still sought reason in the immediate aftermath of completion. It was not that I did not believe His intention would one day be revealed. Rather, it was that my timeline required it to be revealed in a way that I could rationalize following His command. In this, it can be seen that blind faith is often followed conditionally versus unconditionally – and when blind faith is followed conditionally, it is not really blind faith. In truth, blind faith should stretch the boundaries of time and not be scrutinized over the ticking of the seconds passing by in hindsight. For what if the task that was given was to one day create something for one soul that has yet to breathe its first breath of life? And what if the task of feeling led to go somewhere caused a life to be saved that otherwise may have fallen victim to a tragedy without a subtle variable entered into the colossal amount of variables at play in every moment? Perhaps taking a left at a stop sign instead of a right caused one driver to hit his brakes, thus creating a chain of events leading to the divine intervention in one soul's life?

Through all of the examples given, it is easy to see that the fabric of life is threaded through every intentional and unintentional action taken. So it should be seen that the actions tasked by our Father are nothing short of a divine recipe for the betterment of all of the souls along the journey. Nothing should be questioned, though as a child learns to see, guidance is given to help build confidence in learning to trust unconditionally. The moments after delivering the wrapped up book to Lindsey, I found peace in knowing that everything was completed in the most intimate way possible. Having never even used a glue gun before, I became extremely familiar with the Love required in crafting something that at first seemed so simple in concept. The amount of time required to create a single folding box wrapped in blue tissue paper then subsequently covered in white lace is more time than any guy would ever be willing to admit. But the point of the effort is that it was done with every ounce of the soul involved.

And if every ounce of a soul completely humbled on the journey can be seen as the unfiltered doorway of the spirit flowing through, then it should be seen that the book delivered

Wrapping Presents

to Lindsey was not wrapped by hands observed in earthly definition, but rather the hands of my Father, wrapping the package of His words. The delivery of His words in book form was one that – at the time – I still did not quite understand the purpose. I understood it was His command to write, and His command to finish Gravity Calling, but I naively thought the purpose was only intended for the destination of Love that had fallen into view. I never expected it to be a story that would reveal all that these Books of Nine include.

If the story of Gravity Calling can be understood as a Love story in the making, the Books of Nine should be seen as the complete and unabridged version of His version of how a Love story should be told. In the beginning I was introduced to the potential for Love and the hope of Love in another through the interactions with Lindsey. It was a passion that was fueled by His Spirit, igniting an engine to write. And as Book I found its close and was wrapped by His hands with all of my soul, it should be understood that the package was intended to one day be placed under a Christmas tree and opened by me on the day of His command. It was a surprising twist of the story, because I never expected the book that was wrapped up would have carried any other intention than of the delivery of the words to Lindsey.

But the truth is that every effort taken in wrapping the package for Lindsey was truly His Hand wrapping presents for me to open on Christmas during the month of December. In the presents wrapped up in white lace and blue, the story He wanted me to see – and that I was so eager to receive – would

Kingdom

be revealed once He had prepared the eyes of my soul to see His truth. For inside of the package that Lindsey received was the potential for a Love Ever-After if she was willing to receive all that was being offered. But in spiritual terms, it was always about a Love greater, a Love that would not be revealed until my Father deemed that I was ready.

The Love Story was packaged in presents underneath a Christmas tree, foretelling His timing required before I would be allowed to see. The Christmas tree was set out months ahead of earthly timelines since it was spiritually risen shortly after I arrived in Florida. But the tree and the presents were just part of the story, for I was still lost in the honeymoon of wonder in the arrival in Fort Lauderdale. I saw that the package I thought I had wrapped for Lindsey placed under His tree opened a slew of questions I had no answers for. Was it that our souls would still eventually meet? Was it that it just took time for her to eventually see? Was it that there was something else He wrapped up in the presents, possibly just symbolizing the way the book was wrapped up for Lindsey? As a child has to wait in eager anticipation for the day that Christmas arrives so he can open his presents, I had to wait in bated anticipation for my first Christmas in Heaven to see what exactly the meaning in the presents of white lace and blue could carry - especially with no labels to add clarity to the situation.

This book, beginning with Book I, encompasses the days leading up to a grand day of celebration. I understood that His present was guiding me to the destination of Love. Through the eyes of a child, I naively thought I had already figured out what could be held within the present He had wrapped up and left under the tree. It would be a Christmas celebration to remember – my first in the Promised Land. And in that, the foreshadowing of the date's significance began to be unveiled. For Christmas is a day that we celebrate Christ's birth, though it is clearly understood that it is not the date of his earthly birth. The month of December holds a greater meaning in the Divine architecture of the heavens. Through my eyes, it would end up being the month filled with the most spiritual significance. And while I can say there was a Christmas tree risen early upon my arrival in Florida and a gift of lace and white blue placed under the tree, it may even be better understood as the entire month of December as wrapped up in a bouquet of presents from my Father, for the Christmas tree could be understood as representing God our Father, and the presents to be opened, the essence of His word and the story of Christ delivered to a Son who could now understand.

The Christmas Tree

Christmas is a special time. It is a time that involves family, friends, Loved ones, and some people that may be new. It is a time of warmth, great food, and celebration in the company of others. But most importantly, it is a day to celebrate Love. While some may say, "Wait, what about Jesus?" it is important to understand the birth of Christ is the grandest demonstration of Love that those on Earth have ever witnessed: the Love of a Father sending His one and only Son to the Earth, so whosoever believes in Him, would not perish but have everlasting life. There could not be a grander demonstration of Love than that.

The birth of Jesus has long been understood by theologians and historians to have occurred at a time much different than the day his birth is celebrated. Yet, as Christians, there is an adamant belief that December 25th is the day of His birth. An anonymous document discovered in North Africa around 243 CE offers three other dates that could hold truth in his day of birth. One date was September 11th, another March 28th, and the last November 18th. All of these dates were suggested by different bishops based on their own studies of historical records in the early centuries following Jesus's crucifixion. And while it is unimportant regarding which date was the day of

Kingdom

Jesus's actual birth, it is important to understand that there are many dates encompassed in a soul's journey into the light during its time on Earth. This will become more evident by the conclusion of this book. But for now it should be noted that December 25th holds divine significance, for many reasons to be unveiled.

It should also be noted that I can no longer view a physical date of birth as the only day to celebrate birth, for there are many points along the journey that blur the concepts of finite dates into relative points along a much different timeline than earthly eyes could see by sight alone. For as Jesus was born as a man upon the Earth, there would be a coming of age ceremony that occurred around the age of thirty, a birth of his soul in the Heavens, and the day He received His crown. It would take time to pass from his first birth before a prince became a King and the world come to know him as they do now. This does not take away the divine nature of God's Son, but it demonstrates the journey for every man, woman, and child. For just as Jesus walked upon the Earth to give the world an ideal a strive toward, he did so in human form, thereby demonstrating all that is possible through the will of our Father, the Lord.

Others before him paved the way for his arrival just as those in this age are paving the way for the return of the Messiah. And the date we recognize as Christ's birth is a day to take notice of in the signs of the Return. For as all once was, so it shall be once again. In the eyes of humanity, it will always take two occurrences of an experience to add truth to what would otherwise be dismissed. Perhaps this very concept can be explored in the nature of eyesight alone, for a person with only one eye loses perception of depth through the world. Two eyes adds the component of depth to create a three dimensional and tangible interpretation, a required component for navigation.

Christmas has been celebrated for thousands of years, and in some cases the meaning has been marred through pagan cultures that introduced the celebration. But the important takeaway is that the way it is celebrated today should be understood as a reflection of a spiritual theme rooted in divine symbolism. The Christmas tree's origin began in Germany in the sixteenth century in celebration of the feast of Adam and Eve, a day three and a half days removed from the Winter solstice. The tree used at that time was a paradise tree, a tree symbolizing the tree in the Garden of Eden. And while it can be understood that the Adam and Eve hold biblical significance, the question remains why would a tree for Adam and Eve enter into the day of Christ's celebration?

This is a question not easily answered without all that is shared throughout the rest of this story, but it should be understood that the embodiment of Christ through an earthly vessel is done so in the Garden in the presence of His original creation. And while this may give pause to many readers, for now just place this thought on a shelf, for it will all make sense full circle once the mind has journeyed through all of His words. This story is about here and now, there and back again, retreading through the once traveled waters that will require being traversed once again. It is only through the journey across all of the words and returning through them once again that the story will see the beginning meet the end. It is the concept of a snake swallowing its tail and subsequently its head, for that is how His words must always be read.

So with that in mind, it is important to see that the Christmas tree is used in celebration for a much grander meaning. For now it should be observed as a tree of life, a tree of knowledge, a symbol of a seed blossoming from a tiny shell into life that gives life and receives life from its surroundings. It is part of the infinite cosmos and a cycle that is unending. It is the very essence of the blooming of the spirit. For unlike a flower which should be observed for its beauty and role as a support in the world, a tree demonstrates strength from its roots through its trunk. The branches that reach out and cover the ground provide areas of shade for other seeds to take root and grow. It is the embodiment of The One with roots reaching beneath the soil as far and wide as the branches reach above. It is hourglass in form if one takes the time to see it, though this aspect of a tree is usually missed to earthly eyes because most focus on only what is in plain sight.

The Christmas tree that was risen within my apartment when I moved to Fort Lauderdale was one of spectacular glory, one that I would attempt to emulate in earthly form. In years past, a Christmas tree was just a Christmas tree. As long as it was triangular in form and had white lights and modest decorations, I felt peace within its presence. But this year would be different. This year there were standards set on a

The Christmas Tree

spiritual level wherein every action taken required the most thoughtful and delicate approach in action. In every action taken there was always an effort to do so in earthly form as well as in spiritual symbolism. It was important that every action represent heaven and Earth as one, for they always were and always are. The effort to demonstrate the two as one helps the spiritual eyes learn to grow and see beyond the spiritual blobs of light dancing around. There is an undeniable glimmer that requires focus and growth to decipher.

The snow-glazed tree I setup this year felt misplaced in the warmer climate of Florida, but it was important that the idea of crystalline structures of snow adorn the branches to represent the water of the spirit. The tree was seven feet tall (which by now the number should speak for itself) in divine recognition of The All. At the base of the tree, a burlap sackcloth was placed to serve as the skirt of the tree. The burlap was important for a number of reasons, but most importantly in the way it has historically been used to represent humility and God's Love. Sackcloth is mentioned numerous times in the Bible during times of fasting and as a symbol of surrender to the Lord. It is the roughest of fabrics that exists and is an irritant to the skin. When sackcloths were worn in Old Testament times, it was a symbol of repentance, or mourning, and loss. In New Testament times, it is best understood as an outward expression of an inward recognition. In the context of this story, the two witnesses mentioned in John's Revelation are said to be clothed in sackcloth – an archetypal recognition viewed by John to indicate the inward recognition of all the cloth represented. So it was important that the foundation of the tree be covered in this material. The "skirt," as it is known, is the representation of the clothing of the tree.

The tree was adorned with ornaments that carried numeric and symbolic meaning. Upon the tree ornaments in the forms of owls and kings were placed. The number of owl ornaments was nine, the number of kings was three. The owls represented the wisdom of the spheres, the understanding of the whole. It is the divine architecture of All That Is, including the spheres unseen. These ornaments indicated the understanding of His craft represented through the archetype of wisdom. While it would belabor the text to place more explanation here, the entire text of Book VIII is an explanation of this architecture. The kings are symbolic to the Holy Trinity: the Father, the Son, the Holy Ghost. They also represent the Mind, the Body, and Soul better understood as the divisions of ego, soul, and spirit. The kings serve as a symbol to the Christian tradition of the "Three Kings" that visited Jesus in his manger, though no accounts of this are given in the Biblical canon.

In addition to the twelve ornaments previously mentioned, there were thirty-three clear glass spheres placed upon the tree to represent the divine age of Jesus and all that is spiritually represented in that number. It was important that the glass was clear and transparent to represent the purity of the doorway to the Spirit. Like an earthly window can be covered in filth and grime, the window to the spirit must be cleaned and shined. This is the process achieved over thirty-three

The Christmas Tree

years, revealing the unrestricted path for the Spirit to flow through. These thirty-three spheres of clear glass could reflect and refract the white lights adorning the tree causing a spectacle of sorts for the human eye to see.

In addition to the thirty-three spheres, eight metallic glass balls were placed upon the tree. They represented silver, gold, and bronze adorned with a large metallic snowflake on each. The symbol of the metals is easily understood in earthly terms, but in spiritual terms, there is more to learn. The gold represented the purity of the Lord. The bronze represented the metal closest to the Earth. The silver represented the third part of the metallic trinity, tying together the metal that is of the Earth to the metal of divinity. This is the symbolism used throughout the biblical canon, usually appearing in prophetic visions. The metal of brass or bronze is generally referenced as adorning the feet of a person, for the feet are the form of movement upon the ground of the Earth. Gold is used as a symbol of perfection, adorning crowns and jewelry in the vicinity of the neck and head. Silver is used symbolically to represent the pure – colorless for a transition from bronze to gold. The three metals together form another trinity of sorts, and can thus be equated to the Father, the Son, the Holy Ghost.

The number of eight snowflake ornaments might at first seem absent in meaning, but it is important that eight spheres form a cube that hides a ninth within it, representing divinity. The number eight is also symbolic to the journey, for the number eight is tantamount to achieving more than is earthly.

Kingdom

And while the last piece of significance will not make sense until the end of the reading, the number eight is the last date of twelve-hundred and sixty.

There was one more ornament added in companionship to the eight; it was a blue, glass ornament painted for me by my daughter. If the ninth sphere can be understood to be hidden within the eight, the ninth being represented through my daughter's hand could not be any grander in meaning. Again, I know the symbolism may be tough to follow without the full understanding of the divine architecture of All That Is, but once that is understood, it will all make sense.

Twelve more ornaments adorned the tree in shapes of doves, the meaning of peace and tranquility, the twelve days leading to Christmas, and the symbol of Love. On the top of the tree was a star handmade from strips of wood. No lights were included on the star, only the handcrafted strips of wood was intended to be observed. It was important that the star be raw and free from light, for it was to represent the carpenter's cup of Jesus Christ. The role of the carpenter is the role all Sons play upon the Earth, for the world is in constant need of being reshaped and rebuilt with the tools of the Spirit. The absence of material light on the star itself represented the light that was inherent within, a light that would shine brighter than anything made by human hand.

With the explanation of how the Christmas tree was decorated in a way to emulate the spiritual tree that was risen upon my arrival in Florida, the months from September to December fell into focus. These were the months that were the most

The Christmas Tree

important in my spiritual growth. However, it was important to set the stage to better understand the days leading to my thirty-third Christmas and why it was important in the timing of His divine plan. The months leading into December were spectacular in their own rites, but the anticipation heading into the month of December held the trump card to the eyes. For it was the month that everything wrapped in white lace and blue would begin to be unveiled in moments of truth.

September to December

From the time I arrived in Fort Lauderdale to September, I was focused on completing the work that enabled me to move away from Nashville. The opportunity was blessed into my life in a way that could only be described as divine. It was an opportunity that arose in the final chapters of Book I – Gravity Calling and managed to carry me through to the days I arrived upon the shores of the Atlantic Ocean in Fort Lauderdale, Florida. During the time I worked on the project, I witnessed the Promised Land through eyes of a child, birthed from the womb. It was a moment of crowning, learning to see, and learning to speak. The first forty days of the experience were witnessed as a soul being birthed into a new world – a world of spiritual nature, where the body of Earth was second to His divine work.

The melody of the angels singing hymns in the heavens was the sound of the wind. The sun rising over the Atlantic Ocean each morning was a hint of His hand pulling back the veil that separated earthly eyes from spiritual sight. The rhythm of the songs the angels sang were the syncopated rhythms in which all things moved throughout the day. The nights were filled with wondrous communions with the Lord. Sitting upon the shoreline at night and speaking to my Father felt like sitting on the edge of the world. With no one around, endless beaches to my left and right, an infinite expanse of water in front of me, and an ocean of stars above filled with twinkling lights, it was easy to become lost in the majestic wonder of the moment – a prince in the making sitting on the edge of the Earth.

It was the very definition of an event horizon – the edge where two bodies melt into each others' gravity. This was the edge of Earth and His Kingdom, the closest it could be until these two bodies would one day meet. The first days of being in this place prepared for me was experienced like a newlywed couple would experience a honeymoon, eyes of wonder, everything new. But the first months of melting into the splendor of this majestic location was also filled with the intensity to finish the work that had helped me get there. The work engagement with my client wrapped up at the end of August, leaving the months to follow in uncharted territory. Though I had confidence from the beginning that the Lord would always provide, I have to admit it was at first a little scary learning to blindly trust in the midst of this paradise.

But after the first months of the honeymoon faded and the work contract that enabled me to follow His call to the Promised Land was completed, I began to survey the land. These would be the months of stardust settling from the impact of bare feet running across the desert sands. The first forty days were indescribable in the way my Father helped my perspective change and how He opened my eyes to see the Glory of Heaven on Earth. Everyday of the honeymoon in this en-

September to December

chanted land I experienced something new, though it was still partially hidden in the luster of the plume of stardust kicked up during my arrival. The first forty days were experienced as a child learning to see for the first time through spiritual eyes. There was a promise of Christmas ahead and a tree setup for the day it arrived. The presents were wrapped up in packages of white lace and blue, waiting for the day when the child would open up all that had been prepared for him by His Father and the girl he did not realize he always knew.

And though it may seem premature by having a tree setup and revealing the presents so far ahead of the day of celebration, remember how it once felt to be a child. In the days of autumn when school starts back up and children see their classmates again, the air of newness carries an excitement of the school year ahead. The holidays are talked about early on, and when children ask their parents for new clothes or new toys, they often hear the words, "Not now, maybe for Christmas." It is not that there is a desire for something out of greed, but rather the hope and excitement placed into the upcoming days to be able to receive. This is the way the months from September to December should be understood – though the eyes of a child, placing hope upon what would be revealed when December arrived. Though just as a child must learn the meaning of Christmas to understand the meaning surrounding the occasion, so it was intended for me to learn the grandness of His message that would be delivered and the reason I had to wait. During the time in between September and December, there was so much more to learn and experience. These days

Kingdom

encompassed some of the grandest moments of God's work that I have ever been able to witness.

Just as a child returning to school after a summer of bliss and happiness would be tasked with new lessons and new classes, I would experience the same circumstances in this new Promised Land. Though as inexplicable as it may sound, over the years of the journey I have been taken to the heavens, shown the wonders of His hand, and spoken with angels and many of the elders written about in the Biblical canon. There have been conversations with angels where the words shared with me were intended to be understood in hindsight. There has been a swath of lessons experienced creating a story that I would not see in real-time – only in moments following through His Glory. I was following His lead, trusting that it would all make sense in the end. And, as the days of September to December played out, I learned that His grand story had so much more to reveal.

I experienced Heaven on Earth everyday in this new land, but it was not until after the stardust settled that I saw it with so much detail. These were the days I spoke to angels on Earth – some able to be seen by others, though at times others quivered in fear and never saw what I was able to see. There were supernatural occurrences inexplicable to anyone standing near. There were halos in the sky parting the clouds to keep rain from falling down. There were divine experiences witnessed by others around, though they had no idea how to put into words what they saw. But through it all, the most important experiences of these months leading up to December, were how my Father was telling the Love story of life. It was not a story about me, but rather a story told by His Will through this bodily vessel – a story of hope and Love eternal, a divine Ever-After. So over the next portion of the story, it is important to understand that the experiences presented are all shaping a Love story of a Groom and his Bride. It is a story that would blindside a prince, and through that, a story difficult to recount in a linear fashion. So though the story all makes sense in the end, it may seem to journey into tangential side stories along the way. But maintain peace that the story was and is a Love story all along – a story penned by His Hand, the greatest Love story ever told.

White Tigers & White Dresses

When I moved to Fort Lauderdale, I took with me only what I could fit into the back of a towable U-Haul. In the months leading up to the move, I understood the importance to remove earthly possessions from my life. There was a part of me that almost decided to leave everything I owned behind and arrive in Fort Lauderdale with only a bag of clothes and toiletries. In that scenario, I still knew that everything would be provided upon my arrival. Possessions were never a question of attachment, rather just a concept of luxury to make the journey more enjoyable.

It was with that mindset that I began removing any excesses from my life. Fiscally, I have always made sure to purchase the best item that I desired. It was not a price tag that defined "best," but rather a concept of what it meant to me. As an example, in terms of audio equipment, this meant purchasing the highest quality set of speakers and signal chain components to my ears with cost as no object. I would much rather have saved to purchase the audio equipment my ears desired rather than purchase something of lesser value just because I could afford it. There is obviously a fine line in this approach as I also did not allow for superfluous indulgences, but it was always the method of my approach to purchases.

This approach was exemplified in everything I owned. Any item worth owning also required scrutiny in the price versus quality. But never was a cost limit imposed, only the understanding of how much quality was important and from that point, the best price versus quality ratio was assessed. To an outside observer, I frequently heard, "You have nice stuff." As a rule, this was probably very accurate. But, it was not ever an indulgence but rather the polish and presentation to a purchase. Why cut corners if quality suffered?

So when assessing what parts of my life could be left behind there was an obvious cost component to be weighed. I understood that my Father desired for me to remove material possessions from my life, and I had no problem doing so. The challenge became what was considered "material" versus "worth taking." As I prayed for guidance, I also acknowledged that I could easily leave everything behind and start anew, since I understood that taking everything was not accepting the call to shed material possessions. My struggle – as addressed in the prayer – was which items would make sense to take as a foundation (if anything at all). It was during this prayer that my Father offered a solution that bridged the extremes of the two. The solution was essentially taking anything that fit in a towable U-Haul.

It was simple. If it fit in the U-Haul, it would be taken. If it would not, then it would be donated. This proved to be a wonderful exercise in assessing my possessions and paved the way for only taking a foundation to build upon for the move to Fort Lauderdale. It was during this time of shedding possessions, that I decided I wanted all wall decor in my new residence in Fort Lauderdale to be comprised of art from Fort Lauderdale artists. I wanted everything in my new place to be composed of those expressing Him through their art, those already led to this Promised Land. It was inspiring to think that the very essence of my residence would radiate Him through those already experiencing Him in this divine location. Whether the artists recognized it as such through their art did not matter, for art is always in the eye of the beholder. But it was important to paint the essence in the resonance of Him. With that in mind, I loaded up the U-Haul with only a foundation of items.

After arriving in Fort Lauderdale and getting settled in, I began searching through galleries to find the decor for my residence. I spent several days walking through all of the galleries in the city, but kept returning to one specific gallery right near my apartment. It was a gallery called "Paul's Gallery" located in the North Beach shopping center, though it is no longer there. Walking into Paul's Gallery, I noticed that all of the images on the walls were filled with seemingly abstract splashes of color. He used an interesting blend of acrylics and foil over textured canvas to create some truly remarkable pieces of art. It only took the briefest of moments when looking at each painting to see the spiritual inspiration intertwined in his presentation. I knew in this moment there was a reason I had been led into his gallery.

I wandered over to one particular painting that stood out beyond all of the others and became mesmerized at the story he was telling. To some, what would appear to be abstract colors painted diagonally across the canvas, told a story of Creation with an image of a woman that I understood to be Eve. It just so happened I had my daughter that particular week so she was helping me pick out the painting for my apartment. I began describing to her where the image of the woman was in the midst of the colors as well as the spiritual implications of Creation. It was as if the painting illustrated the Garden of Eden wrapped up in the embodiment of Eve. My daughter was fascinated with the story that I saw within the painting.

As I spoke with my daughter, the gallery owner walked over to me smiling profusely. Paul introduced himself to my daughter and me. I saw his divine light and understood that God had purposed this interaction. Paul told me that the name of the painting was "The Garden" and explained how it was one of his most inspired paintings. He began to point out other features in the seemingly abstract image that further built upon all that I was explaining to my daughter as well as how the painting came to be. My daughter also chimed in with some imagery she saw as well. The interaction ballooned into a wonderfully spiritual conversation about his art. Neither Paul nor I pried about each other's spiritual walk – it was obvious through the artwork itself and my understanding of his message within the painting.

Paul went on to tell me that nobody else had ever entered into his gallery over the years it had been open and understood the spiritual story underneath the artwork in a way similar to how I was explaining it to my daughter. He was like a proud father in that moment. We shared in a little more conversation before I decided that this was a painting I must have. My daughter really wanted me to purchase it as well. As it turned out, the price fell right in line with what I was hoping to spend. Overall, it was a perfect collision of two spiritual souls along life's journey. "The Garden" would be the first piece of art I purchased for my apartment in Fort Lauderdale.

A few days later I returned to pick up the painting and bring it home with me. Since I had walked over to the store with my daughter and had to fly her back the following day, I did not have an opportunity to take it home the day we originally saw it. When I entered, Paul and I had another wonderful conversation. He went on to tell me how he was very picky over who he sold his artwork to. He explained that his gallery was not about the money, but rather about the expression of the spiritual inspiration he received. As I listened to him talk, it became clear that this particular painting meant a great deal to him though he seemed excited by it finding a place in my home. Paul also felt the desire to talk to me about my daughter and how he saw so much love between us. Even to this day, Paul still checks up on her and me to see how we are doing.

Kingdom

When I was about to head out the door, I asked Paul if he ever did any custom artwork. He told me that he rarely does any because his focus is always found within. So as we parted ways, I said if he ever happened to do a painting with a lion in it, to let me know – that I would be interested in checking it out. In truth, I wanted a lion for the symbolic purposes of my Father. I did not want my artwork to be identical, or in the same style, so I was not even sure how something with that theme would turn out in Paul's abstract style. Regardless, I was curious and asked him to let me know if he ever carried that theme through one of his paintings.

I stopped by his gallery on a couple occasions to see if he had completed anything new, but he always said he was working on something special, though it was taking some time to complete. Several months later, I received a all from Paul. Since we had never spoken on the phone, I was not quite sure what to expect. After we exchanged pleasantries, Paul said, "Jonathan, I have your painting ready. It is of you and your daughter. When can you come pick it up?"

This was a defining moment along the journey. Though uncharacteristic to the way I ever spent money, I understood spiritually that my Father had prepared something special for me in my life. My Father knew that I was attempting to decorate my apartment with inspired artwork from Fort Lauderdale artists. He also knew I was being diligent about using the money provided into my life for greater purposes of helping others. In this moment, I was not sure if Paul possibly needed money and painted something for me in hopes that I

White Tigers & White Dresses

would buy it or whether this was something truly divine. Regardless, I heard my Father's call and agreed to buy it from Paul, sight unseen.

When we met a few days later, Paul was waiting in a store that was next to where his gallery once was. As it turned out, Paul had decided in the preceding weeks to move his gallery across town. Spiritually, I understood that he had fulfilled his purpose in this area and that the Lord was calling him to his next destination. When I walked in, there was a group of people all talking in amazement about the painting before them. The voices of the people ran together with questions and comments along the lines of, "Are you sure this is not a photograph? It looks so real! I cannot get over how wonderful this is! And you did this? Wow…" At this point I had not seen the painting and had no idea what to expect. All I had ever seen were abstract pieces of art from him… and then I saw it.

When the painting fell into view, I felt a spiritual rush of emotions flood my eyes and pour out in the form of tears of wonder. The painting took my breath away. There before me, was a painting of the most picture-perfect white tiger holding a baby cub. All I could do was walk over and give Paul a hug. I understood everything in that moment, but Paul's words brought clarity to any questions I could have asked. The painting was a portrait of my daughter and me through his eyes. As he spoke, I heard my Father speaking through him. He went on to explain how special I was and how special the Love for my daughter was. To anyone listening from the outside, I am sure it may have seemed like a strange conversation, but it was the conversation between a Father and his Son, distorted to earthly ears through the forms of an artist and a client.

The painting was so different than anything I could have expected from him. For days I studied it thinking it must have been a photograph as well, but it clearly was not. Paul went on to tell me that every now and then – maybe no more than a couple times a year – he creates paintings for "very special people." He emphasized how much work he put into the eyes of the white tiger to indicate all he saw in me. And while I have never shared that portion of the story with anyone that has seen the painting, I have heard on multiple occasions, "Wow, Jonathan. The eyes…" In truth, the face of the tiger is as if my portrait was lifted from human form and placed onto a tiger in such a way that the tiger looked like a picture-perfect tiger to anyone else.

Paul went on to tell me how he saw me as a white tiger and began explaining the significance of the white tiger to him, though he did not open up about the spiritual meaning in words. It was as if there was an earthly conversation going on for those around us to hear and a spiritual conversation going on underneath the words. The symbolism in the white tiger held so much meaning, but Paul wanted to me to specifically understand how "rare" the white tiger was and how it represented a divine strength. He stopped short of any further elaboration on the aspect of divine strength due to the others around, but I understood without words. I was so excited with the artwork, which was also personalized "To Jonathan" in the

White Tigers & White Dresses

bottom right hand corner of the painting. Blindly I showed up to pick up a painting and walked away in a wash of His light.

The symbolism in the white tiger is entrenched in the Asian culture – which is Paul's heritage. In China, the white tiger is said to be one of four divine creatures. It is the guardian of the West. The face of the white tiger was often carved on tomb doorways and passages to ward off the Azure Dragon (one of the other divine creatures). The face of the white tiger often was adorned on the shields of soldiers going into battle to represent divine strength. The white tiger is a holy beast that represents the season of autumn. Though this symbolism will have much greater meaning as more is revealed in this book, think of the white tiger as a holy symbol during harvest season. In Japan and China, the tiger is the "king of the animals" rather than the lion. The face of the white tiger is the symbol of one of the highest military rankings achievable and is representative of a leader among soldiers. And while many additional spiritual connotations exist, they are lost in translation between Eastern and Western cultures. But the greatest symbolism was not just in the Asian expression, but the expression of the entire experience that my Father desired to demonstrate to me.

At this point in time, I saw the world around me as Heaven upon Earth. I understood the meaning in the crown I had received and the Kingdom that awaited. Every day I was constantly engaged in a spiritual conversation with my Father through the world around me. I charged myself with closing the gap in hindsight and the present moment. Even in moments such as receiving the call from Paul regarding the painting, I heard His call even if I did not understand the meaning. And, though there were many times I thought I understood the meaning in His calls to action – such as the moment when I saw the painting from Paul – the Glory of His story was in the seed that He was planting all along. For if the first painting I purchased called "The Garden" could be understood as a portrait of Eve, then the portrait of the white tiger and its cub should be seen as a father and his daughter.

Adorned in white, the tiger is a portrait of a prince holding his daughter. But when viewed in context of the Love story being told, it is like family portraits of two halves becoming whole. In one painting is a portrait of my daughter and me. In the other, a picture representing the ideal woman as God saw her when He first created her in the Garden and named her Eve. And while the white color of the tiger should be understood for the spiritual symbolism it embodies, it should also be understood in context of the purity in the woman. For if one is to understand that Paul is a vessel for Divine storytelling between my Father and me, the two paintings should also be understood in a combined context of a woman adorned in a white dress, uniting a family. And while it may seem like a stretch to see a combined meaning in the two paintings together, it will eventually be revealed how the two portraits were made for one another. The two paintings were paired in a way to foreshadow a couple in the making – white tigers and white dresses in the courting phases of dating.

A Bride's Unveiling

Butterflies.

The unmistakable feeling of a fluttering sensation in the stomach. Sometimes the feeling is so great during a first date with a person that it makes one think the food has made him sick or perhaps he is coming down with something. But as uncomfortable as the feeling of butterflies is, it is also one of the most longed-for feelings to experience. Both man and woman long to feel the tossing-tumbling sensation from within the center of their abdominal region, but what is it about the feeling that invokes such a grand calling within?

I like to think that the idea of getting butterflies is tied to the soul acknowledging a potential counterpoint in another. A person does not get butterflies on a date if there is not chemistry between the two individuals, so there must be an aspect of attraction at the core of the sensation. I like to believe that butterflies are the possibility of forever, wrapped up the immediate moment.

Think of the point of origination in the sensation, then ask any person, "Where does a person feel butterflies within?" The most common answer will be "the stomach, deep within." However, it is the answer rarely given that is the one that

Kingdom

holds the most meaning, for the feeling of butterflies is tied to the naval. The very point that once held life and connected a baby to a mother in the womb is the point that nutrients and Love once flowed through. It is the one specific place on a person that represents life, and of being of the Earth.

But there is much more to the naval than just earthly meaning, for it has long been taught the spiritual umbilical cord connects a soul to the Source. The spiritual umbilical cord is mentioned in the Bible as the "silver cord." Much can be studied about this concept, but at its root, think of it as the connection of a soul between Heaven and Earth. Perhaps in a different analogy, think of the soul as a baby in a womb, connected to its Mother who will one day give birth as the soul begins to crown. The idea of the silver cord has been taught for generations, though most has been lost in translation through various teachings.

So, on Earth, when standing in the presence of another soul that has so much attraction in her essence and so much potential, it should be seen that the soul would react in kind to a newfound kind of spiritual nutrient being fed from the Mother to the soul in the womb. It is a rush of earthly sensations in reaction to this rare spiritual nutrient. It is the recognition of the potential of Love in another being fed through spirit. It is a sensation that defies earthly explanation, but shakes a person to his core. Often the feeling manifests as a feeling of earthly sickness, and would not this be the case? The spiritual nutrients of existence are feeding through the spiritual umbilical cord directly from the Mother to her child in the

A Bride's Unveiling

womb. Just as the potential of Love is a form of spiritual food, the earthly body reacts in expression to this new sensation, creating an uneasy feeling in the pit of the stomach. It is often one of the first times a spiritual sensation is felt in such an earthly rush. The concepts of motion, spinning, and the states of euphoria and bliss of the heavens are wrapped up in a fluttering sensation, defying earthly understanding, thus causing a misinterpretation of the feeling as occurring in the pit of the earthly stomach.

But it is also important to understand why the potential in Love would feel like butterflies fluttering about. For generations upon generations, butterflies have held wondrous spiritual symbolism. Much can be learned from the life of a butterfly. It is one of the only creatures of God's creation that crawls about the Earth after its birth to live part of its life as a caterpillar before metamorphosis. At a certain point in the butterfly's maturation, it spins itself a cocoon removing itself from earthly interaction. During its time in the cocoon, the exterior slowly hardens becoming more impermeable to earthly forces. It can be seen in this very demonstration that the life of a butterfly is like that of a child upon Earth. At some point during spiritual maturation, a cocoon must be created to separate a person from earthly distractions so the soul can further grow through the life-force of the spirit. During this time in a spiritual cocoon, the outer shell hardens, becoming more impermeable to the noise of earthly distractions.

When it comes time for the caterpillar to emerge from the cocoon, first the head emerges followed by the legs. It should be seen as the point along the spiritual journey that the soul begins to be birthed from the womb. It is the point of crowning, symbolizing a prince arriving, a king in the making. But when the butterfly fully emerges it can be seen that the size of this new creation is many times bigger than it once was, even dwarfing the size of the cocoon. In a spiritual sense this should be understood as how an angel's age is represented in form – the larger the angel, the more elder it is understood. Even in popular movies, this is embedded into storylines with few ever taking notice. Think of how in the movie Thor everyone seems to appear as the same size until there is a moment the strength of the King must be demonstrated. It may only be a few seconds of film montage, but in that moment the King is represented as many times greater than that of his son. So it should be understood that the butterfly's emergence is the symbol of divine maturation. The wings cause it to appear to dwarf the size of the cocoon's housing, though the interesting conundrum of the wings is that the bigger they are, the greater the ease the butterfly can fly, but the size is disproportional to earthly mass that limits flight.

The wings of a butterfly fluttering about should be seen as the wings of an angel adorning his back. There really is no better Earthy symbol of a soul's maturation than to study the life of a butterfly to understand how it separates itself from a creature of the ground to a creature of flight. On the wings of the air, the butterfly can flutter about effortlessly bringing joy to everyone who witnesses its flight. Think about how much happiness a butterfly brings to a child. Children love to chase

A Bride's Unveiling

butterflies, to catch them on their fingers so they can watch them take flight. More smiles are created from butterflies than any other non-domesticated creature. It is a calling within for the soul to take notice. And if it can be seen that the evolution of a butterfly is to the maturation of the soul, it should be understood that the ending is Love, and always was.

So in understanding that a caterpillar receiving its wings is metaphorical to a soul growing to understand the fullest extent of His Love, then there is no better way to illustrate the potential of Love within than through the sensation of butterflies fluttering about. For if it can be understood that the spiritual nutrients being fed to the soul are bound in a way similar to a baby bound to its mother by an umbilical cord in an earthly womb, then it can be understood that the nutrients to the soul would be the embodiment of a Love greater than a soul could yet understand at that point in its maturation. The feeling of butterflies is not recognition in the potential of earthly love, but rather the spiritual love that was always intended to be represented through the expression of earthly love. The spirit is the source. The expression of the spirit is demonstrated through the walk upon the Earth. One cannot exist without the other in order for a soul to gain a full understanding of its Creator.

The feelings of butterflies is one of the most beautiful sensations ever experienced. In Book I, my Father's use of the butterfly became apparent when He sent one to light upon my arm on the day I followed His directive to move on from my former employer and follow blindly where He was leading me.

Kingdom

The butterfly at that time was a divine guidepost symbolizing all that would one day become. Early in the journey I still had the perception that I was further along the spiritual journey than I was, even though I understood I was studying just a grain of sand upon a great shore. At the time, I understood the butterfly in the symbolism of spiritual growth, I would not have the context of experiencing crowning in a spiritual womb to add further depth to the eventual meaning. It is as if in every way that God shares a message, two sides of directional understanding unfold. It is only over the course of a soul's maturation that the understanding of His meaning can unfold. What was once the meaning farthest from becomes closest in understanding and the message that was understood best in the original moment (the message closest to) has now become the message farthest from the point it was originally delivered. It is the beautiful art of His delivery. And if His delivery can be seen as art, the expression of His message through the paintings I received from Paul should be seen as the outward expression of His story unfolding – a divine message that would one day be uncovered.

The paintings that Paul had created embodied the story of white tigers and white dresses. Though when I received the paintings, I did not see them as the portraits they would one day be revealed to me as the message always intended for me to see. At the time I received "The Garden," Paul wanted to make sure I understood the story of a caterpillar becoming a butterfly that he was trying to tell. It was the aspect of the painting that was clearly his proudest achievement, though it

A Bride's Unveiling

was not the part of the painting that first caught my eye. But to Paul, it was important that I understood. Upon the canvas, there was a textured worm that blended in with the rest of the painting in colors and abstract form. In the way that Paul wished the story to be told, the worm became a caterpillar and eventually became a butterfly, which is one of the first parts of the painting the eye will see. It takes a moment of studying the path of the butterfly to see how it originated as a worm in the water of the Garden, but once it is observed, it is apparent the beautiful story being told.

This painting held such a grand meaning wherein one day I would look back and understand it as a painting of my future wife, Christ's Bride. It was the foreshadowing to the greatest Love story ever told – one that my Father was always telling me, though it would require further spiritual growth to witness all He intended for me to behold. White tigers and white dresses were Paul's expression of a prince upon the Earth and a Bride-to-be, an expression that demonstrated the life of a caterpillar crowning and gaining its wings. The expression of my Father's message in the paintings ignited my soul in a way that I could not quite describe. It was the spiritual recognition akin to butterflies upon first seeing my Bride. And while this was the earthly manifestation of all that was unfolding to the storyline in the heavens, it was a storyline I had not quite unraveled just yet. Though it is now easy to see in hindsight, even the momentous occasion of meeting Christ's Bride in the heavens for the first time happened through the eyes of a spiritual child, oblivious to standing in the presence of his Bride.

Kingdom

When I first bore witness to Christ's Bride, it was on a morning in September when my soul was taken to the heavens. It began in the same way as the other journeys to the heavens that I experienced so many times over the three and a half years these Books of Nine took place. But this experience was a little different than the rest. When I arrived in the heavens, I was greeted by a beautiful brunette angel where she took me to attend a wedding. We stood in the crowd as we witnessed the ceremony. During the ceremony, the angel continued to change dresses and gauge my response to each dress she was wearing. I understood her dress was different each time I looked at her, but I was naive to all that was taking place. It was clear she wanted to make sure she looked beautiful to me, but I only understood this in hindsight. In the way everything works in the heavens, I understood that she was indecisive on which dress to wear so she kept changing dresses to see which one I found most beautiful. At the end of the wedding she nudged me to get my attention. At this point the rest of the wedding ceremony fell from my view. The only thing I could see in this moment was the beautiful angel standing in front of me. She was wearing a white dress that had a single strap over her shoulder. It was a wedding dress, though I would not see it as such as I stared at her. She was beyond beautiful in a way such that I could not even form words as I stood there mesmerized at the radiance of her beauty.

The day of a Bride's unveiling is an experience that is the Third Revelation identified in my journals. It is the last chapter to Book VI – Rebirth III. But in the context of this book,

A Bride's Unveiling

the unveiling of the Bride should be understood through the expressions of Paul's paintings. For in all of the manifestations of my Father's voice through the world around me, the paintings held the grandest meanings of all. For long before I understood where He was leading me, long before I would unwrap the presents placed under the Christmas Tree, my Father was planting seeds along the way. Through these paintings, His plan was performed in the grandest way. For if it can be seen how the two paintings were paired in a way to foreshadow a couple in the making – white tigers and white dresses in the courting phases of dating – then it should also be seen in the context of the butterflies adorning Her image in The Garden, for they were the spiritual butterflies foreshadowing a Bride's unveiling.

Halos In The Skies

Somewhere in a stranger's eyes, the skies are raining. In another's eyes, the sun is raining lightdrops down on a blue-clear-sky kind of day. Whether it is the embodiment of water or light, the colours of God's palette are flooding down upon the mosaic of the land in the most fantastic expressions of brush strokes from His hand. The water that pours down from the sky nourishes the land in the same way as the sunlight pouring down. In this it can be seen that light is embodied in the same way as water, though most would never equate the two as the same due to the differences in tactile sensations.

But light races down from the sky just as water races down from the clouds, and when these two substances meet in perfect equilibrium, a rainbow is formed. The rainbow is said to be a reminder from God that He would never destroy the entire world by flood again. It is a sign of light refracting at a precise angle within droplets of water above so as to break apart and open up a single droplet of light into the visible seven colors. The rainbow is a sign of wonder that excites the child within the oldest of adults. The rainbow is steeped in legends and myths, even so much as to power stories of pots of gold awaiting whomever can find where the rainbow ends.

Kingdom

The colors of the rainbow carry through to another concept spread across centuries of time. It is said to be the color of the road that runs between the heavens and the Earth. The Rainbow Road as it is known, has been illustrated through stories and media for generations, but why would this theme exist if there was not an underlying truth to its origin? For to study the Rainbow Road, one would learn that it has been observed by the few documented travelers to the heavens. Though it is the road less taken compared to earthly roads travelled, it still embodies the idea of the road to the heavens. It is a road I have seen countless times, though I do not think it would be fair to equate it to anything of earthly design.

So if it can be understood that the Rainbow Road is a road to the heavens, the concept of a pot of gold awaiting the one who reaches the end of a rainbow is firmly rooted in truth, albeit hidden from the eyes of those who have not yet experienced it. And if it can be understood that a rainbow is a perfect equilibrium of water and light, then it can be understood how the idea of a Rainbow Road connects the body and the spirit to the Earth and the heavens. It is a perfect equilibrium of the water of the spirit and the light within the body blending together to create a path to Eternity.

Now think for a moment of the times throughout life that a rainbow has appeared in the skies. Now think how rare it ever is to see an ending to the rainbow clearly formed. Most of the time, it forms high in the sky without reaching the ground. But in recent times the structure of a rainbow has become more perfect. This is not just conjecture but has been well documented. Rainbows have become much more complete in formation, often even forming a double rainbow where in generations past, only a portion of one rainbow existed.

When I moved to Fort Lauderdale I took notice of a new kind of rainbow in the skies. It was a complete circular rainbow initially hidden from my earthly eyes. I cannot be certain if it existed because I noticed it with my spiritual eyes, or if I noticed it existed and it manifested through the skies for others to see. Regardless, one point remained, the rainbows served as halos in the skies preventing the rain.

But before I took notice to this uncanniness, I spent months in the sun enjoying the sand and the beach. From September to December I spent almost every daylight hour enjoying life soaking up the sun. It was the most peaceful retreat from the earthly life I had left behind. But as I began to experience the days in greater length and greater clarity of spiritual vision, I began to take notice of a strange occurrence. It seemed that nearly every moment I was out in the sun, the rain never came in a halo around this new home. I could sit on the beach as rainclouds pushed through, and watch it rain on the buildings to my left and my right while the building I lived in was left untouched and cast in the light.

The first time I noticed this I thought it was too good to be true. Could this heaven I lived in also be immune from the weather? To earthly eyes it seemed unlikely, and as I tried to bridge the idea of heaven and Earth as one, I began to ask others if they ever noticed this occurrence. For months it would rain daily, but only on either side. Many times, when clouds rolled in, the skies remained blue above. It became such a consistent occurrence that it became the talk among the residents. Many had never seemed to notice it until I pointed it out. But one day, as I started to study the occurrence more acutely, I noticed something that was hard to see without sunglasses. There around the sun, was a halo of rainbow light circumscribing the area where the rain and clouds did not touch.

Whether my spiritual eyesight continued to gain strength and clarity, or whether the intensity of the rainbow halos was increasing, over the course of my time in this residence, the occurrences have become more pronounced. In the beginning I noticed the halos in the skies as smaller in size, but as time wore on, the halos became much greater in size. One of my most vivid memories is the recollection of sitting on the beach with a new friend, where we smoked cigars and laughed about how it was raining everywhere around us, but not directly above. It was not uncommon that when people started to take notice of the phenomena that they would call out and get my attention. Perhaps the rain held off as long as my spiritual presence desired the sun to shine down.

But the halos became even more apparent to others. One day a girl I had rarely spoken to came up and asked me what, over the last several days, she was she was witnessing with the moon. This caught me off guard, for I had not paid much attention to the light of the moon when it was directly overhead. But when she described the rainbow halo surrounding the moon, I understood the intensity was increasing from sunshine

Halos In The Skies

to being visible in the light of the moon. I shared with her the story of the special times we were living in and how the halos were the signs of the convergence of heaven and Earth. From that night forward, I paid attention as the moon gained a rainbow halo when it was directly overhead. And while I was not sure whether the halos existed because I was, or because they were already in existence to witness, I noticed that their intensity increased in proportion to the efforts on my spiritual journey.

The days of great spiritual successes would demonstrate more pronounced displays of the halo and a greater width to the blue skies. On days of spiritual distress, the halo could not hold off the rain. So if it could be understood that the journey I was on seemed to have a direct impact on the skies above, it should be remembered for a greater meaning that will be revealed at the end of this book. For even when I was a child, one day I took notice of a similar ability when I pointed to the clouds and demanded it to snow. At that moment, snow fell from the skies – part of the biggest blizzard to hit the south during my days on Earth. Was the blizzard going to happen anyway? Absolutely. It was predicted it would. But the moment the snow would start falling could have happened for various reasons. The command I issued as a child was witnessed by my cousins. To this day they will be able to recall that moment with clarity, for it was a moment so divine in timing. If it can be seen that the clouds held more potential for snow to fall down than would ever have been experienced at that point in my childhood, then it would only take the slightest command from a spiritual child to invoke atmospheric movement.

The spiritual control over water is one that is documented in the miracles performed in the biblical canon. Moses struck a rock for water to pour out. Jesus walked upon the water and turned water into wine. Noah built a vessel to withstand the greatest onslaught of water of all time. Rivers were turned to blood during plagues. Jesus also stopped a storm from destroying the vessel he was in with the disciples. But more importantly the ability to hold off the rain is a sign of the two witnesses as foretold in Revelation – something I understood by careful observation. And while it should be understood that the popular interpretation of an ability is the capacity to show out, the truth of the matter is it happens without thought and hidden from the eyes. So to say I cannot be sure if the halos in the skies existed previously to my arrival or because I arrived, is the same as to say I do not know if the rain held off because I desired, or because it was desired that I observe this occurrence through my spiritual eyes. It is a conundrum that would leave the most cynical left doubting, and those of hopeful eyes still wary of having witnessed anything that defied reason.

To say that the command to snow occurred as a child and that the rain held off and the clouds circled the skies around the beach I was on during the months I spent in the sun, are facts that to this day can be corroborated. It leaves only the question of perspective – will it be observed as truth or bathed in doubt? For I never once brought light to the relationship of its occurrence to my presence, only that it was observed and

Halos In The Skies

discussed in the conversations I had with others. In my days in Fort Lauderdale I witnessed halos in the heavens, halos on the angels around me, and halos in the skies – all embodied in either white or rainbow light. Above us in the skies were halos of the moon, the sun, the clouds, and the rain – halos that separated and joined the spiritual and earthly divides. And in the theme of separation and joining of two extremes, the manifestation of heaven on Earth was a rainbow, breathtaking and heart-stopping when seen.

Angels & Demons

Angels and demons. Heaven and Hell. It is the fundamental concept to existence that has been debated throughout the ages. Nearly every person who has ventured down the road to spiritual growth has had to wrestle with his interpretation of these concepts. Some may believe angels and demons exist, but not in the world around us. Others may not believe they exist at all. Some may believe there are other explanations to the historical accounts of angels and demons upon the Earth. There are a surprising number of Christians who avoid this topic all together when it is mentioned in the Bible since it challenges the mind beyond what is rationally interpreted through the senses. And then there is the question that if God loves everyone, why would there be darkness and evil?

I struggled with my personal interpretation of this concept for most of my life. As a child, I believed in the Biblical canon like a child believes in a fairytales, myths, and fables. I blindly believed for I had no reason to doubt. As an adult, I wrestled with scientific rationale of the angels and demons. It was not that I doubted my Father or that creation is infinite – I was just on a quest to unravel the mystery that had stumped minds since the dawn of creation. But at the age of thirty when my

Kingdom

Father spoke to me in my first vision, my perspective began to shift, even if only a little bit.

Slowly, through the nurturing and growth of my spirit in the heavens, I began to see angels. At first the angels were only in spirit, but over time my eyes were allowed to see angels around me on Earth. For the longest time I did not believe there was anything truly evil, rather just the concept of a soul absent of light. Even if my definition still remained unchanged to this day, the interpretation of that definition may be a little different, for I have seen how some of the angels cast out of the heavens (such as Lucifer and Abbadon) must suffer the consequences of their actions. And while doing so, these souls absent of light overtly oppose our God of Heaven, though I have to believe there must be some ability to repent − however slim of a chance it may seem. That belief has remained unwavering, though the very concept of "perspective" without omniscience means that some part of existence will always fall in the shadows for a period of time.

But when it comes to angels appearing in form upon the Earth, few people seek to understand this concept for the underlying truth. If a body is seen as a vessel for the spirit, it can be understood that the strength of a person's spirit is always the delta between the tugs of angels and demons upon the soul just a marionette would react to the tugs of the strings by the puppeteer There will always be animalistic instincts that serve as the basis of the mind and body, but the strength of the soul is what overrides the expressions of words and actions as it is birthed within. So a person absent of spirit, could easily react

Angels & Demons

to temptation or blurt out hurtful words without even thinking. This person may rationalize his own misguidance in the actions, when the truth is he is being puppeteered by angels or demons. Perhaps a person smiles at another passerby, a reaction that may have seemed instinctive when it was really the angelic light seeking to burst through the heaven and earthly divide and spread Love to another. So it can be understood in this context that any vessel has the capacity to be puppeteered by an angel or demon. The strength of the spirit determines how sensitive the vessel is to the reaction of one side or the other.

The strong in spirit who walk upon the Earth are guided by a light within, where darkness cannot find any place to seep in. The weak are puppeteered by darkness which radiates out through the expressions of their body. The way they treat themselves and others is a reflection of darkness taking hold. To some who walk upon the Earth, there can be conscious decision in spirit to grant access to their vessel to either an angel or demon. In this case, to earthly eyes a person appears real to others – perhaps with an earthly history. But the truth may be that the vessel houses a soul in which the spirit can flow through unimpeded. So it is entirely possible to interact with an angel or demon seen to others as a human.

One last concept that is even tougher to fathom, is what if the soul that once inhabited a vessel passes on, leaving the body for another soul's journey. While this may be a difficult concept to grasp at first, it becomes easier to see through the concept of possession. This is a concept I chose not to believe in for much of my life. It was only through the last three and a half years in conversations with my Father that I was able to witness how this act manifests in life. But even if one chooses not to explore the concept of possession, it is imperative this concept is studied through the eyes of Christ and Baptism. For if it can be seen that Christ is the divine spirit manifesting in earthly form, it goes to show that the willful surrender of the soul to our Father opens the doorway for Christ to enter and reside. This is a concept preached in every religion, but it is often lost in the clutter of metaphors such as, "If He knocks, will you allow Him to enter?" But to think of the spiritual journey as a progression of strength of the soul to a point of complete and humble surrender, then it can be understood that the marriage of Christ to the soul is the concept man is to strive toward. In this concept it can be understood that at any point along the journey it is possible a person is speaking to Christ directly. And while that may seem like a concept that could be rare, if angels and demons are tugging upon the souls of every spirit at all times throughout the journey, then any words have a direct conduit to the Lord.

Every person in passing, every person closest in relationship to you, are conduits to the Lord, and alternatively, to darkness looking for any angle and any ammunition to help it extinguish light. Angels and demons can manifest in other ways as well. As it is written in the Biblical canon, angels can appear upon the Earth without bodily form. In many documented instances in the Bible, people surrounding a prophet who witnessed an angel would cower and hide in fear to the

Angels & Demons

Glory of God. This is another type of experience I have humbly been able to witness, but it still leaves questions in the earthly minds of the others who cowered away. Since these individuals were not worthy to look upon the grace of an angel, how could they ever prove the account of the prophet? It creates quite a dilemma to those who lack faith – to believe in the only man who witnessed the angel, or to introduce doubt since all of the others surrounding the prophet were not allowed to see. What would you believe?

In the final form, the angel appears in a way for others to witness. Though I believe it can happen in a blaze of glory with fire and smoke billowing forth with chariots flying down from the heavens, I have not witnessed an angel appearing in such a manner, though I have seen them manifest in form from nothing. I suppose it is part of the wonder a child longs to believe in – the wonder that Hollywood recreates through special effects in the movies. But this wonder also leads to misguidance in limiting the mind to understanding the true architecture of God's divine hand. Though I have witnessed the appearance of angels in this form when my soul is in the heavens, as of this writing, angels have not appeared to me in this manner through earthly eyes. For this sole reason it is important to leave open the door that prophecies such as the End of Days will occur without anyone ever knowing. It is also how a soulmate can puppeteer many different vessels until a man finds his way back home to her. While the prophecies could very well be fulfilled in a literal version of the accounts written, it is through the lessons my Father has shown me that the

Kingdom

prophecies should be understood in a way similar to a parallel storyline happening where the expression of the prophecies are demonstrated through earthly results, but completely open to the fulfillment in literal expression if that is His desire.

White Leather & Blue

While my exodus from Nashville to Fort Lauderdale has been viewed through my eyes as stepping foot in Heaven for the very first time, there have been many special moments where I understood that the angels all around were tiered in a way for my soul to understand as it grew in strength. My spiritual sight was slowly interpreting the spiritual blobs of colors and light as shapes with meaning and purpose that I could understand. The first angels that fell into view were the ones that spoke the loudest spiritual message. Those were the ones I noticed upon my arrival. The second angels to fall into focus were those disguised as the needy and the homeless.

One particular evening in early fall, I felt a sudden need to leave my apartment and go to Starbucks for a coffee. At that time, I rarely left my apartment at night. But for some reason, I felt a calling to go. But as it turned out, the desire to go was not about the coffee, but the experience that would unfold along the way. After reaching Starbucks and purchasing my coffee, I turned to leave through the backdoor as was my typical point of entry and exit. To my surprise, I found the back door locked – a new policy they had implemented for the later hours they were opened. So, in an uncharacteristic path

Kingdom

of travel, I left through the front door and headed back to my place.

After rounding the corner of the building, I noticed a man sitting on the sidewalk near the back of the building. He was only wearing one shoe. Many things ran through my head, but the overriding thought was to just sit down and talk to the angel I came to know as Scott. When I sat down, Scott seemed disoriented and scattered. His clothing was dirty and he was drinking from a gallon jug of water. When we began to talk, I asked him where his other shoe was to which he replied that it was lost. We spoke for a while – I mostly listened as the conversation should be better understood as more in the form of a sermon. As I listened to Scott, he spoke about the return of the Messiah and quoted verse after verse from the Bible. He was not just quoting specific verses in a preacher-like fashion. Instead, he was racing though how verses were intertwined throughout the Bible. He quoted it all from His mind and it was clear every word, every verse, every page number, who spoke each verse and who replied, was all ingrained in the depths of His mind. He would jump from verse to verse, weaving through the story of the Messiah's return.

After about an hour or so of listening to his sermon, he paused to drink more water. He went on about how he was overheating and had a hard time regulating his body temperature – words that are familiar to those who have traveled to the heavens. I understood that this angel was in bodily form upon the Earth just as my soul travels to the heavens. When I travel, I have to be given water and certain foods to help me maintain harmony. If I overheat in the heavens, I return to my body. In this moment I knew I was witnessing the opposite version of spiritual travels. Though it was a lot to process, and my earthly mind still tried to rationalize his homeless presence as of earthly origin, I decided to take him to a store and buy him shoes and clothes.

Scott continued to talk about a pair of shoes he had seen at a store several miles away. They were white leather and blue – size fifteen – was the only description he could offer. His foot did not look anywhere near a size fifteen, but that is the size he said he wore nonetheless. Since it was Sunday and after that store's hours, we walked to a nearby store where I bought him clothes and new shoes. He was incredibly thankful, but spoke all in spiritual words. He continued to talk about the love Jesus showed the world. After he seemed taken care of, we parted ways – but this was just the first time I would see Scott and come to understand how he would forever change my life.

Days and weeks passed by without us crossing paths again, but that all changed on a blue sky afternoon. On the second day I saw Scott, I was walking to a nearby restaurant to get some lunch. When we crossed paths, he was only wearing one shoe again. When our eyes met he was still a good distance away. I shouted out, "Hey Scott," to which he replied, "Hey Jonathan! Jesus loves you." I asked him about his missing shoe and he replied, "It's okay. You do not understand yet. You will understand soon." His words hit me hard. I knew he was telling me he was traveling from the heavens though it seemed he was not allowed to share that piece of information. I asked him if there was anything at all I could get him, to which he asked me if I was able to find the shoes of white leather and blue. I told him I was not sure if he needed them after the last pair of shoes I purchased him, but I would be happy to see if I could find them. He nodded in recognition and then began to tell me he was overheating again and that he had to leave. His final words were, "Danger is real" before we parted ways. I turned to look behind me to see where he was walking, but he had already vanished seemingly into thin air.

At that moment, in the distance I heard a man yelling from the other direction. To my eyes, the man yelling was sitting alone on a park bench. I assumed this must be the danger Scott was referring to. I watched as the man seemed to go into seizures on the bench though he was still shouting out words like a demon. This carried on for several minutes as I observed. In this moment, I knew I was witnessing my first possession. I felt no fear, but I felt the strength of God course through me. I understood a call to action was the task at hand. I looked at the man, held out my arm in his direction and said under my breath, "Demon be gone." Immediately, with no delay from the words parting my lips, the man sat up and looked around him as if oblivious to how the demon had vanished from him. It should be noted I was well over a block away, out of the sight of anyone who would see this action take place. It was the first time I had ever attempted to will the spirit of God into another body to remove the man's soul from the

White Leather & Blue

torment and torture of the demon. In truth, until that day, I did not even believe in possessions. It only became evident through the spiritual conversation I had just experienced with the angel named Scott.

After I observed the man for a few minutes to make sure he was free of the demon, I walked past him on my way to the restaurant. As I passed him he stared at me with spiritual eyes of recognition. His eyes were wide and glassy in spiritual recognition of the strength of God that had cleansed him. I thought he may have sensed it flowed through my vessel as I neared him, but regardless, I could tell he felt blessed beyond anything imaginable.

When I finished lunch, I decided to go see if I could find the pair of white leather and blue shoes that Scott had mentioned during the last two conversations. After running several errands throughout the afternoon, I found the store I thought he had described. I walked through the store holding onto hope that a single pair of shoes would somehow identify themselves as the ones he was speaking about. As I sorted through the racks of shoes, only one pair of shoes turned out to fit the description of "white leather and blue." It also happened to be a size fifteen. Whatever the spiritual purpose was, I knew I had accomplished the task. I purchased the pair of shoes (and one additional pair for him) and returned to find him.

It had become dark so I drove to the only place I knew where to start looking for him – the place we first met. In spiritual terms, when one travels to the heavens, there are times it feels like two souls can connect by finding the point of origin

Kingdom

from first interaction. It seemed like the same would hold true if an angel travelled to Earth. When I pulled into the parking lot, I did not see anyone around. The parking lot was empty. I stopped my Jeep and got out to look around. No sooner had I, than Scott appeared. I am not sure where he came from since there were not many places to hide. But that was unimportant. All that mattered was that he had arrived.

We exchanged greetings and I handed him the pair of shoes. Scott seemed like a child on Christmas. There was clearly something important about those shoes – or maybe it was just the effort demonstrated – that ignited his soul into a childlike awe and wonder. He put the shoes on and began sprinting about the parking lot telling me how fast they would help him run. It was like a child would describe a gift he had longed for. It filled my eyes with tears, and my soul with an ocean of Love. Scott and I talked for another half hour or so, where he emphasized that it was important I hear everything that he had to say. He told me a story illustrated with directions and movement. He would enact a path of travel and the directions that were key to the story. There was so much to process that I barely understood the words, but what I did understand was he continued to speak about Matthew 25 in verse. When he completed his story, he wanted to share it with me again because "it was important that [I] hear all [he had] to tell me."

After he completed the story, there was no denying I was in the presence of an angel. His story echoed every aspect of the way a message is delivered in the heavens. I asked him,

"Scott, I know this may sound a little odd, but do you travel to the heavens and back?" He looked at me and smiled. His only words were, "And how would I do that?" We spoke a little longer where he did manage to say how he "has a thorn that allows God to communicate to [me] through [him]." We eventually parted ways. In those moments I knew with complete certainty he was an angel, and he understood I knew. It is important to recognize that he would never identify himself as such, though he never denied it. It is the way of the spirit – answers formed in faith to a question rather than through the eyes and rationalized.

The third time I saw Scott was on an evening in late November. I had walked over to the grocery store and passed him along the way. I asked him if he needed anything to which he said, "Some guava would be nice." I told him not to leave, and that I would be right back. In the grocery store in addition to the guava, I decided to buy him all of the toiletries a person would need to clean themselves up and look presentable. I figured that giving him the tools he needed would help him blend in with the surroundings. It was clear that the travels back and forth from the heavens were hard on his body. When I exited the store, I found him, and we sat down at a table. I shared with him all of the items I bought for him. In total there were four grocery bags full of items that could help him. Some of it was food, other items were the ones most people would not think to offer if they thought he was in need. We shared in more spiritual stories before parting ways.

Kingdom

Right about the point I reached the entrance to my building, I crossed paths with a Canadian family that had been so warm and gracious in welcoming me into their family during their time in Florida. They asked me if I wanted to walk with them, to which I obliged. They asked me where I was coming from late at night so I shared with them the story of the "man named Scott," though I was careful in how I presented him. In the end I said, "To me, he is an angel so I want to make sure I do all I can to help him." The family was more than receptive, and it opened their hearts and minds to helping the homeless without questioning why. As we neared the table Scott and I had just recently occupied and shared in conversation, I saw all of the bags I had purchased sitting there unattended.

For a moment I wondered if Scott was only visible to my eyes. And in that moment I wondered what I must have looked like carrying on a conversation with someone who others may not be able to see – especially with leaving all of the grocery bags on the table. As I talked to the family I was with, I pointed over to the table indicating those were the items I had purchased him. They paused in recognition of the absence of Scott and the bags sitting there unattended. Whether Scott was able to be seen by others or not, I closed my eyes and prayed for God to help me not appear crazy. A few moments later after sending up the prayer, Scott appeared standing near the corner of the building, just hidden from sight from where we were walking. I said, "There he is. Good. I was worried." The family laughed as the words cut through the awkward tension that had mounted in recognition of Scott's absence.

After that day I would only see Scott a couple of more times – each time brief, but full of God's Love. He would always tell me how much Jesus loved me, and that I would be blessed, but most importantly, to keep doing what I was doing because Jesus would one day return. There were constant references to Matthew 25 and verses from Revelation. During these last times I saw Scott, he would always mention he "did not know if he'd be returning." He seemed to know that his ability to travel from the heavens to Earth was coming to an end due to reasons out of his control. And to this day, I have not seen him since our last conversation when my parents visited in January of 2015.

Sanskrit Angels

There is a concept written about throughout the ages of how angels can appear to certain individuals causing others to run away, cower at their appearance, and hide. Other times, there are conflicting accounts as to how different encounters with angels took place based on the lens of each observer and varying accounts of the stories. But never is the experience ever questioned as to whether it occurred, for when multiple observers attest to the experience doubt is removed. It is an interesting conundrum since there is a large movement in the world to abstain from religion, when even those agnostics will still rationalize something must have happened to warrant multiple accounts of different experiences. Many will stop short in searching for reason since documented accounts are very limited, which leaves the resolution open-ended.

Seeing angels in any form is an undeniably spectacular experience. But when the angels are witnessed in the company of others, it makes the experience that much more special. Though there are just a handful of angelic encounters written about in this book, it is important to see that no two angelic encounters chosen for this book occurred in similar ways. The various perspectives of how an angel can appear upon the

Kingdom

Earth is what is important to see, which is why these specific encounters were chosen.

No experience was ever more spectacular to my eyes than what happened in late November. It was already apparent through numerous other experiences how angels were all around my home in Fort Lauderdale. Perhaps, only I could see them. Perhaps others would see homeless men or women who I would see as angels. Regardless, to earthly eyes, it should be understood that up until this point, I believed I saw the same experience as others around me would see the experience – if they were allowed to see it at all. It was through the sight of my spiritual eyes that allowed me to see the angels in a visual representation similar to how Hollywood has popularized it. But on a day in late November, I would witness an entirely different experience than a friend sitting next to me witnessed.

Late in the afternoon on November 20, 2014, I walked to a coffee shop with a friend who lived in the same building as me to share in coffee and conversation. Her name is Cheryl and is an amazing woman. From the first moment we met, there was always a spiritual connection. As I got to know her, I opened up to her more about the journey I was on and shared with her a few details about the relationship with my Father. I was always careful to take baby steps in conversation, for it seemed that moving too fast would be a little too much to digest. So when we had opportunities to share stories over coffee or on the beach, I always enjoyed listening to hers and sharing

Sanskrit Angels

the next small baby steps with her about my journey. On November 20th, it would be a similar conversation.

We sat outside of the coffee shop where I shared with her the story about knowing God early in life – being Baptized on Christmas Eve, praying to fall in love and subsequently meeting my ex-wife. I shared with her a story about a prayer I said shortly after my divorce, when I prayed for God to help me feel loved when I thought all hope was lost. The next morning I awoke to an angel's arms holding me close. It was a day of the grandest Love and warmth that I have ever experienced on Earth. I shared with her a story about the first time I saw an angel and how I did not realize it was an angel, but rather thought it was a ghost.

The topics of the conversation seemed natural in context to the story that she shared with me prior to me opening up to her, but I became aware that Cheryl did not seem to want to hear about seeing angels, so I carefully tried to navigate through the conversation. When I shared with her the story about the angel that first appeared in a ghostly manner, she told me to stop. She became visibly scared and shaken. It was an odd moment because it seemed like God was speaking through my vessel in the conversation as I listened to the words He was saying.

At the point when she told me to stop and became visibly scared, two angels walked up to her. To her, I am sure it seemed like a husband and wife as I understood their appearance – but honestly, in all that transpired, I cannot be sure what she actually witnessed. When the couple approached, the man seemed to be speaking quickly under his breath as he told Cheryl how she had the most beautiful blonde hair. The first time anyone meets Cheryl, it is one of the first attributes that is noticed, for her hair is genuinely breathtaking – but it was the first time I had heard anyone make a direct comment.

Cheryl seemed almost taken aback. The scared sensation she was demonstrating caused her to momentarily lock up when the angel spoke about her hair. Her face was surprised, as I was at that time. It is not often a couple on Earth will talk about the beauty of another out of respect of their relationship. But I understood her pause was so much more. She was witnessing an angel in a form her eyes could rationalize, but one her spirit trembled to in fear. As their conversation continued, the man looked at me and said something in a language I did not understand. My initial thought was, "This is what Sanskrit sounds like."

Sanskrit is generally accepted as the oldest language on Earth. It has survived for at least six thousand years. It is a language known as "the language of the gods" and is a language I have heard and seen in written form in the heavens multiple times. It is a language that predates the written form. In the context of the conversation we were having outside of the coffee shop, it seemed extremely out of place. When I heard the words, I just nodded and smiled back at him to acknowledge hearing his words. I listened intently as He again told Cheryl that she was "such a beautiful woman." I looked at the female angel, and she gave me a look that I can only describe as something out of my travels to the heavens. It had the austerity and Love of a great angel.

I continued listening as the man told Cheryl something else in the Sanskrit-sounding language. Cheryl looked at him blankly like she did not hear him. The female angel then said something in the same language to Cheryl as well. Cheryl still did not acknowledge as she stared at him blankly, though engaged in the afterglow of his compliments. The two angels then bid us a good evening in English before they both said something again in the indecipherable language and walked off into the distance.

After the two angels walked away, I spoke to Cheryl as if nothing out of the ordinary had occurred. All she could keep saying was, "That is so odd." Cheryl would then follow up with thought-fillers like, "Interesting..." and "Hmmmm." After I sensed she had enough time to process the conversation, I offered the reply, "Is it?" She went on to ask me what I thought the couple's words meant, but I only replied, "What do you think?"

Cheryl tossed around ideas about potential meanings in the conversation and why this couple would have walked up to us. She continued to reiterate how she receives compliments from time to time, but only from people she knows. It was apparent she understood something was much different in this conversation than she had experienced in the past. She emphasized how she never receives compliments from strangers, much less married couples. Continually she circled back to how strangely timed it all seemed. I just said, "You know, one day I hope you can see everything for what it is and not what it seems."

This comment, of course, prompted further questions from her about my thoughts of the couple. I was careful to not project my recognition of the couple being angelic in order to see if she would arrive at that understanding on her own. Eventually, she exclaimed, "I bet you think they are angels. Stop it! Do not tell me that." I never said anything to cause her to tell me to "stop it." I never even replied. She responded to her own thought aloud as she rationalized what she had witnessed. It was only when she asked me to repeat the conversation to her that the couple shared that I understood we witnessed two completely different conversations.

I repeated the dialogue word-for-word, and pointed out the places the man and woman spoke in a language I could not discern. When I spoke about the different language Cheryl looked confused. She said, "He never said anything else after he said you are so beautiful." I looked back at Cheryl dumbfounded. I said, "Yes he did. He said something to me, then said something to you. You did not answer him. I just assumed you did not understand him." Cheryl became visually disturbed. She became panicked and said with a fear in her voice, "No. No Jonathan. No, he did not say anything. Stop it. Do not play games with me. He did not say anything in another language. And, he did not say anything to you."

In that moment I recognized the absurdity of him speaking Sanskrit to me in the midst of an English conversation, but it never crossed my mind as the conversation transpired that my reality differed from what Cheryl saw in that moment. I had always assumed that an angelic encounter would be perceived the same way to those around. But that thought process quickly stalled as I recalled how just weeks before an angel showed me her wings while others were sitting around us at a patio table. In that circumstance the angel revealed herself to me in playful recognition that I had identified her true form as an angel upon the Earth in the midst of a conversation with others. It was a dinner in which I thought I was dining with other souls in the Promised Land, but would come to understand I was dining with angels. It was one of the most memorable experiences in Fort Lauderdale since I had arrived.

Dining With Angels

"So many lost souls. They do not even know..."

Those were the words that crossed the lips of one of the two angels standing near me. They were involved in a deep conversation, most certainly unaware of how their words were beginning to carry to my ears. Without even knowing the context, I could tell those words were uttered in part to describe the situation surrounding all of us in that very moment – the lost souls that were congregating among the angels. However, this time would be different from other encounters with angels. This time, I would not be experiencing angels during one of my travels to the heavens. This time, the angels were here on Earth. This time, I had been invited to one of their houses on Earth in a dinner celebration. This was the moment, for me, that belief in being surrounded by angels and the reality of angels in earthly form would collide.

Sadness is the only way I could describe the feeling that engulfed my soul when those words registered within. It was a moment that should have been filled with rejoicing – a moment of awe dancing upon the surface of the skin akin to a honeybee lighting upon the petals of a flower, or a butterfly fluttering along the surface of a leaf, gracefully touching down in a way that causes an ignition of splendor to race along the

Kingdom

surface to and from its very point of contact – ripples upon calamity's norm. But this day, the only feeling that I felt was the weight of every soul's oblivion to the days of judgment looming ahead. I did not have to know the context of the conversation to feel the sadness the angels were expressing in their conversation. It was as if there was a single cry from the silence that broke through to my soul's ears, to which my soul responded in kind to the sad chorus their souls sang. Ten thousand times ten thousand souls unaware. Ten thousand times ten thousand that are naively going to suffer the repercussions of complacency's inertia. In that moment, as I digested the gravity of the angel's words, the angel that was speaking glanced over at me allowing his words to trail off. He knew exactly what I had just overheard. It did not take but mere seconds before he reacted and walked over to me.

The house where we were was located in a city named Plantation, Florida. It was a beautiful house, and the name of the location could not have been more fitting for the type of get-together that would eventually be unveiled. The host (and owner of the house) was an interior decorator, so her house was appointed in original design and artwork. Nothing could have told a greater story of her spirit than in the way she had appointed her house through the expressions of her soul. Original artwork – oils, pastels, pencil, and mosaic – ornamented her house in just the perfect way. Only a few weeks prior, I had received an invitation to attend her social get-together. The invitation left a lot to the imagination – all pertinent details were withheld.

Dining With Angels

All I could glean from the invitation to this gathering was through the theme on the card: "Celebrate Autumn – Cooler Weather Is Here." Upon the surface level, the theme to the get-together seemed to be just a seasonal title with a designer play on words. But I suppose it was the wordplay of the theme that caused me to overlook what the event was truly about. The list of invited participants was shielded from every other person's view and no more details were available – just the theme. In truth, I originally dismissed the invitation in favor of attending a football game several hours away. I only saw the surface level, failing to look one step further as every bit of my journey has continued to lead me to do. But over the course of the preceding weeks to the get-together I received several emails from the host strongly encouraging me to attend. Even though we had only met once at a fundraiser nearly three months prior, her desire for me to attend the get-together was masqueraded behind lines like "I would love to introduce you to some very nice people" as well as other soulful tug-of-war phrases. I could sense there was a greater reason for her desire in my attendance, but never would I have guessed what would unfold that October evening.

As the angel walked over to me in acknowledgment of the words I had just heard him say, I was still trying to find the rationalization that I was truly standing with angels on Earth. Up to this point, I was only aware that I was standing in a house full of a seemingly eclectic group of people – each uniquely strong and full of stature. Of course I had noticed in the room the human forms of the angels that I have seen in the heavens, but the moment something of this magnitude first happens, it is nearly impossible to process in real-time. My mind raced at the possibilities. Were all of the attendees angels? Were the couple of angels I recognized from the heavens in human form the only angels among a crowd of others? What was the purpose? Why was I invited?

To earthly eyes, everyone would have appeared to be regular humans. There was nothing special about their outward appearances. There were not wings, halos, or white robes. And though I had been applying the concept that everyone I met in Fort Lauderdale was an angel to improve my walk, it undoubtedly stretched my mind to its limits. However, the truth of the seemingly "crazy" thoughts of seeing angels becomes more rational over time than at first blush. So, as I had embraced this approach in my daily walk, if nothing else, it had helped me continue to grow in all aspects of my spirit. In every conversation I had with another, I viewed it as a spiritual conversation. Would I answer it in a pleasing way to an angelic teacher? Would I pass the test? Would I act in an appropriate, humbled way – one where ego is suppressed out of the response? And while I have had no tangible proof that my actions were anything more than spiritually-lead, this would be the first time the heavenly angels made themselves known to me en masse here on Earth. This was the moment that truth in understanding everyone as angels around me became fact rather than faith-and-a-fairytale.

Since moving to Fort Lauderdale, my spiritual eyes had been gaining strength in discerning spiritual blobs of light into

Dining With Angels

the forms of the angels. When I closed my eyes during meditation and at night, my soul was taken to the heavens where I would speak with angels. During waking moments, the angels on Earth were slowly becoming easier to discern. But what I never expected – and partly why this experience was so grand – was the very same embodiments of the angels I had witnessed in the heavens appeared at this Autumn Celebration.

The angel I first overheard speaking was an angel that has only recently appeared in clear form to me in my experiences in the heavens. In my journals, I refer to him as the angel that looks like Richard from the television show Lost. This particular angel appears to be of Spanish or Cuban heritage with strong facial features. At the house, when he walked over to me after noticing I had overheard his conversation, the angel introduced himself as Alejandro, though he shortened it to Aleph in conversation. Aleph is the first letter of the Hebrew alphabet and represents the archetype of strength. It also represents "the beginning." His name was a clear indication of his spiritual introduction to me. As we chatted, he called a girl over who was his date to the party. They both told me how they did not know anyone there – including the host – but were eager to speak with me.

When I asked them how they heard about the event, they tried to pass off the question by saying "from a friend" and quickly changing the subject. As we got to know each other, the questions Alejandro asked me were clearly directed at my spiritual walk. I think he wanted to see if I recognized him, though I never verbally acknowledged it. Eventually, the conversation turned to talk of a trip these two angels had just taken. The girl pulled out a camera and began showing me pictures of a forest. In earthly conversation, I am sure it would have appeared bizarre. But in the context of the spiritual conversation, it could not have been clearer. The forest he was showing me was of one of the locations in the heavens I have visited many times. It seems to be a place of spiritual strength training. I have written about this location many times in my journals and described the towering trees and waterfalls that fill out the landscape. In the conversation, I acknowledged that I recognized the place (though in vague references). It was at this point both Alejandro and his date were called over to their other angel friend and then disappeared from the party.

Only about a half hour had passed since the get-together had begun and I already had come to the recognition of the angelic interactions occurring in the room. It was after the first interaction with Alejandro that I recognized the theme of party on the invitation – "Autumn Celebration" – was alluding to "the harvest" as mentioned in Revelation. The words I overheard Alejandro speak could not have been clearer. No one in the room had ever met before, and it was only a select group of guests invited to the get-together. I understood that this an invitation for a select group of invited souls to dine with angels.

It was interesting to watch the angels versus the invitees. It became more apparent as the feast wore on. In the beginning everyone was just sharing in small talk. By the end of the night, I found myself sitting out on a patio with another couple that was invited to the party discussing religion. The couple

Dining With Angels

first began talking about how strange all of the interactions had been, still trying to rationalize all I had understood about the angels. The lady who first began speaking with me could not get over all of the "coincidences" of the attendees being connected to each other in ways that defied earthly explanation. In one scenario, two people had grown up minutes away from each other in a tiny town in the rural Midwest.

As the conversation wore on, the subject matter became very spiritual. Whether the lady was an angel testing me in my responses or whether she was an invitee, I was not sure. But, I did take the queue and answer all she asked about me. I never introduced religious topics. Rather, the couple continued asking more questions about me and my faith to which my answers were all religiously founded. I assumed this grabbed their curiosity which led to the lengthy conversation. About an hour into the conversation I noticed that most of the attendees had made their way out to the table and were all surrounding us and listening intently. It was as if this was an opportunity to demonstrate my spiritual growth before the angels of heaven that had descended to Earth. A couple of others sat down next to me and began supporting the answers I was giving. In some cases I noticed guidance, in others support and confirmation. To the person asking the questions, it became a deep conversation about faith and spirituality.

To my left, a girl with short red hair sat down. Her hair was in the form of a pixie cut. I was confident that she was another one of the angels that had identified herself in my travels to the heavens recently. She had such a peace about her and a

Kingdom

vigor in the way she answered the questions. Her answers were eloquent and filled with the perfect amount of spiritual guidance. When the questions were asked by the couple, the red-headed angel would always let me answer and then acknowledge my answer with her eyes before chiming in. It felt like something I had experienced many times in the heavens between a teacher and a student (where I was the student). I suppose I must have let on my spiritual acknowledgement because at one point, the angel glanced at me out of the corner of her eye before revealing her wings to me.

There is nothing that could have prepared me for that moment. Even though I knew I was dining with angels, to see the combination of an earthly vessel with spiritual forms was a first for me. Imagine an earthly body with a ghostly form of wings quickly unroll from her back and spread out behind me. This is the experience I had, though no one else would notice. It was only the briefest of moments that I saw the angel's wings, but it was one of the grandest I have ever experienced. The conversation with the group did not last too much longer before everyone decided it was time to part ways. It was not a gradual ending to the celebration, but as if there was a sudden reason for it to find its end. Perhaps it was in the revelation of the angels wings. Perhaps it was in the way the conversation with the couple was handled that revealed my soul. Whatever the reason may have been, everyone parted ways promising to see each other again.

I know we will all meet again when we find each other in the End. And while encounters like these are memorable in so many different ways, this is just one of many that happened to me since the day I arrived in Fort Lauderdale. It seems hard to fathom how the luster and grandeur of moments like this – moments of dining with angels, and seeing an angel's wings – can fade over time. But even the grandest moments can be superseded by life when it manages to get in the way. Those are the days that feel crushing to the soul – like a ship lost at sea – for there is still recognition that the wonder of the moments that God has allowed the eyes to see has faded into the distance behind something earthly (and more than likely petty). It is when the experiences begin to fade that the soul must seek out our Father and ask Him to remind us again of His splendor – to help the earthly dominance fade so that the Spiritual eyes can retake the reigns. It is one of the most special prayers that can ever be prayed – one that demonstrates the truest recognition of the journey… the humility in recognition that a soul is nothing without the strength of God.

Remind Me Again

Days come and go. As time wilts away and becomes cast off as the forgotten vehicle that governs the actions of our daily lives, it becomes easy to lose appreciation for the greatness that God has bestowed around us each and every day. The craft of His magnificence is the pinnacle of amazing. It is not just a beautiful flower or the peaceful sound produced by the rolling tide of the ocean. It is everything – everything that comprises what we know as life and existence. For just a moment, take the time to think about creating something as beautiful as Earth upon a blank canvas. To envision every intricacy that is part of this experience is enough to boggle the mind.

So as it would come to be, my time in Fort Lauderdale has been surrounded by truly memorable experiences. Every day is a blessing. Every day is another opportunity to take another concerted effort of upward motion toward His Desire. But sometimes, the recognition of God's experiences are pelted at such a fast rate that it can become easy to overlook the macrocosm of this Promised Land in lieu of the microcosm of the intricate daily lessons. It is for this very reason that I have made a concerted effort to ensure one day a week is spent in celebration of the brilliance of the Lord and His creation, without work or daily tasks getting involved out of respect for His splendor.

Setting aside one day a week is not an idea to mimic the demonstration of the Sabbath for my journey. Rather, that is just how it worked out. In the beginning I was not locked into a specific day to set aside. I tried to play it by spiritual ear. If I was on the beach and there was clearly a purpose in conversation in adding light to an otherwise darkened world, I obliged. I would always set aside work and focus only on where the Spirit was leading me. In the beginning it seemed to always happen on weekends, perhaps because that is when most people are not working and have time to be out at the beach. But as the weeks and months wore on, I began to notice that while each and every day I would go out to the beach, it was almost always Sundays that became a day to follow the Spirit's lead. This was not a decision of the mind, but rather one of the Spirit. So, as I came to understand Sunday as my Sabbath, I always made sure to keep that day reserved for praising, listening, and following His spirit. For most of my time in Fort Lauderdale, I did not attend any specific church during those Sundays, but that evolution also began to happen over time. Mostly, the version of the Sabbath I celebrated should be seen as a day I understood how to find stillness, celebrate His spirit, and help bring light unto others in need.

Through it all, as the stretch from September to December neared its end, I found myself over several days of November struggling to find the fire within. It was not that the fire was extinguished nor that I was losing faith, rather it seemed too comfortable of a place to be in and I wanted to ensure I had not fallen from His Grace. Every day leading up to and through these days of struggle had been full of miraculous experiences, but I really felt the need to feel the fire roar inside. And while I would not see it as such, in hindsight, I can see it was the calm before the storm.

From July through the first week of September my life in Fort Lauderdale took root. The work contract that had helped me arrive had ended and was up for renewal. From September through the end of November the renewal to that contract had not materialized. In prayer I found peace that it may have been the end of the ride. There was eventually one conversation with an angel in the heavens where he wanted to bring me peace when he said, "These days are the best days of your life." I felt calm and peace in knowing my Father was taking care of me, though the uncertain future created some anxiety. While I felt I was in limbo regarding work during those months, I knew His directive had always been to complete these books. So as November began to reach its end, I prayed for God to remind me again – to remind me of His wonder, His splendor, His grace; to bring peace of mind to the anxiety that my mind could not put at bay; to see the magnificence of His work in a way that would light the fire within; to hold me close, to help me feel His Love so that I could move through each day without any fear.

I said this prayer on November 13th to help me be reminded how this place I was in truly was Heaven on Earth. And though it may seem like a play on words, I wanted to stay

Kingdom

grounded to Heaven rather than Earth. When I awoke on November 14th everything changed. In every aspect of the day my Father continually showed His face. It began when I awoke to the buzzing of my phone. I reached over and picked it up to discover I had seven emails. If there ever is a way to start a day strong, it is to be awakened by the hand of God. And while it may not appear this is how I was awakened, it is important to understand how I recognize His communication. He speaks to me through a myriad of ways, but early on in learning to hear His voice, I noticed His signature of the number seven was tantamount to hearing His audible voice. Though He will communicate with each person in a manner that is specific to him, for our conversations, the number seven always appears.

So it can be seen that by waking up to the buzzing of the phone, my Father was giving me a nudge and saying, "Hey Son, wake up." As I reached over to my phone groggily in an effort to see why it buzzed, I saw that the buzzing sound was an indication of receiving new mail. When I saw the number of emails totaled seven, it was a moment I opened my eyes and said, "Okay Father, I'm awake." From that moment on, I knew the day would be special.

After showering, I headed to get some breakfast. The day was unusually calm from the typical hustle and bustle. Perhaps my Father was just allowing me to feel peace within, and to everyone else the world was in its routine spin. After picking up a coffee and breakfast, I began to walk back to the beach where I planned to sit outside and enjoy the warmth of the sun

Remind Me Again

on my face and the sand beneath my feet. But as I walked back toward my building to head out to the sand, I saw a flock of seagulls fly overhead. The birds caused me to take notice to the direction in which they flew. In this moment I saw a shape in the clouds as the birds disappeared from my view.

The shape in the clouds was a crown with seven spires. At first it may seem like I am making this up, but it should be understood that the world should be viewed in the context of each person's walk with God. To one person He may communicate in a way that to another He may not. In the context of the clouds, it was so clearly defined. The crown was the only cloud in the sky. The seven spires were clearly defined as if drawn by His hand. The crown was so defined I took a picture and sent it to Bryan. The meaning of the crown should be understood as it has been described through this series of Books. The crown was a way for God to remind me that I was standing in His Kingdom. If I were to have questioned the shape in the clouds as being a chance occurrence, the mark of seven spires was too much of a coincidence to discount. So knowing that I had been awakened by Him, I recognized His first words spoken to me as, "I just wanted to remind you this is the Kingdom, and here is your crown."

When I reached the beach, I enjoyed my breakfast with no one around. I watched the cloud-crown dissipate over the next hour. As it began to dissipate, it remained strong in form. At one point, out of nowhere, two more spires formed. If seen in the context of a fluent conversation, the crown began with seven spires representing the seven divisions observed on

Kingdom

Earth. As the cloud began to dissipate, it could be seen as the Earth giving way to the heavens. And, when this occurred, the seven spires revealed the two hidden. The number of spires totaled nine, the mark of Heaven and the complete number of divisions hidden from earthly eyes. The concept of seven versus nine is discussed in Book VIII – Secrets. But, for now it is important to indicate a footnote for the reader to seek further guidance in Book VIII. For in understanding the concept of "nine and the two hidden within the seven" the significance of the symbolism in the spires becomes much more divine in meaning.

 The day on the beach turned into an even grander conversation with my Father. After spending some time paddle boarding, I returned to the beach and, while sitting alone, a man who I met at the autumn celebration dinner when I dined with angels walked up to me. His name was Jeff and was the embodiment of the blur between angel and man. In every aspect I truly believe he was divinely sent to this land. At the dinner several days prior we had discussed how we lived near each other. But today he decided to walk down the beach to say hello if I was out there.

 When he arrived I was initially caught off guard, for in my eyes stood an angel before me, or an angel in bodily form. As we stood there talking, we began to learn more about each other. I learned how he was once married for seven years before he became divorced. That number related to the duration that I had been with my ex-wife. For from the time we first met to the time we divorced, was right at seven years – a divine punctuation mark. But that was not the only occurrence of the number seven. As we talked about the condo building that he lived in, I came to learn he lived on floor number seven, and that he had inherited the unit from generations before him. He went on to discuss the significance of the seventh floor though he never related it to how I had seen it before. To him it was a number that indicated safety, a floor from which he could be rescued if the integrity of the building ever came into jeopardy.

As we talked, the number seven radiated throughout the conversation. I understood that it was the voice of God that I was hearing. But I suppose I was not the only person on the beach who heard the voice of God, for an older gentleman who lives in my building approached Jeff and me to say, "Hello." This man was named George and I had become really close with his family over the previous months. But, not once had he ever walked over to me. I had only seen him in passing when speaking to his children and grandchildren, and perhaps one other conversation when I walked up to say, "Hello," to him. So it was interesting that George approached Jeff and me, for I had never engaged in any conversation with George aside from normal pleasantries and the occasional, "Hi."

When George walked over, he wanted to speak with Jeff. George is one of the longest tenured residents. And while it would be hard to see it through the perspective I am about to give, to me he appears to be a King of this heavenly Kingdom. He is warm, loving, and always has the presence of a father. Perhaps his vessel is one for my Father. It is clear that he has a great spiritual life in every sense, and that he longs to maintain the beauty of the Kingdom as I have come to see it. When he approached us, it seemed he wanted to welcome Jeff in. As he approached, Jeff made a subtle bow of his head, and George nodded back in recognition. The next words spoken should not have caught me off guard, but still managed to leave me speechless. After George said, "Hello," he said, "This is God's country," as he motioned his hand out over the sand. It was the first time any religious conversation arose with George, though I have had spiritual conversations with his family. But it was another divine mark from God on the day as I asked Him to remind me again of His Kingdom.

After the day wound down under the sun, I returned to my apartment to clean up and try to get some writing done. When I arrived I noticed I had missed a call. It was from my financial planner – another man divinely purposed into my life before I left Nashville. To receive a call from him was akin to God saying, "Hey Jonathan, this is just a reminder of your blessings. There is more to come and reason to plan ahead. So be prepared to expect more in the near future." It was not long after this call that I fielded two more. One was from a potential new client that wanted me to meet with the company executives to discuss using me on their upcoming project. The second call was from the client I had been waiting on a renewal from. It was on this call that we talked about the final details of the renewal and even a potential bonus. So without me ever reaching out for business or calling my previous client, I received two potential revenue streams and a call from my financial planner. The divine nature of the experience should be clear, but the point of two potential streams of revenue should be viewed in the same manner as a sign of double confirmation akin to the sign of two doves. And though everything would eventually work out exactly as God planned with the clients, I understand now that the greater meaning in all that God was saying was, "I've got you son, do not worry about your future." It had less to do about the earthly details of the calls themselves, and more of a symbolic meaning of, "You asked Me to remind you, so I'm demonstrating the Kingdom to you in every way that I can."

After wrapping up the phone calls, I decided to walk a couple of blocks to grab some dinner. But on the way to the restaurant, I decided to stop by an art gallery and visit the owner. Brooke owned the gallery and had helped me find art for my apartment when I first moved. She has been a blessing in my life and, when I pass by her gallery, I always try to stop by and say, "Hello." This time when I arrived, there was another artist in her gallery. After striking up a conversation, I learned she created the same kind of art I was seeking. She showed me samples of her artwork which appeared to fit my decor. We exchanged numbers before she walked out the door. After the conversation ended, I heard Brooke say, "Interesting..." since every time I come in there seems to be a divine reason. I looked over her way and just smiled. I said, "Is it though? Timing seems pretty well aligned each time I walk in." Brooke just nodded in disbelief and said, "I know." So though there was no mention of the number seven in the gallery, the timing was clearly His. As I sought art to finish out decorating my apartment, God allowed the timing of the meeting with the artist to fall into alignment.

Afterwards I walked to a restaurant nearby, where I was seated by the same waitress who had served me the previous time. The dinner was great, though the restaurant was extremely busy. At one point the waitress came up to me and said, "Your patience makes me happy." To many, these words may have sounded earthly in nature, but to my spiritual ears there was so much more meaning. In the context of the entire day, this was God's voice bleeding through her words. Her words made me smile at the recognition of His words. Perhaps she was an angel like all of the others, but it is important that I explain that there is still an earthly component to angels. This component will fool many from accepting the truth as I have been allowed to see it, for to earthly eyes there is only one set of eyes used in the perspective.

After finishing dinner, I headed back to my place. I passed another angel at a bus-stop who I had witnessed before. A few days prior to this day, I had walked to have dinner at the same restaurant I had just left. It was the first time I had ever visited that restaurant. On that particular day, I was experiencing a tremendous lack of confidence in my appearance. I am generally at peace with myself and never really down, but something about that day had me reaching for any boost of confidence. When I had left my house that day I had prayed for God to help me find strength through my wavering confidence. It was in answer to that prayer that he placed this angel into my life.

Remind Me Again

When I walked toward the bus-stop, I noticed an older lady staring at me. I honestly thought she was going to ask me for money. But when I approached her she said, "I just have to tell you that you have great hair! I normally would never say anything like that, but there is something that made me feel compared to share." We shook hands and exchanged pleasantries for a moment, then parted ways where I would not see her again until this moment. At the time of our first meeting, I knew my Father had placed her in my life. I do not usually receive random compliments, so it was obvious this interaction was divine. So in the context of returning from the restaurant and seeing this angel for the second time, I understood my Father was saying, "Hey Son, remember her? Remember how I placed her into your life?" It was a moment where no words were exchanged, there was only silent recognition. As I passed by her we each nodded at each other and smiled. After I had walked a good ways past her, I said, "Father, I noticed."

When I returned home, I said a long prayer thanking my Father for all that he had shared, but as it turned out, He still was not finished. Before my prayer ended, I received a call. It was from a homeless man I have been helping to try to find a job. Though I have not freely provided him with money to spend, I did provide him with an iPad. There are days that we sit together and go through job applications. I have realized my purpose is helping him learn to help himself. And while he had not yet received any responses to his applications, the voicemail he left me was telling me he had his first interview set up. It was a moment of spiritual recognition that the work I have been putting in is helping him in the right direction.

After checking my voicemail and hearing the message, I checked my email one last time before I headed to bed. The last email I received was from a dear friend. It was from Teresa, the mother-figure I discussed in Book I. Without belaboring the details from the first book, it is important to understand the symbolism in her earthly name and as a mother figure to me on this journey. The punctuation mark to God's day of reminders was marked in how he signed off with her communication. As I read through the email and understood the divine timing and the symbolism in the content of her message, it was the first time I noticed the date all of the reminders were occurring. The date was November 14, 2014 – a date that sums to 7/7, a symbolic number to the seven-and-seven moments that have occurred between my Father and me all day. This was the last time I would ever ask Him for reminders, for the days upcoming in December were the start of the next leg of the journey. But before the divine nature of all that was to be revealed to me in December occurred, Lucifer would appear in bodily form to me upon this Earth.

The Day I Met Lucifer

Elevators. At the most simplistic level elevators are vehicles used to travel upward and downward, limited to vertical travel only. Other vehicles can travel along other axes, but only elevators are used to move people, places, and things up and down. When elevators are understood at this primal level, it bodes well to observe them through this pretense when Divine communication occurs as well. This does not mean that every time a person boards an elevator he should think of the ascent and descent on every occasion. But it does mean that when one stands in an elevator during recognition of a divine message being delivered, that the context of the elevator is important to observe. For if the language of the Divine is to be understood in the complexity of the delivery, the body of the message is the embodiment of the setting.

As a child learns to hear the voice of God, the first recognition of the sound of His voice usually sets off an ignition of fireworks inside. It is easy to see how the excitement of the recognition, or even the scrutiny of questioning the message, leaves the body of content hollow in depth, for only the voice was heard and not the entire message. But as a child learns to refine the senses in understanding the Divine language, it becomes clear that His voice is fluid in conversation, spoken throughout life's daily navigation. So when it is understood that He speaks whenever He desires, the secondary question asked should be, "Why now? What other factors should I be observing?" In the divine architecture of all that is spoken, every factor is important, every aspect unspoken.

In November of 2014, I stepped onto the elevator in my residence. I was accompanied by a new friend I had met at the Autumn Celebration Dinner discussed in the chapter "Dining With Angels." He is one of those people for me that is hard to gauge whether he is of earthly body or of Heavenly nature. When the end of my days on Earth arrives, I would not be at all surprised if my Father said, "Yes, Son, he was an angel all along." The man was named Jeff. He always radiated a warm and inviting spirit to everyone around. He is a reiki master in practice, though I understood it to be more of a way of life to him than a profession. Every time Jeff would engage in a conversation with another, he would always bow his head and bless them. For someone uncomfortable in acceptance of the spirit, I am sure it could cause discomfort at the start of a conversation. But, I never saw him waiver. He always began in blessing before a word was ever spoken.

In any experience upon the Earth, there is always greater strength in numbers. In the case with Jeff, I have to think the perception of two strong souls together forms an even greater manifestation of the spirit to other people observing. Others that I have met throughout my journey have always expressed a strong recognition of the spirit radiating from my bodily vessel. Many times people would not know how to place it into

The Day I Met Lucifer

words, but that did not stop them from trying. I heard everything from, "There is something about you" to "You have something different." Many times it was just a person saying, "Have we met before? You seem so familiar. I cannot place it." In my youth, I just assumed I had a face that was similar to one that people saw on television, though no one was ever able to quite identify the similarity. It was a phrase I have heard hundreds upon hundreds of times throughout my life. But in youth I did not understand the eyes of the spirit. As a child of the spirit, I became more aware. And as time wore on and spiritual strength was gained, I understood that very question asked was not of earthly recognition. It was always a form of two souls exchanging spiritual introductions.

So with the understanding that the strength of the spirit multiplies in numbers, the experience that happened to me in November was both the cause and result of the spirit strengthening around us. As Jeff and I boarded the elevator to head down to the lobby to part ways, I carried a paddle for my paddle board in one hand and my bag for the beach thrown across my back. The paddle in my hands was vertically held in a manner so as not to obstruct any others aboard the elevator. For over five months I had ridden the elevator near daily with paddle in hand in this very same manner. But when we boarded the elevator, the darkest presence I had ever witnessed on Earth permeated the confines of the five by six space we were bound within.

Standing in the corner behind two women was a man I had never seen before. He had the whitest hair I have ever seen on Earth. He had a crisp white razor-cut beard with cleanly-defined edgings. He wore dark sunglasses which were as dark as pitch. The arms of the sunglasses were wide and extended around the sides of his eyes. It was apparent that his appearance was important and that no one should see his eyes.

As the elevator descended, the man's voice rang out from the corner of the elevator. "You should not be in here." I knew immediately he was speaking to me, though I did not understand the context beyond the spiritual recognition of what was happening. If one has ever seen the show Supernatural on television, the illustration to all that was happening would be apparent. The damp, foreboding essence that spilled forth out of the elevator when the doors opened for Jeff and me to board was none other than Lucifer himself, standing in human form. I knew when I stepped onto the elevator the feeling was the very same feeling of standing with Lucifer in the heavens. But this would be the day I met Lucifer here on Earth.

The feeling was thick as molasses as he stole the air from every soul in the elevator. As I puzzled over his words, I recognized the descent of the elevator as the supporting imagery to his delivery. I understood the symbolism in the spiritual conversation taking place, but remained without any earthly context to bind the words to a response in the silence following his words. His next words rang out as everyone's breath was held in check in anticipation of the words sure to be spoken. "You should use the service elevator." he said. This was the moment I understood the earthly context. He disliked the paddle I carried with me aboard the elevator. In terms of space taken up, the paddle took up no more space than the space I would have taken without the paddle in hand. It was standing vertically extending slightly over my head.

The silence resulting from his words continued to suck the air out of the moment. As I tried to determine any appropriate response to the spiritual conversation Lucifer was provoking, Jeff's voice rang out in the silence. "I'm sure it's okay! Well, I will not tell if you do not say anything." The other two people on the elevator smiled at the wit in Jeff's response. I laughed inside, but kept my face free of reaction in his retort. Jeff managed to throw out the most playful of comments to offset the serious nature of the words spoken by Lucifer. In a spiritual context, his reply was even funnier to my spirit. It was as if the word of God said, "Petty child, this is why you were banished from my Kingdom. Do you not see your words do not matter? Go away now, and leave alone those with strength in the spirit."

Lucifer's response was terse and voiced his anger at Jeff. He boldly said, "You'd be best not to talk right now." It was as if Lucifer was saying, "Go on your way. It is not your concern. This is between me and Jonathan." The air in the elevator was again syphoned off and turned into sludge. I understood this was Lucifer rearing up his head to try to derail me on my walk. In the surrounding days of this experience it had become clear that God had ramped up His level of communication to me, as if an important moment was upcoming. I understood there seemed to be a great importance for darkness to attempt to cloak and extinguish the efforts of my Father with me.

Kingdom

Nothing could have been more apparent than the manifestation of Lucifer in the elevator that day.

The elevator arrived at the lobby level and everyone escaped to freedom as quickly as they could. Jeff and I parted ways and I went out to the beach to paddle board for a while. While on the water, I prayed for guidance. I understood the strength of my Father was stronger than darkness could ever hope to conquer. If this were an experience, I would have simply called upon the strength of God to ignite a spiritual explosion in the moment which would remove all negative energies from the radius of the explosion. I have journaled about how this experience takes place. Think of the strength of God appearing like a bolt of lightning striking down all darkness in the surroundings.

But having this experience be the first of its kind in my walk upon the Earth, I was not quite sure what was appropriate to ask of my Father. As I prayed upon the water, my Father spoke to me about the difference between spirit and man. It was important for me to understand that the body is a vessel for a soul, and a soul a doorway for light and for darkness. A weakened body and a weakened soul, would give rise to an open vessel for Lucifer to take hold. The embodiment of Lucifer on Earth is to be understood as temporary in nature, likely only occurring during the delivery of the message. In these moments my Father revealed that all that I witnessed was like a possession. The soul and the body that was inhabited during the elevator's descent was likely unaware that anything ever happened. So with the newfound knowledge in

The Day I Met Lucifer

all that had happened, I felt resolved to attempt to absolve Lucifer's vessel of sway. I understood that through touch, the spirit of the Lord would heal the man's soul and vessel which was weakened for some unknown reason to me. My Father would shore up the doors and walls to prevent Lucifer from ever entering again.

The next day I went out to the beach again, and once again found myself standing in the elevator with the very same man. This time he asked a question instead of issuing a command. "What do you do with that thing?" he asked, nodding to the paddle in my hand. My answer was brief. "I paddle board." I said. Silence once again filled the elevator's walls. At this point I heard God's voice asking me to carry on. I asked the man, "Do you ever go out on the water?" to which he gave a most dubious answer. Again, one must see earthly words in spiritual nature, to understand the question I asked and his response. In reply to my question, he said, "I was once a great captain. I've seen too many things. I once saw a man fall in… and a shark. Sharks everywhere."

Every word of the man's reply rolled off Lucifer's tongue. Think of the way he replied in a spiritual response of carefully chosen words. Water is symbolic to the spirit of the Lord. The reply was Lucifer's answer to his fall from the grace of God. Even in the most earthly of interpretations, his response was unfounded for the context of the question. So for this particular experience, it should be understood that this was the moment the words from Lucifer were spoken on Earth, which carried his spiritual reply to his fall from grace with God. Not

Kingdom

another word was spoken as we parted ways, but I felt a peace with the effort as if Lucifer had surrendered his efforts to the strength of my Father's spirit.

A few days later I saw the same man on the beach. I asked a few people about the man's history. I learned that he had recently suffered a stroke, and that he had given up on the world and seemed to hate God. In learning this, my spirit stood up in recognition. I walked over to the man and pulled up a seat beside him. I began a verbal conversation with him which, in spiritual conversation, demonstrated how his words had not deterred me. Perhaps his first words could best be understood as a wall to the spirit. Over the course of an hour, I saw his soul reappearing. In the context of the wall, it was either broken down or a door opened inviting me in. We talked about his situation with his stroke. This is when I learned it was his seventh stroke. The number of strokes held such a divine recognition that for anyone to have survived seven, there must be a reason. This man had held on through a fight that most others would never have survived. It was clear that God had plans in his life.

We never spoke directly about Christ or religion. Rather, I always steered the conversation to his situation. As I got to know the man, I saw how his body and soul had broken down. There was not an ounce of darkness to be found. It was the absence of hope, the absence of light. It was the absence thereof that allowed Lucifer to appear in my sight. But as I spoke to the man, hope reappeared. The pilot light inside of him reignited. Before parting ways he wanted to shake my

The Day I Met Lucifer

hand. When I reached out to his, our hands were held tight, not by his strength or my own. It was the strength of God filling his soul. There was a flash of instant recognition to the connection that had been made. I could tell he sensed the river of the spirit flowing between us.

As I felt the spirit flow within, I silently said a prayer for him. I asked my Father to take a piece of my life and to fill this man with hope and light. After my prayer I pulled my hand away, only to find he did not want to let it go at all. He made comments about the strength of his grip and made references to the strength he felt in my hand. Again, this was not a conversation about the physical handshake on Earth. It was a conversation of the spiritual handshake of two souls.

Over the months after we parted ways that day, I would see this man named John around the building Sometimes I would see him out at restaurants as well. In every case, I always made sure to stop and sit down. He would always want to demonstrate his handshake and strength, a spiritual gesture to help me see his spiritual strength. We always shook hands, and I always said that prayer. To this day I know my Father was always there. This man filled with light, the essence of our Father. He strengthened inside so much that he wanted to share it.

During the last conversations I experienced with this man as the 1260 days drew to an end, he told me about how God was working in his life. It is important to note that I never brought up God or Christ. It was always the unspoken spiritual conversation occurring that reignited his light. The strength

Kingdom

of his spirit bubbled up his recognition in his words. There was always an unspoken conversation within the earthly words. The very last conversation I shared with this man, occurred on a bench inside the lobby of our building. He was waiting for a friend as I was waiting for mine. I walked over to him to check up on his life.

As he spoke, the conversation turned very spiritual in nature. He began to share with me his thoughts on his purpose and reason for living. This was the first time he spoke of God or religion in specific words rather than leaving them unmentioned. The conversation was invigorating in light, for just a few months prior, unbeknownst to him, Lucifer had taken his body and soul out for a joyride. As the conversation ended, he wanted to shake hands once again. It is always a moment I cherish in spiritual recognition with him.

We shook hands in a bond that ignited the river of the spirit once again. I could sense he understood the spirit flowing into him. Earlier in the conversation he had mentioned that he was not feeling well. This handshake was the expression of his spirit asking for help and to be healed. As I held his hand he put his other hand on top of mine as if to draw every ounce of the spirit to help fuel his light. During this moment the words he spoke in closure of our conversation, were words I will remember forever throughout the ages. He said, "Jonathan, I never speak to anyone else about what I share with you. I do not know why, but I know there is something about you. There is something greater ahead and is the reason I am still here. Thank you. Thank you for everything."

The Day I Met Lucifer

With those words, a man named John found the light. Darkness had been expunged to rid the shadows from his life. And while it would be hard for a person to ever believe his soul had ever been puppeteered by the man in rose-colored glasses, the point to be made is this man was no longer encumbered by that darkness. Unto the latter, it was easy to see, a man once hating life had found reason to believe. And so this would be how the end of November found its end. The period from September to December was filled with angels in human form, angels in spirit, angels who appeared in different ways to others near me, demons that temporarily inhabited bodily vessels, and demons appearing purely in spirit, angels that revealed their wings, and rainbow halos overhead revealing His light. All of the experiences were foreshadowing the events of December and the events to come after – the events that would forever change my understanding of the journey and the Love story hidden beneath these earthly interactions. For it would be in the month of December that I would understand the role my Father always intended me to command – a newborn baby crowning in the heavens, a prince in the moment, a king in the making, to prepare the way for the return of the Messiah.

The Messiah Is Coming

I am not sure there is really a way to put the true gravity of the message my Father shared with me during the month of December into words that can illustrate the luster and grandeur of His intention. There certainly is not a standard in this day and age in which any comparisons can be drawn. And, most certainly, there has never been in recent history a delivery quite so spectacular leading to the day my Father wound up and delivered His pitch which would cause the world to stop and take notice in a way that would forever be marked upon this generation's epitaph. The territory of His message falls somewhere within the great expanse of a body of water both uncharted and unchartered. The path leading to His words should be seen as a boy-child wandering through the woods, exploring the unknown. And, somehow in an inexplicable cosmic collision, the wanderer happens through the woods, to the shoreline of the body of water and eventually discovers where our Father was leading him all along.

Was it a destiny predetermined or was it the happenchance of His grand design? The answer is almost certainly "yes" though every decision was followed through free will. For all of the circumstances that could lead a person to a particular destination are what our Father hopes for in each of us

Kingdom

all along, but the choices to take the steps and persevere throughout the journey is what unveils the wanderer as chosen from day one. The wanderer merely follows, increasing the pace of his acceleration until one day He is allowed to become. It is merely the perspective of the observer that associates a definition and an explanation to the spiritual birth of one of His Sons. There is a particular set of circumstances that everyone faces, challenges that test the spirit to the limits. The ability to filter through the noise and decipher His heartbeat pulsing underneath is the test for everyone. For in all that has been described thus far, the classifications observed through the earthly perspective should be understood as the inability to see Heaven and Earth as one.

It is important to understand that the instructions shared with me in December occurred in a similar manner as described above. For in all of the prophecies that have ever been, the circumstances have always been ripe for fulfillment in the sequences given. Think of the world as only that which is observed through the eyes of man, where there is always a constant state of spiritual potential, that when spiritually tapped can begin to spill forth and manifest into the world. This breaks the minds of many, for most see a linear world. The Biblical stories that have been shared for thousands of generations seem like fairytales that could never happen in the modern world. And, if, for some majestic reason, a similar event was to unfold in modern times, the thought would be too much of a fantasy and fairytale to ever be accepted for the truth held within its core. For how would the world receive a

The Messiah Is Coming

message that is at the foundation of every religion's very beliefs when no one is actually expecting to hear the message itself? And how would the message ever be heard, when the deliverer of the message did not appear upon the Earth in the most miraculous of ways? And, even if he did, how would they ever be convinced to believe? How could a person trust the words given? How could the world find truth in all that our Father desires to be proclaimed?

As a whole, it is a large pill to swallow. For how would a person believe the words written or spoken in modern times without thousands of years of hindsight to determine where faith should be found and truth should be trusted? Even in the times that Jesus walked upon the Earth, his very disciples doubted his identity. The most spiritual man of the modern age was also the most hotly debated. Though if he were to return today, it is easier for most to choose to ignore the potential and not even join the debate. During his reign, some of his disciples chose to affirm their faith in private conversations as documented in Mark 8:27-30. In that particular verse, even the identity of Jesus was shown to be debated long before he was to be crucified and his disciples persecuted. And, even after the many miracles Jesus performed, and later as it is documented during his tribulation and crucifixion, Peter (one of Jesus's closest disciples) denied Jesus three times upon being questioned of his allegiance. Though no religion actually debates the existence of Jesus, semantics skew the divide of religious lines. For that, there are more examples of man questioning God's word before Jesus's arrival.

Kingdom

The stories of Abraham, Isaac, Moses, Jacob and Noah all illustrate similar doubts cast by those having to hear the word of God through the eyes and ears of another. These characters are the very foundation for every religion across the globe. They predate Jesus, Mohammed, Confucius, Buddha, and anyone else involved in a modern spiritual ministry. But the stories are possibly even more fantastical than what was witnessed through the most modern Teachers of Man. At a very rudimentary level, the story of Abraham's followers might best be understood as a leader of lemmings unable to make any fundamental decisions. Even through all of the miracles God performed and illustrated in the grandest of ways to all of Abraham's people, they still doubted. Lot's wife – who was rescued by an angel – was turned into a pillar of salt because she did not trust and listen to the angel saving her. That may possibly be the strongest illustration of doubt possible. Whether the story is literal or symbolic, or even what scientific circumstances could have caused her to turn into a pillar of salt truthfully does not matter. The illustration is that there was the voice of God leading her home which she clearly – and repeatedly – chose to ignore even after witnessing all of His miracles in the desert with Abraham. Even hers and Lot's residency in Sodom was because she continually doubted God's word as communicated through Abraham when they lived in his tribe.

The ego is a funny thing. In an instant, it has the potential to destroy everything that ever was and anything that could ever be. Noah built an ark against inexplicable odds. People doubted. In the end, an entire civilization was destroyed. One family survived – God's chosen people. In another story of doubt, Moses was delivered the Ten Commandments from God as he witnessed the face of God's brightest light upon a mountain top. Yet, when he returned from the mountain with the miraculous writing by God's hand, his entire following had already turned to false idols and turned against the words God had spoken through him. All it took was forty days to lose a nation. He had to return once again up the mountain to receive another set of tablets to replace the ones broken from his anger when he witnessed his people's abomination before the Lord. Each time he did so by asking forgiveness for the error of his people's ways. One man – despite all odds – had to ask for forgiveness for the error of an entire civilization's ways. Even as his story continued and the Ark of the Covenant was constructed which led to multiple cities tumbling through the will of the Lord, the world still doubted. The world – as a whole – never believed. And what happened? Civilizations were destroyed. Only the very few who truly believed in those particular moments of God's communication were the ones who were saved.

For over two thousand years, mankind has had the opportunity to digest the message foretelling the end that was prophesied would one day arrive. It would take that long for God to grant humanity the grace to learn how to hear His message for when it would be most important to hear. If one thing can be learned during the thousands of years that His Word has survived in written form, it would be that humanity has always doubted, and in the end, humanity has always been destroyed. But perhaps it is best to view the impending end as a new beginning, for those who hear His word will be saved. For the stories that have survived have always carried one important message: Hope. Within every moment that God has spoken through a person, He has always opened the door for those who have doubted all along. The ones who find their way home in the end will be allowed entrance into His kingdom just as those who have been practicing all along. But it does not mean that man can delay, for no man will know when His arrival and subsequent rapture will occur. We should all be prepared for that day to be today.

So it would take me by complete surprise when the day arrived that God would begin sharing his directive to me in such a clear and concise way. For over the previous three years, my Father has been speaking to Bryan and me in a manner that is still hard for even me to believe. To hear the voice of God once – even for just a fraction of a second – is the most spectacular feeling a man will ever know. But to hear His voice not just once, but through a fluid series of spiritual experiences and conversations spread across twelve hundred and sixty days is such a magnificent story to forever be told. I cannot explain it, and words will always fall short in expressing all that He has allowed me to see. But the most important understanding was that He had spent the previous three years preparing me to be able to share the message He wanted the world to one day see. It was throughout the month of December, 2014, that my Father shared His message in the grandest

The Messiah Is Coming

of ways. If there ever was a time that I thought I was ready to receive His directive to lead others to Him, this was the time that I paused in disbelief. For His message was not just a message of salvation, nor a message letting me know I was as prepared as I needed to be. This was a message that would forever be defined in history.

There is a time when every child takes up a hobby or learns to play a sport. In those times, the child must learn the basic skills to be able to perform the new hobby or sport with any adequacy or proficiency. The same concept applies to an adult with a career. Any new trade takes hours of practice to refine and hone the knowledge required to eventually transition from a student to proficient master. It is said that it takes approximately ten thousand hours of practice at any new trade or hobby to become proficient enough to fully stand alone. But even as a person stands alone, there is still so much more to learn. It should best be seen the moment a foundation has been poured, and a concrete base has taken form. But even as a child learns how to play a new sport, or an adult learns a new trade, the passion from within takes root and wants to run with it like the wind. There will always be moments in the beginning when the ego fools the mind into thinking it is ready to stand on its own. It is like a college student graduating, expecting to be a master in a job he has yet to perform. And while passion fills new graduates with a false sense of maturity and understanding, the truth is that it takes that very passion for them to one day learn how to stand on their own.

Kingdom

It is interesting to calculate the concept of ten thousand hours for any skill or trade and apply it to the spiritual journey I have been blessed to be a student of. For if one is to multiply eight hours a day (the average length of a work day) by twelve hundred and sixty days (the length of time this journey was always foretold to take), the number works out to be ten-thousand and eighty hours... precisely the amount of time it would ever take for a human to perfect the skills required for any earthly trade. And much like a new student learning a trade, in the beginning I wanted to run with the new skills I was learning and share it with others. I wanted to teach all that I had been shown by God, for I was certain I had already learned all that was required for me to get started helping others learn the ropes. It seemed so simple – like the foundation was one that my ability to quickly learn had already grasped. There were countless hours of conversations with Bryan and prayers to God asking what the next step was for me to take – how could I get started helping others find Him. But the answer was always the same. The answer was to wait.

I always viewed myself as a bucking bull, ready to burst out of the gate at a rodeo. The energy and passion raged inside of me, coursing through my veins in an uncontrollable extension of anxiety within. It was a fire alive that I wanted to use to ignite the fuel of the spirit within all in good faith so that I could help others follow His lead. But on the day when the gate was opened and I was instructed to move forward with a full head of steam, I felt a new sensation unfamiliar to me. It was a pause placed upon my soul in recognition of ignition.

The Messiah Is Coming

The instructions He would utter would leave me temporarily paralyzed within.

The pause was not just for the fraction of a second when the meaning of His words hit me. For days the pause flushed my body with momentary helplessness in understanding just how to communicate such a grand message in a way that would forever be remembered in the way He wished it to be told. It was a moment that I can understand only now was like a drag racer revving up his engine to create enough torque for the sudden burst of blinding speed required to launch forward from the starting line. But at the time I was given the "gentlemen, start your engines" message from my Father, it seemed to me like it was all happening in slow motion.

It would take a couple of months to fully understand that His commands to "go" and "run" involved a tremendous buildup of torque so that His message would be propelled at the greatest velocity possible, creating the greatest rip of sound through the aether to grab the attention of those with ears to hear, and the greatest burst of blinding light from the explosions caused by the fire igniting the fuel flushing the engine within for those with eyes to see. And though it had been clear for some time the direction His messages seemed to be leading, never did I expect I was being prepared to share a message that will forever be remembered in history. For on the day of December 14, 2014, God shared specific instructions for me. The message was to "Go!" and to "Run!" And most importantly, to "Tell everyone the Messiah is coming." And how more special could the command have been, for a man of

Kingdom

thirty-three to be asked to paint the path pink preparing the way for return of the Son, who at thirty-three, died for all of our sins?

Thirty-Three

What is it about the age of thirty-three that makes it so special? It is a number that has stuck in the minds of nearly every Christian for thousands of years. It is an age that needs no introduction, for the thoughts it invokes are always the same. Is it not funny how after thousands of years, one number can linger in the minds of generations and generations to come? At this point in the writing of this chapter, I have not even specifically said what it is that I am talking about, yet I am sure it is already known. Thirty-three was the age of Jesus, the Messiah, the Son of God, His Holy Grace.

It is ironic that while the number has no written fact, it has always been understood that the age of Jesus was thirty-three. The way this number has been derived is based on the summation of the accounts of Jesus's ministry. It was understood during the time of Jesus in order to become a leader in the ministry, a person must have been at least thirty years old. In Numbers 4:3, it says "from thirty years and upward, even to fifty years old, all who enter the service to do the work in the tent of the meeting." As Jesus began his ministry, it was most certainly bound within the terms of the canon of their day. For anyone who would speak as a witness to the Lord, still had a set of standards to uphold in a very defined way, regardless if a person's role was just as a witness or the Son of Man revealing the way.

And while the overarching numeric themes throughout these Books of Nine expose the root of the meaning of the written Word that have been hidden during all of this time, to belabor the text with more exploratory definitions of why thirty is important would be a disservice to the embodiment of this specific book. For now the knowledge that should be gleaned is that thirty has been understood for generations to be a shining moment during a soul's rebirth – the moment the womb of the spirit is capable of delivering all that the Lord had already conceived. Call it a virgin birth, or a rebirth of the soul. It is an immaculate conception in spiritual terms, an embodiment in the womb of the spirit, hidden from the eyes but revealed to the soul. It is a very specific point in time, a moment for the world to take notice, a moment the angels in the heavens celebrate and behold.

But it is the age of thirty-three that is so fundamentally well-known. What is it about thirty-three that has left a mark upon thousands of years of generation's minds and the souls? What makes that specific age stand out more during the period of Jesus's ministry than the other years still told? And how can the world even be so sure this was his age? Is this just a best guess, or quite possibly a sign for another generation to find significance in all that would be foretold? Perhaps the best way to understand the importance of his age is to see it for more than the sum of each of the parts, but rather to see it as the whole. For in the whole embodiment, one can understand the

Thirty-Three

spiritual truths placed in another messenger's words, as well as learn how to discern the truth held in these specific words.

On the surface level, the most important point in the ministry of Jesus was when he died for the sins of all mankind. It was the saving moment for the human race. He was crucified before a population that would rather see a spiritual leader killed while sparing the life of a murderer than cause disruption through spiritual divide. It is accepted that the ministry of Jesus at the point of crucifixion had lasted three and a half years in duration. Theologians have studied the stories for thousands of years and almost all can agree on this specific duration of his ministry. So, knowing that he was likely baptized at the age of thirty leaves little room to shake the math in understanding how he must have died and risen at the age of thirty-three.

Based on the written word and testimony of Jesus's ministry, most theologians can prove how the ministry of Jesus lasted three and a half years – a number that will be important in chapters to come. This number can be debated, and it is not the role of these words to change anyone's viewpoints or beliefs of His age. It is just important to know how the number came to be so the rest of the story can be understood. It is up to the reader to find truth in the words and faith in understanding. Could Jesus have been thirty-three when he started his ministry? Absolutely. Could he have been thirty-three when it ended? Absolutely. The only point of reference is in Luke 3:23 when Luke says, "Now Jesus himself was about thirty years old when he began his ministry. He was the son, so it was thought, of Joseph, the son of Heli," In either case, the importance is on the relative numbers and how they have also been demonstrated through all that is written in these books. The age of thirty is significant, just as is the age of thirty-three and the time span of "three and a half" years for his ministry. And quite possibly that is what make the Word so special. For the Word carries meanings that will be uncovered for ages to come. For now it is important to understand the potential, and understand that regardless of specifics, the relative nature of the numbers are what is mentioned in specificity.

The age of thirty was viewed as a foundational age in times of yore and is also the age I would eventually understand as the point in time when this story began its course. Though I would not see how any of this story was falling together when my earthly life seemed to be falling apart just days before my thirtieth birthday, it is now clear in hindsight that the disruption I understood in my earthly life was actually the spiritual ramifications of the Lord firing off the alarm to my spiritual clock so I would rise and wake – for it was time to begin doing the work of His calling. It was His alarm clock that would sound through the ages. I can never express just how truly blessed and thankful I feel to know that my soul took notice. I suppose I could have just as easily have pressed "snooze" and gone back to a life incomplete and full of nonsense. But my soul took notice. And today I understand that this was always my purpose. The steps I would take upon this Earth were always intended to reveal this part of the journey.

Thirty-Three

When I arrived in Fort Lauderdale, it was a time when everyone I met and every place I visited was new. It was fresh. At age thirty-three, I was just learning to see. My Father had opened my eyes. As this portion of the journey began – the beginning of Kingdom as the books are divided – the steps I would take upon the sands of Fort Lauderdale were the first steps taken in His Kingdom. It was the Promised Land I understood was forthcoming. But it would also prove to be the precursor to Heaven and Earth's merging.

As I would speak to each and every soul I met, there was always a recurring theme – a theme I will never forget. For just as the age of Christ has forever been emblazoned upon my mind, so too it would seem that the unique situation of my arrival in a locale uncharted would carry a similar recognition through those I met. For in nearly every conversation the question of my age would ultimately arise. In response to the question, the words "thirty-three" almost always invoked the same retorts and recognition. More often than not, the words replied were, "The age of Jesus" followed by words like "Interesting…" or "Hmmm…" but each circumstance invoked different ways that each soul handled the reaction of its internal recognition.

In all of the situations prior to being asked the question of my age – and also due to the fact that these interactions occurred so early on my journey – I rarely, if ever, talked about any spiritual or religious convictions. The instructions from my Father were only to learn and to write all that He was sharing, for it was not yet time to share the story that now I am sharing.

Kingdom

In the beginning, conversations were just about souls meeting one another. But age and career are usually the topics of choice in any first conversation, so it was almost impossible to not have this kind of questioning arise mid-conversation. These conversations gave rise to the signs that God was continuing to demonstrate to me, though I can only see it now as more of a grand foreshadowing.

With each conversation, the repetition of the responses became etched into my mind. Without a doubt, it stretched across the boundaries of my own comfort zone. I understood I was on a journey and tasked to write all that He spoke, but I still was not remotely clear in the beginning of His intended calling for me. I only understood each step to be an effort to move forward. I was always moving blindly. Talk of any relation to Jesus's ministry seemed sacrilegious and ego-driven. But as the journey continued to take its form, my Father helped me understand that the ministry of Jesus was the ideal to strive toward. For in all steps, I have continued to ask my Father to train me as a King. Though never would I expect all that He would task me to do would be part of a journey to be forever remembered in history.

It is with the utmost delicacy I wish to express that these words are not placing any comparison to the journey I have been charged to take to the ministry of Christ who was and is our Savior and King. But in all cases when seeking spiritual knowledge, the comparisons to be drawn are the ones that will prove to reveal the tie that binds everything together. It is an unspoken tether those with eyes to see will recognize without

Thirty-Three

explanation. It is how the Word of God continues to speak to every generation. The invisible tie that binds is constantly tugging at the soul like a spiritual marionette in recognition of our Father's reigns upon the soul.

So, if for no other reason, the age of thirty-three should be viewed as an age divine. It was the time that disciples of Christ understand as the age of the risen Lord. It is the age when it can be viewed as how one man's journey completed its cycle, and his soul continued into the light. The age of thirty-three was the most visceral and visual representation of the body being cast to the side and the soul becoming fully anointed in the Kingdom however hidden it may have first appeared to the eyes. The divide of Heaven and Earth has always separated believers from the non. It is a divide that is bridged through the words left behind and the fulfillment of all to come. God will continue to speak in the same ways He has spoken for generations. And in every case it will always be unique, though somehow not any different than it ever was. The architecture to All That Is will always be the demonstrable language for those seeking reason.

And while the age of thirty-three is the age understood as divine, it should also be observed as a marker upon the actions in how these words were introduced into the world. For just as Jesus's ministry began at age thirty, so too would the journey of the evolution of these words begin. Though I would not understand it at the time, to see it now ignites my soul with light. The age of thirty-three is when the twelve hundred and sixty days foretold finds its end. And in all that comes to pass, well, that is still to be shared. But at this point it is important to see how three and a half years of prophecy is also embodied within these words and how it will be understood leading up to, and after, the end.

The number "three and a half" is an important number revealed from the study of thirty-three. It is a number that recurs throughout the written Word though it does not carry the same initial recognition as the numbers forty, seven, or thirty-three. But it is a number that exists nonetheless and quite possibly carries one of the most important units of measure for the understanding of the message embodied in these words. It is important to see it as the actionable duration of Jesus's ministry, and perhaps "actionable duration" is the best way to understand it, for that is how it is exhibited in other parts of the Bible as well. The duration of "three and a half" is spoken directly about in both Daniel and John's Revelation. But it is also important to see its application in duration through another's eyes... Paul's eyes, in particular.

Damascus

The road to Damascus is a long and arduous journey. Each step taken is preceded by one step wobbling, preceded by another before it of equal instability. For Paul, in Biblical times, his journey to Damascus was taken while blind. It was a testament of faith, a demonstration of his commitment to the calling. For Paul, he walked blindly toward a city to which he was led after a miraculous interaction with Jesus Christ. During the time Jesus walked the Earth, Paul (or, rather, Saul as the name he was known by at the time) did not believe. Paul fell on the side of persecution rather than on the side of glory. But during his voyage to Damascus, he was met by the light of the Lord and tasked with continuing to the city in order to regain his sight. It was only then that the eyes of his spirit were opened and he became a believer in the Lord.

Perhaps the entire journey on Earth should be seen as one similar to Paul's journey. For even a man of the greatest faith is walking blind. There is only faith in the immediate moment and a rapport with the Lord in the quiet. Sight is a word that humans take as a literal definition for the disambiguation of particles of light emitted into space passing through the lenses of the eyes and colliding with the rods and cones on the back of the cornea. Those collisions create a series of impulses that the brain can interpret as shape and form. The eyes of the spirit function in the same manner, but are activated on a level that is unseen with the human eye. The light of the spirit flows around us like a river, just as the light of the sun flows around us on Earth before becoming absorbed and reflected by the shapes that form the material world. The light of the spirit can be understood by the soul with the same clarity and precision as the human eye. But just as a baby learns to see in a world seemingly filled with muted blobs of ambiguity, the precision in understanding the shapes fall into view. It is at this time a veil is removed and clarity of sight is gained. The eyes of the spirit lack clarity in the beginning. Many of faith may even walk around holding the eyes of the spirit tightly closed. They may not even be aware – and it is not a judgment being made – for one day they will learn to open their eyes and see.

Paul's journey to Damascus, whether seen as literal or figurative, represents the moment a person is granted sight with the spirit. It took a journey into the wilderness, absence of comfortable surroundings, and a divine encounter embodied through a great flash of light for Paul to understand that he was blind. It would be three and a half days of fasting later that the spirit would allow the obstructions to fall from his eyes and his sight to be "restored." Again, the words chosen are important because restoration of sight, even in a spiritual form, indicates that something had to be taken away in order for it to ever be found. It was never absent from birth, but should rather be viewed as a metaphorical mute button pressed on the spiritual channel for understanding.

Damascus

Paul's fasting was another example that should be used in both physical and spiritual forms. During his era, fasting was viewed as a way to remove impurities from the body in order to allow the body to heal naturally. In spiritual form, fasting removes any biological sway of the body that keeps the soul pinned to the human form. During healing, the soul is an open door to the river of the spirit flowing all around. Think of a window that is covered with grime and dust. The window is so dirty that a person cannot see out – much less feel the warmth of the light trying to pour through. Cleaning the window from all of the sediment and filth allows the light to flood through the glass while also granting the observer of the light a new perspective to a world outside the bounds of the pane of the glass. The light gives warmth. The spirit heals.

When Jesus spoke to Paul, he became the biggest proponent for the Lord. Perhaps he is the greatest reason faith has been able to hold so strong. For, if it were not for his writings, much of the New Testament would not exist. A non-believer in the days of Christ became a believer after the crucifixion and went on to share the doctrine that so many have come to know as the testament to their faith. A man did not believe at the time of the Messiah's arrival. This man was led on a journey into the desert that he did not quite understand all it would entail. But by the end of the journey, this man had heard the voice of the Lord and was blinded from the light. Sight was restored after fasting for three and a half days, ridding the body of all impurities that would hold a biological sway. And whether the story was symbolic to spiritual eyes from the beginning, or whether it was literal to human sight, it is important to understand that his journey to Damascus ended with sight to all forms of light.

So, if one can see the demonstration of faith that Paul left for generations to come, it is important to also understand all that has been foretold will come to pass. For just as Paul was a non-believer and had to be granted sight, no one questions the deliverer of his messages, though mankind has had decades upon decades to recognize this in hindsight. But in the days he walked the Earth, think of the way his story must have seemed. One day a non-believer, the next a believer and the largest proponent of the unseen. How would a man's words be accepted in this modern day and age? Perhaps they will not until after the grandest of moments foretold comes to pass. Perhaps the books left behind will be the only way for people to ever know. For those who are left behind due to their own wavering faith at the end of this cycle's culling, will be the ones eventually tasked to share the story for generations to come. For there is always hope for those who learn to see. An end to one generation's cycle opens the door for new beginnings.

So as my journey to Damascus began twelve hundred and sixty days prior, it should be understood in relative terms to Paul's demonstrable example. For just as Paul had to wander through the wilderness in search of the destination as instructed by the Lord, so has the journey I have been on been guided and shepherded by the word of the Lord. Paul fasted for three and a half days. The story of Paul's journey was the demonstration of earthly fasting in relative terms, so as to be

Damascus

understood for generations to come. The story of my journey embodies the same demonstration of earthly fasting, but in years versus day and of earthly sustenance versus edible nutrients. Three and a half years is tantamount to twelve hundred and sixty days. It is also important to recall the duration of the ministry of Jesus for his ministry is also the embodiment of this very same number. The architecture is a divine sign to forever be noted.

In Daniel and Revelation, the reference to twelve hundred and sixty days and three and a half years is referenced repeatedly. It is referenced in terms of "time, times, and a half time" where "time" is the representation of a full cycle (in earthly terms, a year) and "times" is a representation of twice the duration of a full cycle. The sum total to the embodiment of the journey holds a duration of three and one-half years. In the architecture of the spirit and the relative nature of its math, the division of a year is divided by twelve, and the days are understood as holding one-twelfth of the embodiment of a year. The embodiment of a year was held by the number of degrees in a circle. A year was understood as having three hundred and sixty divisions, or rather twelve months of thirty days. So the sum total of three and a half years is twelve hundred and sixty days. And while this extrapolation of the divine architecture of All That Is shall not continue any further just yet, just take note that three and a half is one-half of seven, a number that one should never forget.

And while the end of this journey will end with a physical fast for three and a half days, there is much more to the rest of

Kingdom

the story before that portion can be fully understood. For now, it is important to see the journey to Damascus, and how the Lord led Paul. To understand the story through Paul's eyes is all that most will ever be taught to know. But to see the story through the eyes of how Paul must have been observed is the most important part. For every person who walks upon the Earth is standing in those same observer's shoes.

To hear the story of the Messiah's return is no different today than it was thousands of years ago. But to understand that this generation has been given thousands of years to understand how to learn to see the truth upon His arrival, gives little understandable wiggle-room for the introduction of any doubt. Think of it as a giant "heads-up" from our Father since it is understandably a hard pill to swallow. He has essentially said, "Children, I know it will be hard to see. That is why I've given you thousands of years to come to understand the importance of this moment. His grand return is the end to this generation. The next cycle to begin will be one of Heavenly salvation. So go on and help share the Word, because upon His arrival, I have a place prepared for your return and will welcome your own arrival. I just hope you can see through the noise of the world. Be strong in spirit and have faith in the Word. For all that has ever been written has always come true. This time will be no different, and My heart breaks for my children who cannot see. Please see. Please see Me."

And with those words, our Father has left his story to be shared for generations to come. Over six hundred thousand words comprise the Old Testament. Over one hundred and eighty thousand English words comprise the New Testament. One hundred and forty thousand words comprise the Apocrypha that many may never read due to it not being included in the mass-distributed Biblical canon. Through all that has been written, thousands of years have been allotted to consume the meaning of the words. Some may get it, many will not. But it is imperative to know that His return and the culling of the souls destined for the Heavenly land will have to once again be understood for generations left behind. And though I have not been shared any specifics about those left behind, I have been shared that there are continual cycles that occur. Could it be the last cycle to occur? Possibly. Could these words only be intended for the final days of this generation? Extremely possible as well. Generations have come and gone before us. Cycles have previously passed. It is just the hint of the possibility – the unknown in all that has been said – that this cycle could be the last cycle of all, at least in the way that has been observed and understood by man. Which side of the dividing line will you stand upon when this cycle reaches its end? Your soul will live on forever, for it has no beginning or end. The question is if you desire salvation and light, or the darkness of the abyss.

    The time is now. This cycle has met its end. This part of the story could not be more clearly illustrated through all that the Lord has shared. If it is not through the words that are written and – if you are reading this – currently being read, then see it through the words that have been accepted for thousands of generations and generations upon end. Find truth in those words. Seek out the words not included in the

Kingdom

popular Biblical canon. Find truths in all faiths, in all religions. Seek to decipher the meaning before it is too late. This I ask. This I plead. Words in any capacity are just guideposts along the journey. It is the intention of these words to offer a concise explanation for those who continue to seek truth. These words were brought forth into existence to help open the spiritual eyes for everyone to see... light.

...

Shapes. Form. Him. The Kingdom. Home.

...

Letter To Bryan

The road to Damascus is the portion of the journey that should not only be understood as the three and a half total years of the first portion of the journey, but it should also be understood as the closure to three and a half months in Fort Lauderdale from September to December before hearing God's instructions. These were the days leading up to His great reveal, His grand instructions. These months should be seen in the same light as when a child is most excited for the arrival of Christmas. As this book began with the crowning of a prince in the heavens, first steps were taken, and preparation for Christmas began. Presents were wrapped, a tree was put up, and a period of celebration with the angels began in the months preceding Christmas Day.

Leading into December, I had experienced a whirlwind of travels to the heavens that had left me speechless. Bryan had been busy with all of his schoolwork, and I knew it was not my place to intervene in his journey, but I feared he was being sucked into the earthly side of the journey. Perhaps that is how God intended it for him at this point, for his role in a hospital is important. But as the experiences mounted and he seemed continually unavailable to speak with, I searched for a way to grab his attention. Though it will not be discussed in depth in this book, the experiences during the first week of December helped define the roles he and I are tasked to play. So as the gravity of the instructions from God pulled upon my soul, I sought guidance in how to bring it to Bryan's attention.

I sat down in December and began to write him a letter. I thought about emailing it, but as my Father would have it, Bryan called me on December 6th just after I completed the letter. Though I had not sent any message his way or indicated any reason we should talk, I have to believe that my Father pulled upon his soul to reach out to me. Earlier in the week, Bryan had sent me a much delayed response to something important God had shared with me. Over the last three years, Bryan and I were in constant communication – I for him and he for me. But in his response I could sense something else going on, so I chose to leave it unanswered until I determined how best to respond.

On this day we were eventually able to connect and talk, Bryan began apologizing profusely for his absence which allowed me to see God's action on his soul. So instead of sending him the letter, I read most of it to him on the phone in an effort to ensure I said all I intended to say. After beginning to understand there was a tremendous possibility that Bryan and I were being called into position by the Great Commander, and that our roles could be much more specific than just two souls shown God's favor, it became important to share as much as I could in a short and concise manner with Bryan. So even though the letter may seem long and begins with a reference to a previous conversation, think of it as the abbreviated version of the previous week's experiences – just as these Books of Nine are still minimal to all that could be shared from the last three and a half years.

...

The Letter to Bryan

...

Man, I've tried to figure out how to respond to your text and at first I was without words. I thought I'd go with a comical response, but I figured it could be taken the wrong way. So I'm going with this...after having time to reflect on my thoughts since you posed that particular question to me, here is what I've arrived at:

You text me about a cliffhanger a day later, but you do not have time to hear about it today. You ask me if I am okay with you not speaking today when ultimately nothing I could say would really matter in the context of your question. For posing the question was only an effort to find peace within your own actions. So any response I could give would only serve as an affirmation in your chosen actions, veiled under the pretense that I am not upset with you. Therefore I chose not to reply back directly. But since you asked what are my thoughts (aka am I cool with it?), here they are from my lens of perspective...

It all boils down to this. I do not judge you. I empathize. I do not let your actions, or anyone else's actions affect me. I'm at peace. I see you working hard. I see you doing all you can. I see you giving the world your all in the ways that only you can. I see you conquering the steps of a new life, a new marriage, a budding career – all while balancing all things possible and succeeding. That is all to be celebrated and praised. You have so many blessings in your life and each one deserves the attention you show it...Which you do every day, until your tank is empty.

Kingdom

I've seen you in so many visions recently that I have not been able to share. God has spoken to me directly and through His Angels so much recently that sometimes I am worried it pushes you away and into your earthly efforts. He has shared with me things I'm instructed to share with you, but I cannot impose that upon you as you balance your time. It will happen when you desire it to be. And truthfully, if you asked me today what I was supposed to tell you two days ago, I'd have to go reread through my journals to tell you – which would not be efficient for your time, or respectful on my behalf for consuming your time.

Over the last week alone I have had around fifty experiences, and we barely have time to talk about one. Our conversations (which I am thankful to have even the briefest of conversations with you) are constricted in time and/or focus, so I know those are not the times to share the messages with you. So I'm left hoping that completing my writing and saying, "Here. When you are ready, it is all here" is the best option. In fact, that is specifically one of the things God tasked me to do (verbatim). So I know that taking up your time to discuss any of the visions is not what I've been tasked to do, so I will not. They are going to have to be read in their context, in the order you will receive them. Over the last year, I have journaled 280k words. To put that into perspective, the New Testament is 188k words. I'm not saying I have written another portion to the Bible by any means, but what I am saying is that there are 280k words of Divine inspiration, instruction, and truth in those pages. This does not count the 150k of other words in my other books or the drafts I've been working on. I say all this to say that in all of those words, a truth has been unveiled in the recent days.

God showed John a vision of seven lamps upon seven lamp stands as someone resembling the Son of Man knelt down. The man had bronze feet,

Letter To Bryan

blazing like fire. The seven lamp stands represented the seven churches (in Asia). In Revelation 1:20 the verse reads "As for the mystery of the seven stars which you saw in My right hand, and the seven golden lampstands: the seven stars are the angels of the seven churches, and the seven lampstands are the seven churches." Further understanding is that the Greek word for ANGEL is angelos, which means "messenger." In the New Testament, the same word is used to describe John and other disciples who carried God's divine communications to others on Earth. So the reference to Angels in revelations means "messenger" possibly of earthly origin.

God showed me, an image of myself in the same position as the son of man. I asked "how I could see" and the angel of the Lord responded "take the brass vessel to my temple." I raised a lamp to my forehead in gesture of his instruction as I knelt in white linen. For the lamp represented the knowledge and light of God's word housed in a brass vessel (of earthly body). In this, I have been instructed to take my brass vessel (my feet, the earthly embodiment of God's message in my writing) and share it with "the church." At the very minimum, I know I have been called upon as one of the seven angelos discussed in Revelation. But I think God has been indicating something even greater – something you and I have discussed over the last three years. In Revelation 11:3-4, it is revealed to John that two witnesses will appear before the return of the Messiah to prepare for His arrival. The very description of the witnesses given to John was the same imagery I experienced in the "anointing." Though I stress this should be explored with great caution, there have been numerous other experiences in December that support this same possibility. So at the very minimum, I know that God has called upon me as one of seven, with a very great possibility that you and I are the two witnesses.

Kingdom

How can I be sure? Well, buried in the fifty visions of this last week and countless more over the last several weeks, I was also told about Uriah on multiple occasions – a word not found at all in any interpretation of the Bible except for the Septuagint...also referred to as LXX. What could that possibly mean? That particular version was translated from Hebrew to Greek by seventy Jewish scholars around 30 AD. It is the oldest translation. Does "seventy" sound familiar? That's because I shared with you in brevity about God telling me about the seventy Angels. I could go on, but most importantly I have also been directly instructed to begin sharing his message with my sister, who I know will deny me at least once if not twice.

...

So while the message carries an air of frustration, it is important to see the underlying motivation was the understanding that God had begun sharing with me enough to decipher the upcoming possibility that the role Bryan and I had been tasked to play could potentially be one of the two witnesses as spoken about in Revelation. But even if that possibility was just a misinterpretation of all that had been communicated to this point, there was clearly a directive to begin preparing the church for some upcoming message. In the preceding weeks I had been instructed to send Bryan a copy of all of my journals. For three years we have spoken for hours upon hours on the phone about our experiences, but if I had to gander a guess, I would bet we had only spoken about two percent of all of them.

Letter To Bryan

At this point in the journey with each of us pursuing the paths that God had guided each of us to take, the urgency in my message to Bryan was one that he probably is still unaware of the importance. The truth is I was not even sure if my time on Earth was ending in the coming days or weeks. When I had been tasked to send him my journals, I could only surmise His reasoning. So, even if we had not spoken, I understood His message needed to be carried through to another person. But now, I understand the greater aspect of His directive was to plant the seeds while I raced on to the destination. It would be a task that required two people to pursue, and in the end, we would both do all that we were intended to do.

After our conversation wrapped up over the letter, I felt resolution in all that was shared. For while our conversation was filled with a defined urgency without a defined reason, in the coming days, my Father would help me understand the meaning. Over the next several weeks of experiences in the heavens, my Father would offer insight, guidance, and specifics to His directive. It was everything I needed to understand the urgency I sensed in the conversation with Bryan. Though I would not be able to share with Bryan all of the details through December for some time to come, there was still a greater reason and purpose that would still need to be understood.

9th of December

How is a man to deliver a message of such magnitude that God has asked to be shared? How is it to be communicated in such a way that carries every bit of majesty and wonder as the words left upon my soul? How can a vessel deliver the message without leaving a little of His Glory inadvertently behind? These are the questions that raced through my mind at the sheer brilliance of the divine words that began lighting up my soul throughout the month of December. For over the course of my experiences in the heavens in December of 2014, I would learn specifically the role that I was being prepared for all along as well as the message that was to be delivered. And what a grand month it would become.

For over three years the Lord had been speaking with me in a way that ignited my soul with a vigor to run and spread His word. For over three years the manner in which He had communicated with me was more than I could ever hope others would believe, though I longed to tell them about His glory. I would sit through sermons in different churches where pastor after pastor would tell their respective congregations how they never expect for anyone in this lifetime to receive the level of communication written about in our most ancient scriptures. Leaders of churches, inspirational speakers, and those who teach His word all introduced doubt into His message. All I could do was listen and know that one day the world would one day witness all of the grand splendor of His word. But I had been told to wait, to listen, to learn all that was being taught until I was given the instruction to go. Throughout these three years leading up to His specific directive, I had only the anticipation that I would help lead others to Him. Never did I expect that the directive was to include more than the prime effort itself. For why would I expect that the role I would be tasked to play was any different than every other person in the ministry had played before?

And perhaps that is the greatest conundrum I would experience. For the role I had been asked to play was certainly no different than the call that every person of faith is charged to do. The revelation of His directive was to be received with delicacy and grace. The action in the delivery was to leave a mark upon the generations left behind. But at this point in the story, it is important to talk about the message itself, for that is how I first received His directive. Through the refinement of the directive, the vehicle became more clearly revealed. But in both cases, the moment that the understanding of His message and the role that would be played touched my soul, the world would be ignited in a glorious harmony of trumpets sounding and orchestral chord.

On the 9th of December, God began sharing His message to me in the most fantastical way. It began with Him explaining to me that the Beast's arrival was upcoming – even by sharing a specific timeframe. But the message carried an addi-

9th of December

tional meaning – a meaning in which I would understand the role I was to play in my Father's legion. If anything should be understood as to the manner in which God communicates, it should be that every message contains layer upon layer of meanings. A simple word transcends dimensions of understanding. Sentences stretch the bounds even farther. Entire motifs and experiences will be analyzed for generations to come. In the case of all that has ever been Biblically written, mankind is still attempting to make sense of the stories written thousands of years ago. At this point in mankind's growth, only the highest levels of His message have been discerned. It is the layers upon layers and depth of His word that leaves churches divided and fuels religious wars. The importance is all that has been spoken carries a greater message, one of unity and Love. But those who have attempted to discern His message have allowed the ego to cause divisions and prevent any understanding of how all of the parts sum to a message greater as a whole.

The directive that God would begin sharing with me on December 9th would be housed in two separate communications of the antichrist's impending arrival. This was not the manner in which I expected to receive His calling. But it was His delivery all the same. It was a moment when the reality of and reason for His call had to be presented in such a way for me to understand all that the role would involve. It was a role that had been foreshadowed, but the revealing of the Beast's impending arrival meant it was time for His message to take shape. For the single greatest step I have strived to take along

Kingdom

the journey in His direction has been to understand the directive in its purest form. It involves not having any assumptions, but rather continually asking questions, seeking help and finding clarity in His desired form. The messages received are all too often formless in definition, but hold the potential for all that will become.

It takes a spiritual kneading of His message to begin to understand His intention from His word, "Go." For this reason, I sought my Father for further guidance and direction before moving without preparation. As it turned out, the scriptures that the angel named Scott had been adamantly speaking to me about weeks before were the most important verses I needed in getting started. Everything is so divinely timed. I did not know at the time I first met Scott what the true reason would be in sitting down with him and listening to him speak, but as I came to see, it was always about Matthew 25 and the verses he wanted to make sure he shared with me.

Matthew 25

In a matter of one calendar month, my Father had shared more directives and guidance than I could possibly sort out as quickly as I desired – and it was just in the first few days. The idea of the bride that I was continually seeing in the heavens permeated my being. I knew that she and I were destined to be, but I had not yet grasped the concept as to why I would be getting married in the heavens. Though it was more real than anything I had ever known on Earth, the Love of my life was not of this Earth and had a grip on my soul. It was a magnetism that pulled across time and space in a way that confounds the idea of existence. How could it be so real, yet we were separated by the experience?

And, on top of the idea of Love in the heavens, there was also this little tidbit of His grand directive. In the midst of all of the other aspects involved in the communication, the one that was the most confounding was this new directive where the Angel of the Lord said, "The time is near, and it is now time to share it with others." My mind raced through countless possibilities of the meaning. But at the heart of the message, I always had a sinking feeling. It was not a feeling of personal sadness or shame, it was a sinking feeling regarding what every man, woman, and child was about to face. Though on December 9th, the definition was not spoken in clear words, I understood where His message was already leading. The apple of the eye that he has been teaching has all been how the end of days is a period of time mankind is on the verge of breaching.

In the midst of all the new communication, I sought clarity through scripture. Matthew 25 was a chapter I was led to study when the concept of the bride became apparent. I was not sure where all of the references to a "bride" in the Bible were located, but I recalled that there were several places that Jesus spoke of this concept. In finding my way to Matthew 25, I began to read about the role of the bridegroom. As I made my way through the chapter, something special happened.

In the preceding months, I had been helping a homeless man get back on his feet. In doing so, I knew I was being tasked with learning how to help him as God helps us – by providing tools instead of solutions and asking him to meet me halfway through his actions. It meant that there was a greater importance focused on the delivery of how I helped versus merely the idea of helping. Instead of freely giving money, I provided an iPad to help this man begin applying to jobs. Instead of offering cash, I occasionally called him up and took him out to breakfast or lunch where we would review his progress with job applications. Over the months prior I felt like we had bridged a tremendous canyon from where he was once standing to where he was attempting to reach. During this time, we got to know each other spiritually, and I had begun sharing with him my story.

Matthew 25

In the days before reading Matthew 25, this man called me to chat. This was not uncommon. Some days I would receive eight or ten calls from him, though I was not always available for conversation. But during this one particular call, he was coughing on the phone and obviously battling a sickness. South Florida does not really get too cold to be outdoors, but he had been sleeping in his car as the coldest week of winter hit. His health was heavy on my heart, and I had been praying to my Father for guidance on how I could help him. In the prayer, I acknowledged having just finished read Matthew 25 for reasons to help me have a greater understanding of how Jesus described the Bride during his ministry. But as I had read through Matthew 25, I recalled there was a particular portion of the chapter around verse 34 when Jesus shares a parable to his disciples about being sick and offered shelter from the cold. I did not think too much about it at the time, but during the prayer, it bubbled up to the surface of the conversation as I was praying about the homeless man. I explained to my Father that I had never invited anyone into my residence since moving to Fort Lauderdale and wondered if it was the correct gesture and/or risk to invite the man over to help him recover from his sickness.

No sooner had those words fallen across my lips in the prayer I was saying aloud, when the phone rang – it was him. Before I answered, I could only smile as I said to God, "Okay, I get it. I'll invite him over. Please work through me to help him get better." I answered the phone, and we talked about his sickness. It was apparent he was still struggling to get better, so I invited him over for the evening. He seemed very thankful and said he would come over promptly. When he arrived, I had already picked up teas and coffees to help his throat as well as a few foods for him to eat. He did not turn anything down and began consuming the food.

As the evening wore on, his voice became noticeably better and his demeanor seemed to improve. I know it was the hand of God at work and not the food and hot beverages nourishing his body. As we talked, the conversation turned more spiritual in nature. There were certain points in the conversation that he openly cried as he talked about the challenges of his life from even the earliest days of his employment, to his parents passing, and eventually finding himself homeless in the streets. He talked about his brother and how they had not spoken in years. He went on to share how he was ashamed of his situation and did not want to tell anyone for fear he would be judged and admonished.

It was a hard conversation, but the warmth of the spirit filled the room. There was not a time I did not feel as if God's hands were holding him close and giving him a hug. We discussed his feelings about how he felt God ignored his prayers and was making it too challenging for him to get by. It was at this time that I role-played the conversation of how he would pray to God.

In the prayer, he spoke about how God "should give him a descent lifestyle." He went on to use the word "give" quite frequently. He also used the phrase "I deserve" multiple times. After he finished I shared with him how that exact prayer would sound in human conversation. In essence it would go along the lines: "Hey. I'm having a hard time because you will not give me anything. You have more than I could ever imagine. Give me some of it." It was a hard pill for him to stomach, and one that he never seemed to grasp in the conversation. I explained how God is always providing if a person is willing to listen. It may not be in the way a person desires it to happen, but God is always offering test after test for a soul to prove themselves worthy of an inheritance. It is not just about a place in the kingdom, but how it manifests on Earth.

The points I raised were continually met with retorts of, "Yeah, but I deserve to be making at least seventy thousand a year." I continually reiterated that a person deserves nothing and the desire to not accept the work offered when it does not pay high enough is basically saying, "God, that's not good enough. Give me more. I deserve better." It was one of the most difficult conversations I have ever had with another, but it is one that led to an even greater conversation later. For as we spoke about his challenges and ways to take the next steps forward, he began asking me about the end of days, and if I thought it was upcoming.

Matthew 25 continued to be a source of truth in our conversation. In one of the other parts of the chapter, Jesus explained the parable of the talents to his disciples. This was another parable I chose to use as I began figuring out how best to answer his question about my thoughts on whether the end of days was nearing. I shared with this man how God gave each of the men in the parable a talent of gold and a warning.

Kingdom

The message is clear in the parable that the men who worked with what they had in order to produce more from the fruit each had been given were blessed by God. The man who did nothing with the fruit so that he would be able to one day return it in full was a man who was admonished in judgment.

I explained to the homeless man how the parable could be applicable to his life and the opportunities presented, but the Lord spoke to me in these moments as well. It was like a flash of brilliance that ignited a pathway in my mind leading to a divine directive. It was in this moment of teaching that I became the student and surrendered to His will. It was a moment that God shared with me how the parable of the talents was directly applicable to all that He has been communicating with me over the years, but most importantly, the directive to begin sharing all that I understood was upcoming with others. I understood that while I may stumble out of the gate, retaining the knowledge versus beginning to share the knowledge and help it grow though others was what was truly at stake. It was at this time I opened up to the man about all that God had been sharing with me. It was as if God gave me the green light to begin using the talents that he had been seeding in the garden of my mind during the past three years.

The conversation was received much better than I could have imagined. The man went on to tell me how he had always believed that God sent me to him for a specific reason. It was during this time that the conversation grew. I chose to use the other resources at my disposal to help share all that I knew was intended to be spoken. We watched two movies that he had never seen which carried God's message hidden within. They were both movies that were spiritual in nature, but could be used for a greater purpose by following discourses with each other.

When the movies finished, he was filled with questions with the excitement of a child. It was as if a new starting line had been formed for this, and each subsequent conversation. We spent the evening talking about the flood of Noah and the divides of Heaven and Earth. It was in this conversation that I was able to start sharing with him portions of the architecture of the spheres. This is a topic that I have not really discussed throughout these first three books in the Books of Nine, but it is the underlying architecture to All That Is and is part of the entire message that God desires to be shared. This concept is the sole topic covered in Book VIII – Secrets, but it is unimportant to belabor it here. For this book, as well as the first two books, are meant to be the story-driven version of the journey for easy-reading. But it was in the way that our conversation progressed that God ignited a path of metaphors to help a seemingly simple conversation carry a great ocean of depth. It was here that I was led to explain how the motion of the spheres are the underlying mechanics to the world that is experienced here...and in that, introduce the concept of an eclipse.

Eclipse

In earthly terms, there is a concept of an eclipse. It is a subject that is well known but rarely experienced. The concept of the eclipse is one of three metaphors used to form the foundation to illustrate how the End of Days will occur without most people on Earth ever knowing it occurred. But wait, what was just said? What concept just slipped into this discussion? Unfortunately it is part of the message included in this disclosure. Those words were not misspoken, for it is important to understand how the world will remain oblivious to the ending even after it has already happened.

There is a concept in the book of Revelation that leaves many people in disbelief as to how God could be absent during His destruction of Earth in the End of Days. His absence is highlighted by a point in time that the reign of the anti-Christ is said to begin before our Father promises to return. Purely in the written context, this clandestine figure is referred to as the abomination of desolation, rather than by name. It leaves many people scratching their heads as to why He would allow this to occur. Why would our Loving Father leave a world to the wrath of the abyss? Fear not at the meaning in this prophecy, for part of His will in the delivery of this message, is to ensure this mystery is unraveled for this and future genera-

Kingdom

tions. For those who have not yet heard His call of their name during this portion of the journey, there is still time to understand and enter the Kingdom for all Eternity. For those who have been left behind, consider this chapter the key to unlocking this great mystery.

In exploring the concept of an eclipse, the premise is very simple. When the light goes out, the Earth is covered in darkness. The darkness is temporary as the paths of the moon and Earth around the sun eventually return through the point of intersection in their respective orbits. Though the elaboration in Revelation is open to interpretation, to understand the idea behind the eclipse is part of the foundation. For when the spirit inside is understood in the concept of light, it must be understand that each soul is a conduit for our Father's light. Each body is but a vessel to distribute this light and this goodness to others in need of the warmth of the Savior.

The closer a person is to God, the brighter this light shines. It is acknowledged by the soul through the sight of the spiritual eyes, but is not necessarily quantifiably identifiable to those still bound by sin. It is just recognized as "something different." The ability to radiate the light inside should be seen as the strength of a spiritual muscle. This muscle is what keeps the mind, body and soul in balance. The greater the light shines, the more it should be understood as the depth of a person's egoic surrender. It is a muscle that keeps a person cast in the light when darkness is raining down all around him.

In understanding that the soul is like a muscle to a spiritual calling, it is important to re-explore the concept of the

Eclipse

marionette-nature of the spiritual tugging upon the soul. For in every action taken in bodily form, it is always under the push-pull force of an unseen spiritual chord attaching the outpouring action of the body to an internal spiritual calling. Think of the way in Gravity Calling, it was indicated how the man in rose-colored glasses puppeteered a friend of mine who was unaware of all that was happening. It was easy to see through spiritual eyes that his actions were not of his doing, but rather inspired by a force hidden beneath the sight.

The puppeteering action upon the soul is a concept experienced by everyone. No one is immune to it, which is why the removal of ego in pursuit of the spirit is the most important effort ever taken. Think of this push-pull motion upon the soul like a pendulum weighted on either side as servitude of self versus servitude of the Lord. When the understanding that the pendulum is weighted in the direction of the strength of the soul, it is also easy to attach positive and negative connotations and see how the ability to gravitate in one direction or the other becomes part of the embodiment of the soul. These are not just words to paint an idea of how a world could exist around us. Rather, these words are the very definition of the push-pull motion. In the description of the pendulum, the weight that directs a soul in one direction or another, is a passive force with a pulling motion. The concept of the marionette carries the same connotation. Whether the soul is gravitating to light or darkness, or whether it is actionably puppeteered by good and/or evil is one and the same. The parabola between the two sides is the definition of strength gained.

Kingdom

Think of the concept of an old analog radio, the kind that had a big knob and dial. Unaided to the ear, stations are constantly blasting out songs and talk shows into the air. Even by turning on the radio, this is not necessarily clear. It takes the action of seeking out the station with the monstrous dial to be able to hear all that is veiled from the ears. Think of this radio as a spiritual dial of sorts, where the concept of becoming a Christian and furthering the role of becoming a disciple is only the definition of acknowledging this radio exists and flipping on the power.

The desire to seek out His Voice is an exercise that can be refined for the rest of the ages. The precision to seek out His Heavenly Station is the challenge to everyone of faith. To hear His Voice is not the definition of becoming a Christian or finding salvation. Rather, it should be seen as progressing from a student to a master of the tools that have been given. And even in the concept of a becoming a master of the spiritual trade, the master is actually a greater student than he began when he chose to pursue The Way.

When a person turns the knob on this analog radio for the very first time, it is an exercise in frustration for finding a station that plays to the tune of the soul. The majority of the locations on the dial present only white noise and snow. The first actions taken when attempting to find the desired station generally begin with large, swift turns to scan the entire band of the radio spectrum. It is a process of refinement that occurs. In the large swift turns, it is possible that nothing is ever heard. It is extremely likely that any station that was passed over occurred too quickly for the mechanics of the radio to produce any audible sound for the ear's recognition.

Many passes of the dial will yield to slower and more guided efforts until stations come into focus and are audible enough for the ears of the soul to listen. But in the beginning, precision is a rather dully guided action. Muscle memory does not exist, nor does the technique used on the dial. As a person's understanding of how to use the dial progresses, it becomes almost second nature to change stations to the one desired. The turns and precision to finding the station become more of a reflex-action and committed to muscle memory. But to understand that the strength of the soul that surrenders to the tug of good and evil is still subject to a greater acuity and precision, it should be noted that volume has not yet entered into the equation.

Just as tuning into a spiritual station is a skill that must be developed and refined, the volume of the information plays an even greater role in the spiritual muscle's definition. When a muscle is worked for the first time, it has to work to keep up with the task. The ease at which it can perform the task takes endurance to be built up through increased strength exercises and repetition. So when the volume of this spiritual station is understood, it must first be viewed as subtle in nature with only momentary glimmers of sound. If the work required to find the station is viewed as getting up and going to the gym, then learning how to keep the station volume loud enough to be heard is akin to continuing to use the gym's equipment. Just showing up counts for something, though working out is what leads the soul in guided direction to the destination of the journey.

So when the strength of the soul is put into an audible radio signal perspective, it can be understood that some people may be hearing His song and singing along, while others may just be humming to a tune they heard while seeking the station. To those who do not hear the stations being broadcast, there is at least faith in understanding the power is on in case something is to be heard. But for those without the switch flipped on, they may never know His Voice ever existed. It is a myth and a fairytale story easily reserved as fantasy since the Voice of the Lord is not readily apparent.

When a person is acutely tuned into His Heavenly Station, the voice of the spirit is heard throughout every aspect of the journey. The idea that the sound is like the glow of His Light is how this analogy gets worked back into the definition of sight. If one is to assume that most people never look up to seek out the light that illuminates the day or how there is still a glow of light in the dead of night, it can be easy to see how when darkness arrives, few will seek out the source of light or seek any reasoning. If an eclipse were to happen during the day, most people unaware would passively think of the darkness as shade or a precursor to night. If the eclipse happened during the night, few would ever realize the darkness no longer had any light.

But to those who are aware enough to look up and seek out reason in an eclipse's occurrence, they would observe the source of the confusion was a shadow that passed across the

Eclipse

source of the light. It is a shadow to some, complete darkness to others. For those who looked up, the understanding of a temporary muting of light would be apparent. But most would never know. Most would never understand that the darkness was part of a cycle occurring that would extinguish the light that gives life to the soul.

One last important point to be made about the separation of darkness and light is to understand that strength of the spirit is the fuel to life. Everyone hears the song of the spirit whether it is actively heard or passive in nature, though most may never be aware of its existence. Think of those tempted to surrender to the ego or the darkest of actions. This desire to fall completely out of His Grace is always held in check by the dimly lit pilot light ignited within, the melody of His Voice. Whether it is understood as a song that is being hummed to or a light that is providing warmth within, the potential for goodness keeps darkness at bay even at desperation's end. But the moment the light goes out or the volume to the station is nearly extinguished, every person is subject to losing a portion of the guiding light within that helps steer actions to goodness instead of surrendering to temptation.

To those who have strengthened the eyes of the soul or are at least aware enough to look up and seek reason, the temporary darkness that can be observed is surrounded by a halo of light dimly bleeding out, illuminating the borders of the darkened season. Even those who are highly attuned to the light will notice a dramatic shift to darkness and should be relied upon as leaders and guides. Some will find themselves on

Kingdom

the cusp of understanding the light, and the eclipse will swing them to darkness. Others will never have been aware at all. Those are the ones who will have no fear at the destruction they can cause. This is how a group can come together to wage war. It is how laws get passed that cripple the religious foundation to existence. It is not that I am advocating unity of church and state, but rather I am saying that they are one and the same, acting upon the same plane. Though laws are used as a form of judgment and/or acceptance, the greater call to action is to help everyone get to the destination, regardless of past successes or mistakes.

But I suppose the greater question remaining for those first digesting this explanation is how could an eclipse of the spirit occur at all and affect every nation? How would an eclipse affect the journey for each person, and does it lessen the resolve in understanding the End of Days prophecies such as those spoken about in Daniel and Revelation? To the latter portion of the last question, there must be a resounding "no" expressed, for the purpose of this explanation is to help those be prepared for the day of judgment and desolation.

Shamain

The definition of the eclipse was one was of three pillars to understanding the End of Days. Perhaps it is best understood as the result of the actions that take place during the days of desolation. For as the eclipse begins, the light to the spirit dims. In this motion, darkness and evil take root for this generation.

The End of Days is a harvest cycle. It is defined in this way in numerous references throughout the Bible. In ancient cultures uninitiated into Christianity, there are written records of celestial alignments, calendar-driven markers for dates and cycles. In both of these examples, truth is to be found. And though many may steer away from concepts such as the Four Blood Moons theory, this foundation is also sound. For the motion of the heavenly spheres is still based on an underlying architecture. The movement is in cycles, and souls are the fruits to blossom in definition of heavenly nature. For just as a field of seeds is planted and begins to take root, the growth eventually leads to a time of harvesting the fruit. The seasons change in a timely cycle, and the fruits adapt and grow with this knowledge.

Some fruits will bear seeds so more fruit can be grown. Other seeds may have never even taken root. Some seeds also may not grow into a fruit chosen for this harvest cycle, for the definition of a perfect fruit is different and unique for each situation. If the souls are seen as seeds of this generation, then it stands to reason the cycles continue forward from generation to generation. It does not mean the cycles are endless, as this could be the very last, but it does mean that for generations before us, other cycles have passed.

Think of the mysteries and history of the Earth. What happened to the Egyptians, the Mayans, and the mythical civilizations from before? In every ancient discovery thus far, the written text has been fully supported in truth. So, again it stands to reason the history of mythical cultures that draws criticism and lacks support, could very well have withstood a harvest cycle before perishing from the Earth.

In the written testament of the Bible, there is a recurring theme – those who pass away before the End of Days will be harvested when the end of the cycle reaches time for harvest. There could be no better example than the last chapter of Daniel where he asks God what he is supposed to do with all of this knowledge. God answers him by telling him not to share it with anyone and to live out the end of his days with peace knowing when he perished he would rise again when the harvest time came. For many, this idea breaks the mind. How could someone pass away before us, but be raised at the end of time? This was a question that I had for a long time as well, until God unraveled this mystery for me to tell.

The heavens are multi-dimensional, different levels in different planes. Each heaven is spectacular in its own unique

Shamain

way. My Father showed me many of the different places and locales. Of particular note, I spent a lot of time in what I would come to know as Shamain, or First Heaven. But for this unraveling let's start with the heaven that surrounds the Earth. For when each body perishes, the soul moves on. Some will suffer the wrath of a version of purgatory or hell. Others will arrive straight to the Kingdom of the heavens surrounding this Earth. This heaven is occupied by those closest to us and those of Biblical fame. These are the souls that have achieved favor in God's grace. These souls help each and every soul on Earth continue to grow. They are the voice of God guiding us, appearing in dreams, and the world that we know.

This does not take away from the Divinity in God's nature. Rather, it amplifies the masterful design and glory of His grandeur. Those who have passed before us are helping lead all other souls to salvation. Those who have no hope have been doomed to desolation. There could be no better visual illustration of this concept than the movie Astral City, which is a little known Brazilian movie subtitled in English. It is the story of a man most of the world does not know. He communed with the angels and ascended past souls. The illustration in the movie may be hard to believe in its presentation, but I can also honestly say that I have also visited this heaven. And for those who may not believe these words, I suggest they explore all three books of the Divine Comedy by Dante – another invited visitor to this world. Though Dante had to masquerade his adventures in prose and pretend the three written works com-

Kingdom

posed a play, the truth is that it was as inspired as these words that are written today.

The concept illustrated in the movie is the embodiment of heaven and Earth in a sphere. It moves together in harmony, though other heavens exist and are accessible to those who can hear. This is where the illustration in the movie stops, but it is the foundation of this chapter. For when a person thinks of heaven and Earth as two entirely separate bodies, the understanding to the architecture to all becomes disjointed. So think of heaven and Earth as a sphere. This sphere is moving in two simultaneous directions while we only see Earth as circling the sun. Both of these directions are important to understand, for they form the other two pillars required to understand.

One direction the sphere is moving should be visualized in the following way: Think of a circle approaching the outer corner of a square. The square is much larger than the sphere, which it is approaching at a 45° angle on the outer corner. When the sphere reaches the corner, it must divide to follow its intended journey. The journey will follow the path around the square, hugging the edges until it reaches a new point to divide again.

When the first division occurs, this is the end of the harvest cycle as mentioned in Revelation. Those who are judged in the eyes of the Lord will continue onward and upwards in their ascension. Those who have not yet grown in the eyes of the Lord will be cast back into the abyss for eternity. Now this is the point I want to offer a biased opinion for clarity's sake. For if these words have survived for generations, the opinion offered will have proved to been founded in fact. But I must say that it is entirely possible that the words in this book are only for this generation's cycle. And if that is the case, there can be no greater purpose placed upon each person's shoulders than to share these words, for this is the message my Father called on me to deliver.

Every word ever written in history that foretells the End of Days all deem the end to be finite in nature. But once it is understood that we are all part of All That Is and that All That Is is eternal, then it should also stand to reason that all cycles repeat and recycle. There is potential that those cast aside will be given a new chance to find the light. And if that is the case, then it can be seen that God never truly destroys His Creation, but essentially just sends the unharvested souls back to be recycled. But even with that being the case, it should be mentioned, the darkness, filth, and suffering my Father has allowed me to witness is one that no soul should ever desire or put at risk for potential. For every soul will fall upon one side or the other, and if everyone was aware of the true risk of the outcome, no one would ever surrender to that torment or torture. But, again, I want to make clear, the contents of this specific paragraph are an opinion of the outcome for those left behind and cast into the abyss. It is entirely possible that the road will end finitely for those left behind. It is possible that just as a fruit may not be fit for harvest, a soul really no longer has a purpose. Perhaps it is cast aside where it will decay. Perhaps it will still seed offspring that will have the same genetic deficiencies. Regardless of the view of how those left behind

Kingdom

remain, the basic premise is that a darkness will have fallen upon them, and the strongest lights will have been taken away.

Two As One

The third pillar is the final arm that creates a structure for defined understanding. It is the second direction in which the sphere of Heaven and Earth is moving. If the first pillar is understood as an eclipse, and the second pillar a divide in linear motion, the third pillar should be understood through the idea of implosion/explosion. This third pillar is a motion that is impossible to recreate on Earth, though the idea can be easily illustrated. The western world has a word for this motion, though its definition and popular understanding only serves to confuse a mind from truly understanding.

To think of this motion, let's return to the concept of a sphere. Now think of a sphere that is much smaller, in the center of the first and larger sphere. For this example, imagine them both to be semi-translucent. Though the colors should hold no meaning other than to help add definition to the illustration, think of one sphere as tinted blue and the other red. At the very root of this illustration is the way every heavenly body is defined. Elementary school science teaches a child that the Earth has a core, a mantle, and a crust. And every child knows that the stars contain cores of burning fuel. Higher levels of academic science propose the weight of the core affects the gravity of the body. And while it is irrelevant to discuss the science of cores in this space, it is important to understand that the basic principle illustrated is one that is at the heart of the existence of everything observed.

So without this example being marred by science and reason, just think in simple terms of two translucent spheres – one tinted red, one tinted blue. Now for this example, let's think in terms of equal motion. As the sphere inside expands, the other contracts in reciprocal fashion. I suppose the example could also be understood by just thinking about how the internal sphere expands beyond the size of the other, but it is important to grasp the duality of the motion. As one sphere expands and the other contracts, there is a point that the exteriors of the spheres align before switching positions.

This is the moment the red sphere becomes the blue and the blue becomes the red. As this very point of intersection manifests, it is important to see how the two spheres become one and the lensing creates a purple appearance. In Revelation it says Heaven and Earth become one, and without a doubt, this is how the heavens surrounding the Earth and The Heaven are formed. If one of the spheres is viewed as The Heaven – and by The Heaven, I mean a heaven greater than just the heaven that is bound within the same sphere as Earth – and the other sphere is viewed as the embodiment of heaven and Earth as one sphere, there is a point of transition that souls enter The Kingdom.

Think of how a train arrives at the station. It is just a temporary stop along the journey to its destination. And while the train slows down and stops to board all passengers who have a ticket, this should be seen as analogous to this point of transition. All of those who receive the Mark of God, is tantamount to receiving a ticket. And those with the Mark of the Beast would never make it through the doors of the station. Those who receive a ticket will consist of those chosen who are upon the Earth at the point of transition, as well as those who embody the surrounding heaven. Those in the embodied heaven will be those like Daniel, Elijah, and the Messiah. Those left behind will be cast into the abyss of desolation.

When this transition happens, it will occur in a lensing effect. When the two translucent spheres begin to intersect, there is an event-horizon created on either side of the intersection. Think of it as the point of no return, the point of judgment. The event horizon is the cusp of the eclipse; it is the moment darkness will begin to take reign. It is a necessary moment for the salvation of those who will ascend. It is the last test of will and faith regarding each person's walk upon the Earth.

At the point of the eclipse, the spiritual volume is turned down. The light burning within is dimmed to a level that introduces fear and doubt. This is when the last anti-Christ will reign. It is not one person, but the embodiment of darkness. This is a period that will last three and one half years. It is a halfway point of the seven year period of transition before all that remains will be left for destruction. And for those who think, "Oh, well, I must have at least seven years," it is important to note that this period is already upon us.

When the transition occurs after the lensing of the spheres, the ones left behind will be absent of light and

Kingdom

doomed for destruction. Those who ascend will be filled with the light of Ever-After. While there are several potential outcomes in the way this will manifest, my Father has shown me the truth in the principle of how it will come to pass. It is possible that when the lensing occurs, the Earth will completely divide in two. It makes sense in context, for a divide of this magnitude would usher in chaos and destruction. It would be a moment two planes of existence are bridged, with neither version of the Earth ever knowing the other happened. When this occurs, those left behind will likely not notice those who were taken. For out of 7.2 billion people upon the Earth, very few will make it. In this situation, those who ascend to Heaven during the harvest could arrive in a completely different locale/plane. But it is also possible that the Earth will appear the same. This concept makes sense, for it is how the flood of Noah happened. The only difference is that Noah was tasked by God to transcend generations. By surviving the flood upon the Earth, Noah was able to continue to spread the word of God for generations to come. It is with certainty that the story of Noah is the written occurrence of how a previous version of the harvest cycle ended. It is also important to take note of the significance as written about in my journals (Books IV – VII) that many of the messages my Father has shared with me, continue to reiterate the symbolism in Noah as well as the directive I have been tasked to follow.

Whichever side of the split Noah transcended may be the greatest question of the story. For was it only the story left behind which transcended cycles of generations? Or was it possible he was tasked to continue the harvest cycle to help those left behind grow stronger in spirit? Perhaps the world at that time was not ready for anyone to ascend. But it is also possible that Noah's survival of the flood is also the way in which the survival of the End of Days will occur. For when destruction takes its toll on the darkened souls, all that will be left remaining will be a New Earth, filled with new light and the potential for eternity with God's chosen few.

It could also be seen that the Earth would remain the same – only the souls of the bodily vessels would change planes. Perhaps those who were not seen fit in the eyes of God's judgment would have their bodies re-inhabited by those that have passed away before us. Or perhaps a person would become more like a spiritual zombie, soul-less and void of the potential for eternity. This seems like the least likely scenario of all, but it is important to expand the mind for the potential. In all honesty, I can only speculate on how the outcome will manifest. But regardless of the outcome, the archetypal principle still exists. It is the principle He has shown me and tasked me to share, for the time is upon us and the spiritual results of the outcome remain the same. For even if everything were to still appear exactly the same, the souls of those chosen will be able to move on after death and those left behind would never exist again. Whatever the case, whatever happens, the emphasis on the journey could not be more important. For whatever egoic desires consume us in these days have the potential to sway the scales of judgment in the End of Days.

Kingdom

With the knowledge of the three pillars, Revelation can be unraveled... as well as the prophecies of Daniel, Habakkuk, and Obadiah. The explanation of the three pillars is what I used to explain the answer to the question by the homeless man regarding my thoughts on whether the end was near. It was a wonderful discussion. Though it took three chapters to elaborate upon it here, in conversation, the principles were much easier to share. In the words of this book, it is important that care is taken so that no generation is left misguided or words left too open for misinterpretation. But even with all that is said, after all I shared with the homeless man that evening, God revealed further clarity in His directive. While I used this explanation of the three pillars as the starting point in His directive, on the evening of December 11th, he offered further clarity in how He desired I begin sharing His message.

Next of December

The directive I received from the Angel of the Lord on the 9th of December seemed so clear and full of splendor. Though the directive did not spell out any specific message I was to share, it was obvious that the directive was to start the engine and begin to prepare. The day I received the message it was put into practice. And while I did not think much of it when I invited the homeless man over to help him get better and find shelter, it did set the next phase of His plan into motion. The next day I shared the message again with another person purposed into my journey. Again, the conversation was similar in delivery. I began with the explanation of the pillars as we discussed how the end was nearing. It seemed the message was well received again, though I was left with the same feeling of an imperfect delivery. It was as if I was somehow not sharing the complete story. I was not sure what I was missing in the pitch, but both conversations seemed more doom-and-gloom than filled with anticipation of acceptance of the roles to be played.

Looking back, I suppose that is the way anyone would have taken the message based on the way it was delivered. Though I did not see the delivery as such, it was more like the opposite of uplifting. It was as if there was a moment near the end where each of the two people expressed the same sentiment of, "Oh, that actually makes sense. I can run with this interpretation," but it quickly gave way to, "Oh wow. This just got real. I do not think I want to handle it." In the moments following their transitions of thought, I could feel the impact.

In truth the reality is what it is and cannot be affected. For thousands of years God has given a giant heads-up for this generation. But somehow a warning of thousands of years has gotten lost in the shuffle. And with an eclipse approaching, the shadows of darkness have been creeping ever closer. So after the second time I delivered the message, I turned to my Father in prayer seeking further guidance. I asked Him to help me understand the best way to deliver all there was for me to share. I explained the scenarios and my assessments in the two reactions, though I knew he already was aware of my thought process. But it was more important that I own up vocally to my interpretation, so that he would hear my voice and guide me by my verbalized questions. So, it should not have come as any surprise when the morning of December 11th, He spoke with great clarity and definition.

On December 11th, I was taken to the heavens and stood before seven angels. I understood the seven angels were the same seven angels from Revelation. The angels were enormous and more austere than any of the other angels I have ever seen. In the experience, I was told, "The time is near, and it is now time to share it with others," before I was led to a grassy, green bank with a large tree to our left. We sat on a blanket where we looked at the stars above. There were five

Next of December

objects that formed the focal point of the view. I understood the objects to be the five objects Bryan was shown a few evenings before, which represented the four horsemen and Wormwood. After being shown the objects in the sky, one of the angels took me to a parade where I was told, "The Son of God took office after seventy weeks." As I heard the words, I witnessed the Son of God being paraded through the streets, but not in the manner as it would occur on Earth. This parade was regal and refined. The angels and I all slow clapped His arrival as he walked down the streets of white.

After receiving the message from the angels, on December 13th, I began a three day absolute fast on Earth where I immersed my soul in prayer asking for further guidance in how best to deliver the message as God intends it to be shared. During the morning hours following the first evening of the fast, I was once again taken to the heavens where I received specific instructions on how my Father wished for His message to be shared The message was delivered in four parts consisting of visual imagery to illustrate the directive. In each circumstance, the Angel of the Lord closed with the directive to, "Run and tell everyone the Messiah is coming."

The experiences on the 14th of December added further clarity to the message received on December 11th, which in turn added clarity to the directive issued to me on December 9th. When all three are taken in context of a dialogue with God, the following conversation ensued:

God: "The time is near. It is now time to go share it with others."

Kingdom

Me: "No problem! I'll get started."

God: "Son, let me help you out with your delivery. Your first two attempts seemed a little doom-and-gloom, but good for you for getting started immediately. This time, tell them about the five objects in the sky and the seventy weeks."

Me: "Thank you! It seemed like both people understood your message, but it just hit them hard. You know, I'm pretty sure I understand how You want me to approach it, but I'm going to fast in demonstration of my desire to hear the message as You would like it delivered, because a message this important should not be colored by the deliverer's interpretation of Your instructions."

God: "You are correct. The message did hit them each a little hard. Though you delivered the message with clarity and taught a complex subject very well, let's change up the pitch. Instead of teaching how the end will occur, instead share an uplifting message. Tell the world the Messiah is coming. That is much more positive and gives hope rather than taking hope away when teaching about the end. Oh…And one more thing. Do not forget about the Jewish families either. They are the foundation of this faith. So here are four parables that will speak to everyone in the way I wish for the message to be delivered."

Me: "Thanks again! I'll make sure to deliver the message specifically in the exact words and imagery as the message was delivered to me."

With that, the exact method and words of the delivery of His message were shared with me so that I could share them

Next of December

with others. There was much more involved in the grand picture of the effort to be undertaken, but most importantly the directive was clarified to inspire and provide hope to all of those open to hearing the message. The fast ended with a punctuation mark to all that He wished to be shared. On December 16th, I was taken to the heavens where I witnessed the destruction of the Earth as foretold in Revelation. The imagery was never how I would have imagined it, but it was clearly the imagery that had been described throughout the ages. The hours away from Earth that my soul spent experiencing this destruction and desolation left behind in the wake of the divide was essentially the exclamation point marking the end of the directive. If the message on December 14th is understood as a message without punctuation, it now had an exclamation point added. From this moment forward, days and dates would not be the markers of each step taken in December, for every step forward would be understood as the Next of December.

...

"Run and go tell everyone the Messiah is coming!"

...

How To Tell Your Family

I am not sure there is ever a way to tell your family anything as substantial as the message that God had tasked me to reveal. His message was not even in the same ballpark as the topics that people potentially keep at bay or use caution with when speaking to those they love most. As a child, it is easy to see the topics that could bring love into jeopardy. These topics are treated with the utmost care and delicacy in delivery, if not avoided in their entirety. Though it is never really a question about whether a topic will stop love from existing, it is more of a question about whether a topic will introduce judgment upon a person.

Children tend to hide topics they fear may cause stress to their parents. In fact, adults may be even more selective about the topics spoken about around family. Though I am not saying selective disclosure is a blanket-rule for all families – for there are families that are extremely open and accepting of any and all topics that a family member may face – but the majority of families that I have interacted with during my time on Earth tend to not speak about topics that could introduce judgment upon another, even into an unbiased family.

My family, for generations, has experienced its share of treading lightly among certain topics for fear that the bond everyone has in each other would be divided. As a child I never quite understood the reason for secrecy or the delicate wording around seemingly benign topics. But, as an adult, I have come to understand how strong-willed all of my relatives are. It is not anything negative for it is likely a trait that introduces more strength than otherwise would be possible without that trait. However, the fact remains that any topic wherein a family member could form a strong opinion is one that should always be treated with the utmost delicacy so as not to create a divide or rift in the strength of our family. It is what it is and how it has always been.

So when I was tasked by my Father to speak to my family about all that He has been sharing with me, a certain amount of trepidation entered into the equation. I was not fearful, but I knew that the moments ahead would likely create a divide. It was quite possibly why my Father tasked me to speak to my family in the first place. Families instinctively react in one of two ways to their relatives. They either blindly believe anything a family member says – especially in times of judgment – or they cast aside the family member and side with their mind. There really is not anything in-between for most families. Open acceptance is rare.

The topic I was asked to introduce to my family is already one that requires a certain amount of open-mindedness to hear. But, more importantly, there was an extra element introduced with my mother, father, and sister due to their having watched me grow up. It was not that my past was filled with missteps and terrible mistakes, rather it was filled with many demonstrable wonders of His grace. But as a child learns to walk, he can stumble and fall. Sometimes he needs to be picked back up. Other times he has to pick himself up. No child is born into the world and begins running without first learning to crawl. Regardless, the popular opinion of a person is typically based on judgment of their past and anyone who speaks of God is held to an even higher standard. So many things in that previous sentence should demonstrate the greatest flaw in mankind – the judgment of the vessel rather than seeing the spirit inside.

The judgment of the vessel is the very first element of reaction a person demonstrates when ego is in control... and it occurs without any foundation. As an example, imagine someone randomly walking up to you in the street. They say, "The Messiah is coming," and turn and walk away. The very first thought that runs through the mind is, "That person is crazy,"... but why? Judgment was cast on just the fact that the person approached another to discuss a topic that requires care and delicacy. Their history has not even been observed to form the opinion. Now imagine the person was not a random stranger. Think of having seen this person on other occasions. Now when the words are spoken and the person walks away, the mind will generate the same thought, but attach every aspect of the history with that person. Perhaps at this point, the opinion is that much more strongly formed because the person that approached has left more room for support. To some, knowing a person will generate a higher level of trust. But to the vast majority of mankind, greater hesitation in trust is formed. Now imagine that a family member says the same thing but then walks away. If a family is not completely open-minded and built upon a foundation of trust, an opinion is formed. Maybe the door is open to the potential of truth just a little bit wider than a random person would have been able to manage, but the truth remains that there is a robust history that adds a greater potential of support for either side of judgment to be cast.

However, the most important aspect of this example is not that judgment is cast upon the deliverer of the message, but rather so much scrutiny goes into the deliverer that the message being delivered is missed. One cannot exist without the other, and judgment should never be cast upon anyone, but it is the reality that a man battles when tasked with delivering a divine message. Truth should be sought, the message should be explored and opinions formed based upon the message itself rather than judgment of the deliverer cast. This does not mean to ignore the source, for if the source is chosen by God, then His light will shine through in all aspects of his life. Rather, demonstrable actions of the deliverer will always support the message and further support the truth behind the words delivered. The line of judgment is difficult to define, but if it casts an obstruction in hearing the message, that moment should be seen as the line.

How To Tell Your Family

So when it came to talking with my family, the challenge of overcoming thirty-three years of history of seeing me as a brother or son was going to be a challenge. With my father, my sister, and her husband all receiving Masters Degrees in Divinity, the other hurdle was overcoming the headstrong mindsets that run in my family. Every person on Earth has some amount of pride in his accomplishments in life, so encroaching on the academic side of religion could also be seen as a territorial line. In all that I have just said, nothing negative should be seen. It is just an illustration of the unseen. All I could do is hope that in sharing the story, His words would be all that was needed. I had faith in the delivery, but whether the place of outpouring was open to receipt filled my soul with a burden of inexplicable size. Imagine the ones you love most in your life being placed in the position to choose whether to be open or closed off in receipt. It is not a moment of judgment, nor was I seeing it as such, but to understand that my Father wanted them to hear His words was a feeling of helplessness in whether they truly heard.

Every aspect of how my family could place doubt in His words was introduced into my thoughts. Again, it was not anything I could control, it was just the understanding of all that was at stake. To receive is all that He desires, for in open receipt the Spirit will do the work required. Open receipt of a message not divine will not manifest in work or deeds when true discipleship in the walk is performed. Stewardship of the words through discipleship will clearly separate darkness from the light. But before any separation can occur, open receipt of

Kingdom

the word is required. To receive means to do so without bias, without judgment. Only in receipt can true discipleship of light be stewarded.

Christmas Dinner

When I arrived at my sister's house for Christmas dinner, I made sure to arrive a day early. I wanted to take the time to share with my sister and her husband the message I was tasked to share without family impeding the delivery. The relationship I have with my sister has never been very close, but I love her in every way possible and would be there for her at a moment's notice. To spend time together has been rare. Over the years, even further distance had been introduced. So, to arrive a day early was a special occasion. The dinner we shared together was one of the most spectacular moments I have experienced with my sister. It was possibly one of the first times I had ever felt that we were two adults enjoying the moment rather than two children. To share in the company of her family and her husband was one that I will always hereafter remember.

When dinner completed and the children had been put to bed, we sat at their dining room table sharing in great conversation. I knew in this moment that three years of conversations with my Father was going to be put to the task. It was a moment of excitement and a moment of sadness wrapped up in one. I understood that after the Words were put into conversation that everything else was out of my hands. The delivery of the message would set everything else into motion. And though the conversation went better than I could ever have imagined, I had no baseline to understand a measurement of success. The words were heard and great conversation was shared, but one moment stood out above all others. It was the moment that my sister said, "I believe you believe all that you are saying."

This was an unexpected reflection of the delivery of the message. Whether they rejected or accepted belief in the message and the experiences shared did not matter. This was the moment that I knew I did all I could do as a vessel. If every aspect of the delivery radiated truth and belief, then it was upon their souls to choose to receive. But even as the conversation seemed to be a task performed as a steward of His word, I came to understand it was so much more. Instead of the delivery of the message being seen as a pastor delivering the message, it should be observed as a thought that served as a catalyst. The amount of verbal content delivered was minimal compared to the length of the conversation. Instead, it became a lesson where I played the role of a student after a theological thought was placed as the subject of the conversation.

It was in the role of the student that I learned just how difficult the journey ahead would be. I knew that regardless of the acceptance of the message the feedback gained was truly the task my Father had envisioned for me. After the initial fallout from my opening salvo dissipated and the theological and philosophical sides of the conversation began to take shape,

Christmas Dinner

the conversation realized one of the most startling realities to the state of Christianity. Even as a child I had understood that "to be a Christian" had become a label. It had become the definition of "if there is a heaven, then I want to go there." The label of being a Christian is different for each and every person, though it is rarely as Christ ever envisioned it. The label at its point of origin defined the disciples of the word and believers of Christ. They were stewards of the message that Christ left behind, based in Judaism and actively performed in action. There was a standard of life and a will to follow every written commandment. But over the last two thousand years since the crucifixion, the definition has become more of a safety net – in the event it is real.

There is so much more than attending church on Sunday and donating money for religious reasons. In fact, those two aspects can be completely removed in the definition of being a Christian. And if those two aspects are completely removed, think of how much smaller the body of the Church would become. In some cases entire denominations would be struck from the list, but it does not mean these people will face judgment due to misguidance, for many are doing what they have been taught through the leaders in their lives. There is something to be commemorated for seeking guidance in recognition of the light. Though it does not mean that after two thousand years of warning of the End of Times that this level of misguidance is acceptable in the eyes of God. And perhaps that is the reason that the fire must be re-ignited, for the Church as a whole is not prepared. In many cases the Church is further from the source than it was at its inception, though it may be broader in reach and social acceptance. The majority of people in the world claim religious affiliation, though one must wonder how many would know if the Messiah had returned or even how to listen and seek truth and acceptance at the potential?

This was the very question that bubbled up in the conversation with my sister and her husband. As the pastor and minister of music for a rural church in a sparsely populated area, it made for a great perspective. The question that we focused on was how could a person deliver a message of God's intention in a manner with the widest delivery. The conversation was more on the hypothetical nature, so it allowed them to think openly about the delivery. I began with just one denomination. Since they are minsters at a Baptist church, I started with their denomination. In almost all churches there is a pyramid structure of leadership in the nation. For example, in the Baptist denomination, there is a large group of churches that participate in the Southern Baptist Convention. Just as a hypothetical starting place, I asked my sister and her husband if the leaders of a Convention of this nature would be a good starting place to share a message so that it could bubble down to the masses. I proposed inviting all leaders to an all-expense paid convention. The response I received was surprising. It seemed the opinion was that most pastors would not be open to listening, much less attending. While this was based on their opinions and certainly was not applicable to every member in

Christmas Dinner

the convention, it was more just an illustration of the idea in getting fellow pastors to attend this type of meeting.

I continued to whittle down the size of the groups. Eventually we reduced the size of leadership to just the pastors in the county. In my sister's county, they figured there were probably around fifty churches – all with smaller memberships. Both my sister and brother-in-law knew most of the leaders, so it made for even greater perspective. I asked if they thought they could assemble just the church leaders in their county so that a message of this nature could be delivered. Again, it was hypothetical and philosophical in nature, so it was not a defined task or directive. In their response, I heard the same reply. They both stated that most leaders would not make the time, and most would be resistant even upon hearing the message. This response surprised me, but to add further emphasis to the subject of the conversation, I posed an even more defining question. I asked my brother-in-law and sister if their church was prepared.

The response I heard was quite possibly the most interesting perspective I never expected, for they both replied that more could be done in preparation for the End of Days. The question did not require them believing the message God had tasked me to deliver, it was just a way to drill down to this answer. So, if the root of the message that my Father has asked me to deliver is to prepare for the Messiah's return, and churches are admittedly unprepared yet unwilling to listen, how does the deliverer of the message overcome this conundrum? Even though the conversation ended with the comment directed toward me, "Quite frankly, I do not believe you," there was an outright admittance that more could be done by everyone to prepare for His return – and in that, His message was heard. Now, for a moment imagine being the deliverer of this message and knowing that the time is truly near for the Messiah's return. This is the truth through your eyes, the reality you have been allowed to see. Now imagine the weight carried within the delivery of the words, for those left behind will be left to the torment and torture of the Earth's desolation, never the wiser that their opportunity to find favor in the eyes of God had already passed them over due to their own errors.

The majority of the New Testament is written by Paul, a disciple who was not initially a believer in Christ though he lived upon the Earth during the same time. It took hindsight and a divine experience for Paul to be ignited to preach the word. Think about that for just a moment. In the days that Jesus walked the Earth, his very disciples doubted him, turned him over to authorities for crucifixion, and denied him when their livelihood came into jeopardy. A large portion of the foundation to Christianity is based upon those who recognized his divinity in hindsight. And though Jesus was Jewish, there is still a stark divide in Judaism and Christianity. Now, understand that our Father gave mankind over two thousand years of leniency and grace so that people could understand that one day the Messiah would return. He gave a defined set of rules in what to look for. He did so through multiple prophets whose testimony is included in the Biblical canon. But, today, the Church is unprepared to even listen for His message,

Christmas Dinner

much less discern and decide how and when to follow His instruction.

For just a moment, think of how small the number mentioned in Revelation is that receive the Mark of God. This number is 144,000 and seems so small compared to the number of people upon the Earth. 144,000 out of 7.2 billion souls upon the Earth is so small they will not even be missed when their time has come. This does not mean that only 144,000 will be saved for there is still a little room in interpretation of the written word wherein 144,000 are firmly sealed as the stewards to the others who will face judgment. Either way, in any defining moment of judgment of His grace, we should all strive to be one of the 144,000. This number is bound and true. At first the number seems so tiny, so small. But as I have come to realize over the course of sharing His word, the number is actually extremely large and relatively unfilled. Think of how few people will tell another person they had a dream or a vision that defies explanation, though God gave them warning of the end upcoming. Think of how few will watch a video of someone's testimony. Think of how few people will risk opinions placed upon themselves for delivering His word. Even in conversations with those I trust the most, in describing how "my soul was taken to the heavens," I have been met with criticism and judgment. Those who believe in the possibility that God has been speaking to me have asked that I rephrase how the experience happened when I share the story with others. Think about that for just a moment. Those who believe in the potential of God speaking to a person fear judgment of accepting the message because it is explained as it truly happened, in ways that are supported in all aspects of the Biblical canon, yet would be seen as unfavorable in the eyes of the ego of man. That is quite the situation.

The latter example was not expressed by my family, but it is still another aspect in how the message is shared and why it is included here. The overall action to share a message that will likely be met with resistance is the divide that separates a disciple and a person claiming faith through a label. Certainly, when the view is seen through the eyes as I have been allowed to experience in sharing this message, an unstoppable shattering of the heart happens every time the words are not openly received – especially by those who truly believe the Biblical canon. And though my heart may shatter a million ways each time I attempt to have the conversation, imagine how it must seem through the eyes of our Father. Here is our King, our Creator, sharing with the world everything to help them get to the finish line before it is too late, and few will choose to listen. Most will be too fearful in making a mistake in discerning truth that avoidance becomes the answer. Alas, the fear is introduced due to ego controlling the mind. In removing the ego, the spirit becomes the river of the mind.

So as I was tasked to begin introducing this conversation with my sister and her husband, I became a student in learning how to see two people's reactions of whom I deeply Love and respect. Their reactions spoke wonders to my soul, though their reactions should neither be judged as good nor bad. Though they may have chosen not to believe the message, the

Christmas Dinner

introduction of the question about whether more could be done was achieved. For the role I have been tasked to play in delivering the message was never intended to procure leadership over each church's people, but rather introduce the questions so their leaders can take the reigns. The very foundation of the church as it stands is based on leaders knowing their congregations, and congregations assuming the role of students to their appointed teachers – the ones they have placed their trust within. And though it has been lost throughout the ages, the role of the teacher should always be seen as that of a student of Divine nature.

There should never be a disruption to this equation because in doing so, doubt would be placed upon leaders and individuals. Provoking doubt is another demonstration of Lucifer's hand playing marionette to a divine message being delivered through the body of a man. Every one of every faith, every denomination, every gender, every race, with orientations placed aside, are all brothers and sisters in Christ trying to reach the destination stride for stride. So to disrupt the church is, again, not the approach to ever be taken. The approach is in determining how to help everyone learn to listen. The fire that once fueled the light of the church has been allowed to smother into faintly glowing embers, smoldering out. This was the lesson I was blessed to understand in the conversation with my family. In the role of a messenger I was a student to His divine plan.

Why would a person be tasked to deliver the message to a family before all others? It could very well be for every reason

Kingdom

just written. But there was one more component to the conversation that was every bit of divine. Though my brother-in-law and sister would not expect it as such, the greatest part of the delivery of the message was in another part of His Word they unlocked in conversation. For quite some time I had been receiving imagery painted in pink during my experiences in the heavens – pink flowers, pink clothing, and pink candles. The latter was a topic brought up to lighten the intensity of the conversation. Since I was without clarity on the color's meaning, I felt led to ask about the meaning of the pink candles in the advent wreath. After all it was Christmas time and the lighting of the candles had been mentioned passively by my brother-in-law during our conversation. The prompt to ask the question was the moment I saw God's divine teleprompter of the spirit signaling for me to ask my brother-in-law about the pink candle's meaning. In response to the message delivered, his answer was the message my Father intended for me to receive.

Pink Candles

There is a tradition during the time of Christmas for churches to light a series of candles – called the Advent Candles – on each Sunday leading up to the Christmas service. For many, this tradition is not one of the first memories when Christmas church services come to mind. And, for those who it does come to mind, even fewer would be able to explain why this tradition exists. It is something that seems more like an antiquated symbolic gesture that has somehow slipped through the cracks from older churches into modern times. Lighting the candles is just something that is done in the weeks preceding Christmas, but seems to carry very little impact in the way of modern-day understanding in its meaning.

Some churches use the lighting of the advent candles in each of the preceding services to Christmas as a way to introduce new families that have recently joined the church. As a child, I can recall my family being called up in front of the congregation to light the advent candle on a particular Sunday leading up to the Christmas service. At the time, it seemed only to hold in it the gesture of welcoming a new family into a role of active participation in the church. I am sure that for many families, this is a similar circumstance that has been experienced. But ask any family the meaning of the action performed by lighting the candle and few would be able to expound upon it beyond it being anything other than an old tradition of lighting candles leading up to Christmas.

But the action of lighting the advent candles holds within it a meaning richer than ever imagined. It is a meaning that has only partially survived for generations and is a symbolic meaning that was not even on my radar preceding one very specific moment in the heavens. It would take a tremendous amount of research and understanding to begin to see all that my Father was telling me all along. It was an exercise in uncovering the meaning to the history of the church and how this particular symbolic action came to be.

It was in December that my Father commanded me to "Run and tell everyone the Messiah is coming." Questions filled my mind in trying to understand all that was held within the commandment I had received. I understood the impetus to move forward, but I was just beginning to understand the definition of the role I had been tasked to play. In prayer, I would turn to my Father asking Him for clarity in understanding all that he desired from me. It was at this point I was beginning to understand that I was potentially one of the two spoken about in Revelation that would precede the arrival of Christ. But, quite honestly, having that identity attached to the role I was tasked to play was an exercise in humility, for the hardest task a human is ever charged to accomplish is to learn how to humbly receive.

Giving is an action taught from childhood but, even so, some may never truly understand how to give unconditionally.

Pink Candles

It is the focus of Christmas and learning how to become more Christ-like – as is the charge in Christianity. But, too often the concept of receiving is overlooked. It is the hardest action a person will ever learn to accomplish because it is the completion to the action of someone humbly giving. Typically, most people who become contentious in understanding how to receive choose to react in one of two ways. The first way is to just smile and say "thank you." The second way is to build a wall of humility by saying things like, "Oh you should not have," and, "I cannot accept this," and sometimes, actually refusing the gift. In truth, the greater a person becomes in understanding how to receive, the more pride in humility arises. It seems like a contradiction, but it is the last surrender in learning how to receive in humility. Far too often as a person begins to understand the true action in the giver and the meaning carried through the receipt of the action, the receiver will refuse to accept the gift. Think of the times that people refuse to allow another person to pay for dinner or pay for tickets to an evening out. The one who is the recipient feels they are unworthy of the receipt and will continue to seek ways of repayment. The reciprocal action seems like it would be well received, but it is more frustrating to the giver because the person will not allow a gift in humility to be received.

As I began to learn how to receive in humility to my Father's blessings, I refused to accept blessings when they seemed too generous. Think of the way a particular job or opportunity is blessed into your life. It was times like these that I felt His blessings were too gracious and that it would potentially distract me from my walk and cause me to be lost in materiality. In some circumstances, I would vow that if I accepted a contract or a particular opportunity that I would use the whole sum of the earnings to give to others. I always wanted to return the blessing in full to others in need. Honestly, I still do not believe there is anything wrong with this action, but it should be understood that while our Father is trying to take care of each one of us through His blessings, He is also entrusting us to continue to do the same for others. Becoming the middleman in a giving/receiving situation is the true definition of receipt in humility. The blessings my Father provided during my walk were entrusted in me so that I could use the blessings for the betterment of others. I was a vehicle and a vessel, being taken care of by His hand in the process. But for fear that ego or greed could sneak into my actions, I was left in an all-or-nothing mentality. I would not accept anything from my Father if I did not understand how it could be used in full for the benefit of others. And, when it came to the definition of the role I was tasked to play during the journey, I would rather have assumed no definition than accept a role for fear that identity would invoke the ego to seize control.

The hardest struggle I have ever had along the journey was understanding how to decipher the difference between a test and a blessing. To accept the role that he chose me to perform, and in understanding that the symbolic nature of the role includes the expression of the inheritance bestowed upon a prince, is one that did not arrive without much push back and refusal to accept. Truthfully, the pushback I expressed

Pink Candles

should best be understood as the recognition that I had already been blessed through His Grace and how even the thought that I had somehow defied all odds along the human journey and could possibly be asked to receive His anointing for this role, was more than I could possibly comprehend. For when man looks back upon history and understands the roles that have been played in the spiritual story spanning thousands upon thousands of years on the Earth are only bestowed upon a very limited number of people (though it is important to understand that everyone has the potential for the opportunity), the possibility of ever hearing His Voice, much less receiving a crown and His anointing, seems slimmer than is a rational possibility at the time of its occurrence.

During the course of my journey, I dismissed any and all possibility of the journey being anything other than spiritual growth and understanding. Bryan and I discussed the roles of the two witnesses mentioned in Revelation quite frequently, though it never remotely involved either him or me in the discussion. It was always a conversation discussing the topic, "I wonder who it will be that will return." But as it turned out, it would take three and a half years of the journey to fully understand this role was always intended for each of us from the beginning.

Books IV- VII of these Books of Nine are the books of my journals. As the journal entries occur, it is easy to see all of the details I missed along the way, though if someone were to start reading on Day One without any understanding of the subject matter that would be unveiled, the reader would probably miss the details as well. As for me, I missed them all along... that was until December when I asked my Father for clarity in helping me understand how to "Run and tell everyone the Messiah is coming." In submission to His will, I fasted for three and a half days surrounding this prayer. I did not consume water, food, or come into contact with any liquid to my skin.

It was during this fast and in response to this specific prayer that my Father took me to the heavens and clothed me in a robe of pink. At the time, my mind fought the idea of being clothed in a pink dress. For the past several years the color of pink has been a recurring theme in the heavens. Most recently, I have been shown pink flowers, have witnessed a select few others in pink attire, been shown numerous pink candles, and most recently have been told that a "pink candle represented me." In earthly terms, the color of pink can be embraced in masculinity, but when it is expressed by another in a man's direction, it is generally an expression of femininity. So, with all of the indications of pink being representative of my role and purpose – and having experienced this particular scenario of being clothed in a robe of pink in response to my prayer – I had to go back and try to understand all that He was attempting to tell me all along.

The experience in the heavens ended with an angel taking me to witness the end of days for this generation. I experienced it in years of linear time, though it would only be hours that had passed upon the Earth. As others bore witness to the robe I was wearing in the heavens, they stopped and stared in

Pink Candles

amazement. Some quivered in fear and retreated in disbelief. It was through this encounter in the heavens that I realized that the color of pink held the meaning of the role I was to play. But it would not be until after I spoke with my brother-in-law as instructed by my Father, that I would understand the complete relationship of the color pink to the advent candles and how it applied to the journey.

After the experience in the heavens, I researched all I could about the color pink and its symbolic meaning in relation to faith. In almost all circumstances I was led to the symbolism in the advent candles, though the definitions were very minimal at best. It was clear that the white candle represented Christ in the advent wreath. The symbolic nature of the pink candle lacked any definition that would relate to my Father's response to me. The pink candle, by most accounts, represented Joy or Love (depending on the source). At the core, this made a tremendous amount of sense in how it could be applicable to my role. There were also references to the pink candle holding a meaning symbolic to its origination when the Pope would hold a pink rose during lent. Again, this was interesting but did not seem relevant. So after struggling to find clarity, I turned to the definition of the purple candles. My thought was that if I could understand the white and the purple candle meanings, then the pink candle's meaning would be revealed.

The struggle continued. In fact, a Google search on the internet yields little in the way of definition to each of the candles, with the purple candle yielding the least information

Kingdom

available. So, with little to go on as I began my directive to share with my family how the Messiah was returning, I tabled the idea of a pink candle holding any relevance. In the days following the experience, when I arrived at my sister's house, we sat down to have the conversation I was led to share with them. During the conversation, it became evident that the role I was to play involved listening more than speaking. It was as I heard my sister and my brother-in-law speak, that I realized there was a greater reason I was led to speak to them. To lessen the intensity of the conversation, I phrased a question to break away from the present topic. Since it was Christmas time, it was an easy sidestep into the question. I asked my brother-in-law what the meaning was regarding the color purple in the advent candle wreath.

It was in this moment he began explaining to me how there is a tradition understood more in spoken terms among ministers rather than in written form for a congregation. He explained how the first two purple candles represent darkness. The deep color of purple is the closest color that can express the absence of light without light being fully removed (as the color black would represent). After the first two purple candles are lighted in the weeks leading up to Christmas, the pink candle is lighted. Following the pink candle is one more purple candle, followed by the white candle of Christ.

The first purple candle is called the prophecy candle, or the candle of hope. The second purple candle is the candle of preparation. The pink candle, which is called the shepherd's candle or the candle of joy is used to represent the light illumi-

Pink Candles

nating the darkness. My brother-in-law went on to explain how the pink candle represents a messenger that illuminates the way for the arrival of Christ (the white candle). The pink candle is followed by another purple candle that shows that darkness returns before His Arrival. It is a candle referred to as the candle of love or the angel's candle. My brother-in-law went on to explain that the pink candle should be understood as an indication that a greater light is to emerge out of the darkness lighting the way for Christ's arrival. The white candle is symbolic of Christ, his purity, and holiness.

It was in these moments when I understood the reason for my Father's instructions for me to first share the message with my family was so that the concept of the pink candle would be uncovered. For, if the pink candle could be observed as a spark of light in the darkness preceding His return, then it is also to be understood to be the embodiment of my role with His message – and in this there was further understanding in the potential of being one of the two witnesses. Though I would not understand it as such completely at the time, it was a moment of reflection that held an important definition. For if pink is the color that is the embodiment of my vessel, then the role of preparing the way for the Messiah's return holds a much more divine nature. It was in this moment I began to understand the gravity to the possibility and the potential of this role. But it was of utmost importance to further explore all that has once been foretold. These were the days I was beginning to understand how the number 1260 applied so perfectly to the timeline of my life and His story. It was also then I would un-

Kingdom

derstand how the combination of these two items began to clarify his expectations for my journey.

A Far Away Land

Just after New Year's Day in 2015, my mother and father came to visit me in Fort Lauderdale, Florida. This was on the heels of a visit over Christmas where I travelled to see my family. Leading into the holiday season, God had tasked me to share His message with my family first before I stepped into ministry to share the message with the world. It was not that my family was more important than anyone else, it was just that there was still much more for me to learn in the delivery of the message to my family.

While Christmas was a joyous occasion and celebrated in the company of my family, I was only able to talk to my sister and her husband about the message. My mother and father wanted to come down to visit my new place in Fort Lauderdale, so I thought that would be the best situation to share the message with them after the holidays. A week would pass, and I would see my mother and father again. This time I would welcome them in to the place my Father had prepared for me in Fort Lauderdale, Florida, along the most gorgeous stretch of beach. And while the days that followed were unexpected through my eyes, the angels all around chose to reveal themselves to my parents' eyes. Though my parents would not see their visit to Fort Lauderdale through the same eyes as I would witness their journey, the experience could not have been more magnificent and filled with His glory.

As it was described in the beginning pages of this book, the embodiment of Fort Lauderdale as a divine location is only as such when witnessed through the eyes of the beholder. Think of a doorway that opens up into a room. When a person walks in, the location has changed. In terms of this example, everyone who enters through the door would be in the same location. But now imagine that door opens the eyes to a different perspective. When one person with spiritual eyes enters, Heaven is revealed. Though when others enter through the same door, their eyes may only reveal the Earth. It is a multi-dimensional concept of existence, but one that exists nonetheless. It is impossible to begin to explain how Heaven and Earth exist as one to those who have eyes to see and been blessed by the Lord.

When my family arrived they witnessed a beautiful city, a beautiful location on the beach full of hope and potential. Though my Father had explained to me how others I know would not see the world as I saw it unfold, it was important to understand that they would be blessed within my presence, for they would one day come to understand all that they unknowingly witnessed. To know two locations as one is a truth that had to remain unrevealed until the day it was intended by the Lord for these books to be shared.

When my parents arrived, I showed them around the building. And as evening began to set in, we decided to walk to a restaurant for dinner. We walked over to a Greek restaurant

A Far Away Land

that is one of the most popular in the surrounding area. It is the kind of restaurant that without reservations, the wait can run into the hours. On the way to the restaurant I walked next to my father. And while I had a feeling of what we would witness along the way, it is hard to put into words how grand the moment was even to this day.

As we walked to the restaurant we walked past an abandoned shoe upon the sidewalk. My father took notice of how in mid-conversation I observed the shoe. He understood I saw something that did not make sense to him, though he did not quite put it into those words. As we walked a few yards further, the angel named Scott appeared in the bushes along the sidewalk. I smiled at him and said, "Hello Scott!" My mother and father looked startled at the gesture of talking to the man, for he appeared homeless, dirty, and disheveled from their perspective. As soon as I said hello, Scott lit up with a smile. He said, "Hey Jonathan. I see you are with your parents. I hope you all have a great meal!"

To my mother and father it was an unsettling moment. They heard him identify them and even where we were going. It was not a location I have ever seen Scott before, so it even caught me a little off-guard. Without having ever met my family before, Scott made sure to tell them hello. As we exchanged goodbyes and headed on our way, my father asked me if he was one of the homeless men I helped around the city. I did not quite know how to answer the question directly, so I took a leap of faith and told him directly. I said, "You remember the shoe that we passed along the way? That was a

Kingdom

shoe I purchased for him the other day. Though you may not believe all I am about to say, the reason the shoe was off was because he was overheating. He was an angel who appeared to you in bodily form. So when you ask if he is homeless I would have to say definitely not."

My mother and father were not quite sure how to reply. To them, he appeared as a homeless man with something odd going on with his mind. They each asked again if he was homeless to which I replied, "In a matter of speaking that is how it would appear to your eyes. But honestly, though it may be difficult to believe, the man is not homeless, he is an angel sent here for me." The conversation became a little uncomfortable as I would expect, so we continued on to the restaurant. And while they would not see the magnificence of the moment, an Angel of the Lord was sent to say hello to them. We went on to the restaurant and were able to get a table without waiting. By the time we left, there was over an hour wait. And while again they would not see it as such, this was the second experience of divine welcome. For the truth through my lens of perspective would see it differently than chance. We walked right in to have our meal because that is how it was prepared for us by God in advance.

When we returned to my apartment, I took the time to share with them part of the message I had been tasked to share. But since I knew they would be with me for the weekend, I wanted to introduce the concept slowly. And while the conversation was met with opposition, it was a loving conversation and went better than I expected. It was an evening where I began to bare my soul to their eyes, but I had to begin a little at a time.

The next morning we headed down to the beach. In my building, there are chairs for the residents and others that are paid for in reservation. The freely available chairs are all the same color. They are always treated as first come, first served, and when they are gone there are no more. This has been the case since I arrived in the building, which at this point in time was just over six months in the making. But when we arrived on the beach, all of the chairs were taken, except for three I had never seen. I was so confused at the three chairs stacked up that were untouched, that I sought out a staff member to see if they were available for use.

When I spoke to our beach manager all he could do was smile. He said, "The chairs are for you and your family to use." The chairs were unlike any I had ever seen since the day I had arrived. They were not radically different, but enough to stand out from all of the others on the beach. More interestingly was the comment of the staff. He mentioned how the chairs were intended for me and my family without knowing they were even in town. So while my parents would not see the third experience as prepared for them by God, they did enjoy the beach and time in the sun.

While we enjoyed the warmest day Fort Lauderdale had seen in the past month, the beach seemed to be filled with everyone I had ever met over the past six months. Being in a vacation state, my building is almost always below thirty-percent full. Most of the people I have met have only been in town for a week or two at a time. From an outside perspective, it would appear as second homes for many. To my eyes I saw it as a special place where angels arrived when they were called upon by God. But to my family that day they witnessed a beach full of angels. Nearly every angel I had met over the past six months made a point to go up to my family and welcome them into "their home."

My parents were not quite sure what to think. To their eyes I am sure it seemed like I was just social with my neighbors. But they would not really be able to understand how rare it was for me to see all of these people. Everyone was so eager to welcome my mother and father into this home. To my eyes, I saw the angels pour out an abundance of Love upon their souls. Several of the people who met my parents even volunteered to fly back from their home countries the next time my family comes to visit. One couple even told my parents how they "saw me as their son" and continued to give my parents peace of the heavenly destination they would one day come to know they experienced. It was a day of wonderful community and Love from the angels. My family was left speechless and in awe of the warmth they received.

The conversation with the angels was the fourth experience they unknowingly witnessed. But it was the next several experiences that were even grander in presentation. After the beach I wanted to treat them to dinner. I took my mother and father to a restaurant on the intercostal river. It is a restaurant that again commands reservations to be made, but I thought

A Far Away Land

we would give it a shot after they agreed they would enjoy the types of food they served.

When we arrived, the very first parking spot closest to the building opened up just as we pulled in. This was the fifth moment they unknowingly witnessed. When we went into the building, we were able to be seated outside as they desired. We were given the very best table in the entire restaurant. Call this moment number six of divine intervention. Through my parent's eyes, it likely just seemed like coincidence.

And while I will skip ahead to the seventh divine intervention to make sure it is mentioned, we will return to the conversation I shared after dinner with my family. The seventh heavenly moment occurred the following morning. After my father and I were walking back from breakfast at a local restaurant, a car passed us by on the street. It honked several times to get our attention. When the car began to honk we were about to walk onto the grounds of my apartment building, but just as we took the steps into the drive, the very same car pulled up and stopped. As soon as it stopped I recognized another one of the angels I have met here in Florida. He immediately hopped out of his car to my meet my mother and father. His words were divinely placed through my lens of perspective, but I am not quite sure how my family received them. The man said, "I just want to tell you your son is in good hands and not to worry, we are keeping him here." The conversation was brief. He hopped back in his car and drove away from us as we returned to my apartment.

Kingdom

My parents would only see the heavens I had come to understand around us through their lens of perspective, which was only embodied through earthly concepts. And while I say "the heavens" it important to note how Heaven on Earth is still just a part of the bigger story. Perhaps it is better understood as the Promised Land on Earth, for the multidimensional concept I am describing is a tough concept to grasp. How can one person see an angel and another see a homeless man? It does not mean my earthly eyes manifested something different. It was the spiritual eyes that opened the soul to understanding just how everything upon the Earth is relative to each person's journey. Absolution is a fallacy created by the mind through the overwhelming nature of the earthly senses, which limit the mind to being open to the spirit. The seven moments my parents witnessed during their journey to Fort Lauderdale were divinely marked by the hand of the Loving Spirit. Though heaven surrounded them upon every step of their journey, it would seem like a far away land without the eyes of the spirit. But the most important part of their journey to the heaven I have been allowed to see was the conversation we had during their last evening.

Seeds

During the second and final evening of my parent's stay in Fort Lauderdale, my mother and father wanted to watch a movie before bed. I have a collection of over several hundred movies that almost all contain a spiritual story within the story that most would see. Over the years I have learned that just as writers of books and artists around the globe are divinely inspired, so too are the writers and directors of movies. Most people scoff at the idea, but the truth is a movie is just another form of art. So with that said, I knew any movie that my parents wanted to see would carry a message that could be discussed if needed.

There were several movies that were chosen as options, but since they could not decide I chose one. The movie we watched was Edge of Tomorrow, one that was not as popular at the box office though it was well reviewed and well received. The plot of the movie is about a soldier who wakes up and repeats the same day over and over again. The theme of the movie is that he must help the world survive through an ending he continues to witness though he keeps dying in each experience. The overall effort that must be made is to convince people the end is coming and how to avoid the fate.

Kingdom

The movie is said to be based on the idea of playing a video game where a person continues to die over and over until they figure out the pattern to reach the next level. In truth, it is very possible that the author's book originated with this very idea, but the divine nature of all that is expressed is the part of the story that fascinates me. In the movie, the lead character is viewed as crazy even when he is able to foretell each and every circumstance that is about to happen. The people around him never give him the benefit of the doubt, which results in him realizing he is on his own (for the most part). There is a secondary character that comes into the picture. She has also previously had the same types of experiences. Between the two of them they take the journey together, trying to prepare the world from ending, or figure out a way to save them without them ever knowing.

The lead characters eventually figure out how to survive just a little longer each day as they learn the best way to try to save mankind. There is one particular scene where the lead characters have a heartfelt conversation with the leader of the army. It is one of the most detailed moments in the movie. It is clear the lead characters have repeated the moment over and over and have exhausted nearly every idea they have to get the General to believe them. They went as far as foretelling every event, every disturbance such as a phone ringing, that would take place in their conversation. The end result being that the General never believed them. There is a specific line that is stated from the lead character to the General where he says at the end of their conversation, "You're not mentally equipped to fight this thing, and you never will be." It is a quote that leaves a resonance within the soul for it expresses the very issue facing mankind in the End of Days.

My family and I watched the movie and after it ended, I asked my mother and father for their opinions. Before the movie began I had shared with them about how I liked the spiritual theme that flows through the movie, so I was curious if they understood the message as I saw it. It was my hope that they did, because it would help the rest of our conversation about the Lord's message I had to continue to share. But while I was surprised to hear neither picked up on the storyline, I realized in hindsight that this was the best possible scenario. When I first shared the story with my brother-in-law and sister, it was a struggle to find common ground for a balanced conversation. But eventually my brother-in-law and sister were able to see that the church as a whole was not prepared for the End of Days. Within the context of the conversation with my mother and father, I did not have the same common ground to go on. But with the movie having just finished and the theme able to be discussed, it was the perfect collision for the conversation to start.

I led with the comparison of the soldier's challenge of having to share with the world how he knew the end was coming to the demonstration of God sharing with me his warning. It was an easy comparison to be made and one that we were able to discuss without any disconnect in delivery. But in the end, there was still a lot of questioning the method of my delivery rather than the message itself. Though I knew this was how

Kingdom

the conversation would have to start with my mother and father, there really was no better way to say, "Hey, here is a message delivered straight from God."

Perhaps the greatest part of the experience with my family visiting me in Fort Lauderdale was in all that I was able to witness. I saw the angels upon the Earth pour out their Loving Spirit. I saw the way that God welcomed them into the Promised Land though their eyes were not able to see it as I saw it through mine. Perhaps their Promised Land is in another locale, one that they will one day be able to see, and I will have to figure out. Regardless, either way it was a very special three days. And once again, the role of teacher became that of a student to my Father's wondrous ways. Though again the words of His message were met with disbelief and closed off in receipt, it was through the discussion of the movie that His message was heard. The words did not have to be believed literally in that specific conversation. It was through the modern day DaVincis in Hollywood that a greater spiritual and philosophical conversation could be started.

Perhaps this is one of the greatest principles in the calling upon of a teacher, for in every situation it is figuring out a point of entry in another for the spirit to move about freely. The role of a teacher becomes the role of a student in every situation. Every experience is a lesson in learning how to deliver His message. But it must be noted that His message must also be delivered in the form He desires it to be shared. One method of delivery cannot exist without the other for the task to be completed in the eyes of our Father. Think of His words as seeds, and the deliverer of the message as the gardener who must dig a hole to plant the seed for the message to take root and grow. Some places the gardener plants his seeds could have infertile soil. Other places may have rocks that obstruct a hole from being dug. It takes time and care to find the best location for the seed. But once it is found, the location can allow for a seed to blossom into the beauty it holds within. Through further watering of the seed and tending of the weeds during growth, the results of seeding His Divine Word is its beauty it beholds.

It Didn't Work Out Too Well

After taking the previous month to share the story of the Messiah's return with my sister, her husband, my mother, my father, and some of the immediate people that God had placed into my earthly life, I was still left with more questions than answers. I lacked confidence in how to move forward, though I heard His directive loud and clear. Maybe to the ones I shared the message with, it did not come across as lacking confidence, but rather inexperience in the delivery, for the passion I had to share His message was evident. But in the conversations it became clear that I was still playing the role of a student rather than that of a messenger or a teacher. And perhaps this was partly how my Father wanted me to experience it. It would only take one meeting with a specific pastor for this concept to become apparent.

There is a particular aspect in every portion of the journey where a person understands his role as a student or a teacher. This is a principle discussed in Gravity Calling, but it is relevant to mention here because it is the foundation for the lesson I was learning. In the role of a student, a person is primarily learning from another who has an abundance of knowledge to share. But even as the student learns, there is a minor role played as a teacher. It is usually a passive aspect of the division in roles, but it exists nonetheless. This aspect of "teaching" is mostly performed through the questions asked and the way answers are handled to questions directed from the teacher. And while the role of the teacher would be presumed as one who is already learned within the subject matter being taught, the teacher is still a student in learning how to improve upon his role. The teacher gauges feedback and reactions from the student and may even receive questions that cause the teacher to pause and explore new avenues for answers.

The role of a student that the teacher plays does not mean that the teacher is untrained for the delivery of the subject matter nor unprepared for the task. It means that a teacher is constantly learning, constantly improving, and constantly being challenged to expand the mind and improve at the task. The student, on the other hand, while absorbing all that is being taught, is subtly learning how to teach the lesson at hand. For the questions and interests in the subject matter at hand are the basis for learning how to teach the lesson once the student absorbs all that is to be said. So if it is to be understood that everyone plays the role of teacher/student or student/teacher, it should be understand that one role is always greater and primary to the other, until the day arrives where the roles are reversed.

It Didn't Work Out Too Well

The basis of the idea of being a teacher versus being a student is a philosophy that permeates every person's walk regardless of how aware he is to its existence. But the divide between the concepts is the divide that separates the acceptance of performing a divine task versus one of earthly origin. For most, the assumption would be made that if a person has been assigned a task – whatever the task may be – the assignment of the task would have been based on that person's proficiency. A person hired to coach a football team would understand his selection for the role would have been based on his proficiency in the game and the skills required to manage a team. In another example, when a game is on the line, the player chosen to receive the last catch of the game on a last second play would understand he has been chosen in recognition of his performance in the role. It would be expected that there is a level of confidence understood in recognition of his skill, or sometimes (though less common) the opportunity for that player's potential to be revealed.

It is an idea that generally has no afterthought, nor is typically explored philosophically. It is just human nature in passive acceptance of a role given to take this thought process for granted. But, it is important to note that this passive thought process is the divide that separates how to perform a divine task versus one of earthly origin. This was the lesson I was to learn when my Father tasked me to "Run and go tell everyone the Messiah is coming."

After having pushed through the first experiences of telling my sister and her husband, my mother and father, and select people involved in my life at the time, I had become overwhelmed in spiritual anxiety. Imagine, if you will, being entrusted with one task during a special occasion. Think of Thanksgiving. Now imagine that you were asked to bring the centerpiece dish for a large family dinner. Extended relatives, some you have likely never met, are going to be attending the feast. Maybe it was a ham or perhaps a turkey that you were asked to bring. Either way, it is the main dish which all of those invited to the dinner are looking forward to. Now imagine that you are still learning how to cook. You understand the basic skills required to make a ham or turkey, but a large family is going to receive this food. If the food is not properly prepared, it will be overlooked and cast aside at the dinner. Those who were looking forward to the meal will leave disheartened. If it is not spectacular, no one will talk about it afterwards. It would have been received and eaten as expected, though without any substantial memories left in resonance. It was just one piece of food like all of the others ever eaten.

At the most basic level, providing the main course was the task placed upon your shoulders. As long as the food was cooked and provided as requested, that could be considered successful execution. But what if is not good enough and cast aside – dismissed and talked about at its lack of taste and sustenance? Even if it is just to one person's disliking, that is enough to introduce an onslaught of judgment and criticism. But what if the dish is the hit of the dinner? What if no one can stop talking about it, even for days and weeks after? Even

It Didn't Work Out Too Well

in the event that a few people dislike it, the vast majority's praise will ring out much more loudly.

So at a basic level, to fulfill the task would to be to perform as expected, but the fate of everyone's hunger rests in the balance. Now, let's take the analogy of the main dish and place the same scenario on the task of delivering God's message. The stakes are no longer about hunger, but about Ever-After. Now the task just got real. The importance placed upon the preparation and the delivery can no longer be seen as striving for par-for-the-course execution. In fact, being new to "cooking" but proficient in the principles places even more importance on not having any failures or mishaps in the delivery. There are no second chances to impress the taste buds of the guests again. The hours of preparation are for one moment, one shot, and that is it.

The gravity of the task that my Father had placed upon my shoulders caused me to turn to Him in prayer seeking help in refining my execution. And while there would not be a specific process that I was asked to perform, I came to understand that the task was to be performed like an artist would be asked to paint a picture. The delivery and execution was supposed to be unique to me, but the importance was placed on not missing the celebration, or being tardy. Though the open answer to my question did not leave me resolved in planning my next steps, the anxiety continued to build. Every day that passed, I realized that it was one day closer to the last supper, and one day lost to those who may listen. But as I would learn in the next steps I was about to take, the reason I was given the task by my Father was not because I was a teacher just yet, it was because I understood how to be a student when given a divine task.

In the days following I decided that I would begin speaking with every pastor in the nation, but I knew I had to begin with one-on-one conversations. It would only take the first, to realize it would be my last, for there was a great lesson learned that would refine the execution of my task. I assembled a list of nearby churches and began driving. I had no intention, nor plan other than arriving at each church and seeing if I could speak with each pastor. The reason I would give for my meeting request was simple: "I have a message to deliver."

Surprisingly, the first church I visited invited me right in. I was able to schedule some time with the pastor and speak directly with him. When I entered his office, we exchanged cordial introductions. I abstained from giving my last name, which seemed to leave him a little confounded. But the message placed upon only giving a first name was important. I wanted him to see the message through God's voice, and not that of someone of earthly origin. It is a concept fundamental to the delivery of a divine message. For, the message is God's voice where the first name alone is reserved for the vessel.

After he seemed to warm up to the idea that I would not share my last name, I began sharing with him all that I had planned to say. I began by making it clear that this was the first time I had shared the message with the pastor. I wanted him to see that I was still learning how to best deliver the message. He was very open in receipt of the message I had to

It Didn't Work Out Too Well

share. I began with explaining in general terms how my Father had been preparing me over the last three years to deliver this message. I explained that my intention was not to disrupt his ministry, but rather to share the message from God so that he could determine how – or even if – it was to be used in his ministry.

He asked me specifically what he should do with the message I had shared, to which I only offered him advice that it was not my task to share his next steps, but rather he should turn to prayer. With that answer, he seemed to find a peace in the conversation, however dismantling the message may have seemed. He asked me a few more questions about my next steps and intentions. I did not have to speak much, but rather all I had to do was listen. He expounded upon his thoughts that it seemed like I did not care about any other person's judgment or perception.

Hearing his thoughts that I seemed headstrong in performing my mission left me inspired, but only for just a brief second. As he continued to ramble on about his thoughts about my approach to the delivery of the message, I heard the words, "It didn't work out too well for John the Baptist, did it?" He paused to let his question sink in. I paused, flabbergasted in the question. For just a brief second I had to decipher what it was he was truly asking. Was he asking my thoughts on how John the Baptist received judgment? Was he testing me on my will to perform the task in the wake of my life incurring an unexpected and abrupt ending? It was in these moments, it was like a game of chicken was being

Kingdom

played. He was driving headstrong into the delivery of my message to see if I would bend or I would swerve away. But when I held strong and did not budge in the face of death, neither did he budge in his question. I understood in that moment it was not a question he asked, but rather the embodiment of a message.

From a leader of a church and the shepherd to the countless numbers of those who seek faith in God through his ministry, I was hearing the words of judgment placed upon John the Baptist's delivery. It did not take much for me to decipher how his question was a message. For all I had to do was sit in silence. After he paused for just a brief second, without time for me to reply, he continued on in his thought process. The subject of John's beheading arose and soon there after he turned to me for a response in his repose.

In the only words I could muster, I spoke in strong stature in the message. I explained to him the outcome of my life did not matter. In brevity I shared how the command to deliver this message was my reality and, just as anyone of faith should do, I accepted the task, the outcome, and the judgment incurred in the eyes of earthly perception. I only had to speak a few more sentences before I could feel his pushback and desire to end the meeting. It was as if he heard the message that was to be shared, yet somewhere in the process, his mind reacted in a knee-jerk reaction. This does not mean I think the message went unheard or unaccepted. In all actuality, this went much better than I ever expected. But after leaving the meet-

It Didn't Work Out Too Well

ing and heading back to my Jeep, all I could do was think of the message in his question about John's beheading.

In the moments of hindsight, I wished that I had had a quicker wit and reply. I wished I had said, "I think it worked out just fine." Now for just a moment, think of the words in the pastor's reply. A man of the cloth proposed that John the Baptist's ministry ended in tragedy. I tried hard to digest how a man of faith could have this viewpoint, for the lines have become blurred through which perspective my thoughts have vision. I wondered if I could have once thought the same about how his life ended? And though I could not decide where I would have once landed on my thoughts in reflection of John's life, I knew that I had complete faith in my current view. For as a man of Earth sees finite beginnings and endings while questioning the impossible nature of infinity, I realized that through the eyes of the spirit, I no longer questioned the infinite expanse, but rather questioned the earthly rationale in finite endings.

The eyes that my Father helped open for me as I learned to see has changed my perspective of earthly life and eternity. It was in reflection of this in the moments following, that I realized I had to return to the drawing board to find a new place of starting. In the beginning, Bryan and I had discussed the idea that a video should be the delivery method of the message. Initially, I resisted the idea since it would attach identity to His message. And while I desired to represent the words I was tasked to share, I did not want there to be an assumption of ego when viewed from afar. But it was in these moments that I understood the reason that God led me to this particular church and this pastor to begin sharing the message. For as well received as I believed the message was, there was a moment of the recipient's questioning that gave him room for doubt and pause.

If every time the message was delivered it began one-on-one questions about the source of the message and the role I have been tasked to play, then it would overshadow the message itself. It was a tricky question to navigate, just as in the analogy of how one delivers the main course that would leave an impact with everyone. If the delivery to the leader of a group of people left room for question, chances are great that the message would not continue to be delivered. And, if the eyes of the leaders assumed the ending of John's life in beheading meant "it didn't work out too well for him," then it would mean they would be unlikely to take the same risks that I was taking. So back to the drawing board I returned, as I once again realized the execution of a divine task is the acceptance of the role as a student.

The Proclamation

In the beginning, it seemed clear from the instructions to "Run and go tell everyone the Messiah is coming," that the only way to spread the message to the world would be to do so through video distribution. In the age of the internet, it seemed like the only way for any message to take root globally is for it to be as publicly accessible as possible. This means distributing the video through social media channels as well as through video sharing sights online. But, when I received the directive, I was at odds with the idea of producing a video. At the heart of my pushback was the concept that an identity would have to be attached to the words delivered.

Through the eyes of the spirit, any attachment of identity to an action performed generally indicates ego in control rather than the spirit. For over three years, I had worked to remove any potential ego from entering into any actionable equation. Even in the context of these books, it is important there is no last name attached, for the effort to spread the word is not to give rise to the ego of the earthly source of the act.

Nearly a year preceding this specific call to action, my Father had blessed me with a suite of video production equipment. At the time of the receipt, the white screens and lighting were put into use in a video series for a Christmas fundraiser. At the time it seemed like a perfect collision of resources and divine call to action. But it could also be seen as divine foreshadowing. For if one is to look at the tools in the toolbox of any workers He calls into action, it is important to understand their strengths and weaknesses and how they can execute the tasks requested. In the case of the resources at my disposal, I had everything needed for global video distribution.

But I fought the idea as I prayed for alternative actions. This was the time period I met the pastor with a disheartening view of the life of John the Baptist. But I can see now that it was necessary through my Father's eyes, that I exhaust all possible methods of delivery in order to recognize that a call to action holds the worker accountable to the execution. If the task is not completed in the best way it can, the one performing the work is subject to judgment of the game plan. So as I turned to my Father and prayed, He spoke to me in a grand way.

He instructed me to seek out others with similar messages and see how they approached the task they were given. My first search on YouTube produced a man from Botswana, who called into a radio show to discuss the vision He had received that evening. The specific way he worded all that he was shown was unmistakable in truth in all I had come to know. The man spoke with conviction and an effort to tell the world all that he was instructed to share. I knew God was showing me how another man moved in his call to action. With just a

The Proclamation

little bit more research I saw the day of the recording. This is where coincidence becomes execution in Divine story.

The day the man from Botswana was shared his vision, was the very same day that I witnessed a wedding in the heavens. It was the first time I understood in clarity the destination of the wedding. It was also the last chapter in Book VI – Rebirth III, entitled "Third Revelation." This was a moment of splendor and awe. It was the divine mechanics to the Lord's work across the globe. And whether the man's call would be heard by the world as instructed, his very action gave way to my next effort. For as soon as I saw the video I understood. I turned to my Father in acknowledgement of the next direction.

Over the next few weeks I would put together the video, but I was told to wait to distribute it until the time of His calling. It would appear that the video was a call to action, but it could also be seen from another perspective. For as He called me to tell the world all that He has been preparing me to share, another action would take place through the eyes of Love in a girl.

In the days wherein the video was created, another storyline was equally at play. It was during this time that I understood the call to action was greater than just the words, for it was in the identity that I had been given. It had taken over three years for the understanding to sink in. To think that the story to be shared would hold the significance it would have was greater than my mind could grasp. It was in these days that my Father unraveled the mystery of all that He had shared. He revealed the cord I held in one experience was the measuring rod from Revelation. He went on to reveal the lampstand was not one of seven, but one of two witnesses to pave the way for the Messiah. And while there was much more that He revealed, these two are the most important to disclose in this chapter. This was an occasion between a Father and a Son sharing the most special of moments.

As I heard the call to action and understood the role I was always placed on the Earth to play, I cried out a prayer like a battle cry for my Father, every angel, and every soul with ears to hear. The prayer cried out should be understood as the proposal to my Bride. In was in the guise of a soldier preparing to fight. And while more is written about the proposal to my Bride in a chapter upcoming, the video that was being made should be seen as the formal engagement announcement.

It is a video entitled "The Proclamation," and while I would not understand the name's significance at the time of creation as the announcement of an engagement, I saw the title as the embodiment of the message to the world that my Father wished to be told. The script to the video is spoken word-for-word as said by the Angel of the Lord to me. It is delivered wearing cloths of sackcloth for all of the world to see. And while the concept of sackcloth adorning the two witnesses is important in demonstration, it should also be understood the meaning at its foundation. For the two witnesses adorned in sackcloth should be understood as two people humbling themselves to nothing in the eyes of the Lord and maintaining silence until directed to stay humble to the world.

The Proclamation

The video was created, the battle cry was shouted out, yet I was told there would be another to precede this one to remove all doubt. I understood March would be when my call to action would take place, though I was not given any more indication of a specific time or date. But in the way the Lord works there would be no doubt, for during the first days of March, I received a question from a friend asking me to watch a new video she had just seen. My friend had no idea I was waiting for this sign, yet her question was the delivery of God's second sign. The video was of an Italian girl sharing with the world a message. She was visited by an Angel of the Lord forewarning her of the end of days. And while there are times she spoke in tongue in the message, it was the complete embodiment that was the message. Every word she spoke unlocked the next action of my soul. Another sign hidden in her message was the day it occurred. Her video was delivered for the world to see on Valentine's Day, 2015. It is a day the Earth shares in the celebration of Love. It is also exactly one year to the day Book I – Gravity Calling was printed for Lindsey. Her book is the only book to have been printed on this day in the series. And if it still exists for others to see, the last page is the page dated by the printer. It reads "Proof February 14, 2014."

Within the words that were spoken and the date the Italian girl received her vision, I heard my Father's call to action to release the "The Proclamation." But before I could release the message I first had to share it with the leadership of the church I attended. They had no idea it was coming and as the stewards of the message they were unaware was coming, they deserved to know first before it was delivered for all to see. In order to inform the church I understood I had a two week window. This opened up time to speak to the pastor at his leisure. The day set for the video to be released would be a day that summed to seven, and if possible would sum to sixteen before reducing to seven. I glanced at the calendar and saw the only date available in the two-week window was the second Saturday of March, the fourteenth day. It was a day that summed to sixteen and reduced to seven. And while most may not understand the importance of the number, it is also the way the date that marked the revelation of the Beast's arrival in the world was delivered. It is a way that our Father signs His messages and the way that must be mirrored in the delivery of this message to the world. For others of spiritual minds to understand the significance, it must be embodied in the way He intends for it to be delivered.

But there was even more significance wrapped up in the date it would be delivered, but this was not revealed until days before its disclosure. On the day that I met with the pastor of the church, it was revealed to me that the Saturday upcoming was none other than 3/14. It is a number at first glance I saw summed to sixteen (3+1+4+2+0+1+5). But without thinking about the year, I saw in this moment, the date was none other than the number that represents Pi, 3.14. To mathematicians this year holds even greater significance than to others. But it is important to indicate that 2015 is more special for this date than any other year, for it is the only time in the next one

The Proclamation

hundred years that the number Pi would be represented by more than three digits. It is also the only time in the next ten thousand years that the date sums to sixteen, which reduces to seven. The month, day, and year extend Pi to one digit plus four numbers. For if one is to attach the year to the date, 3/14/15 becomes Pi to four decimals of precision: 3.1415.

So in the context of this story and how the engagement announcement was delivered, it was announced on the day of the mathematical representation of the holiest of numbers. It is the date that signifies the representation of God, the perfection of His creation in the imperfection of earthly understanding. Pi is a number that also occurs in specifics to Book I – Gravity Calling. For as it has been said, the day of it's first printing was one year prior to the day when the first video appeared, it should now be observed that the engagement announcement is the date of the number of pages of the first book: 314. Regardless of the commandment of when I was called into action, I could not hand select a date with any more divine significance. For if there was an announcement to the world of a wedding of the most divine kind, it would be announced on the day that was the most divine.

I understood the two videos that preceded the one I created, should be viewed in a similar way to the two witnesses preceding the Messiah. And just as I have written throughout these Books of Nine, the concept of two confirmations is one of His divine signs. Many who see the videos preceding "The Proclamation" may have doubted their authenticity at the point of their originations. But now it is important to understand through these words, that the videos were placed into the world as part of His Divine works. At this point it should be apparent that it is the sum of His works that are part of the greater story being told. The words in this book, while a summation of many, are still part of an even greater story He is penning. It is a Love story most important for this generation to know since it is The Proclamation of the Messiah's return. But it is also a Love story for those left behind to grasp, for it is the light and the way for generations beyond the last. So without further adieu, here are the words to the engagement announcement's publication, the script to the nine minute video, "The Proclamation."

...

The Script

Intro

...

How would you tell the world that God, Our Father has delivered a message for everyone to hear? And how do you think the world would respond? Would they look at you like you were mad? Treat you like a fool? Would they take the time to hear? Or would they say, "Why should I listen? Why should I care?" Would the world's religious leaders, in all creeds, in all divisions, come together for just one moment to hear the message that God has instructed to be shared? Would the leaders of His Word actually give His Word a chance or would they only see it all after it was all too late? Let me tell you a story. This is the truth through my eyes.

The Proclamation

Prologue
...

For over three years, The Lord has been speaking to me in ways that most people might assume to be impossible – fantastical maybe – though it has all been impossibly real. And through all of the wonder of His ways, He has been preparing me so that one day I could serve as a vessel to begin sharing His intended words at this specific time. The messages I have been asked to share may be difficult to accept at first. For how would the world receive a message that all religions actively claim to believe in and teach, when no one is actually expecting to hear the message itself? Hindsight paves the way for reason and understanding, with few acknowledging faith at the present time. But in this case, hindsight will be too late. For now the time has arrived to begin sharing His message and have everyone of faith, regardless of divide, carry the greatest weight of it all. It is a very special time upon this Earth. A time when we are all called to hold everyone's hands and help them get across the finish line as best as we can. So through it all and in each of the chapters forthcoming, this is His Story, His Proclamation, His Gravity Calling.

Chapter One
...

On the morning of December 11, 2014, God would begin sharing His instructions to me in the most fantastical way. It was on this morning my soul was taken to the heavens where I stood before a great angel. I heard a trumpet sound. Not a trumpet as we know on Earth, but rather the sounding blast of an indescribable harmony of brassy tones, similar to the timbre of French horns, constant and unending. The angel spoke. "The time is near and it is now time to share it with others."

Kingdom

The angel repeated this line twice to make sure I understood my directive. I was then taken to a shoreline with seven angels, who again told me, "The time is here." We sat on a blanket looking up at the stars in the sky where a particular pattern of five objects was the focal point of the view. As I bore witness to the star-like objects in the sky, I was taken by one of the angels to witness a celebration. The angel told me in no uncertain words, "The Son of God took office after 70 weeks." With great fanfare and acclaim, the angels and I all slow-clapped His arrival during His celebration parade in white, just before the angel returned me to Earth.

Chapter Two

...

The morning of December 11th was truly one of the most memorable experiences of all. But this was just the beginning of God's instructions for me. On the heels of the message shared with me that morning, I would again turn to Him to seek help in understanding how best to deliver His message. For over three years, He has instructed me to be patient, to learn, and to write down all that He has shared with me. During this time, I was instructed not to speak, nor share the words written. So as I sought guidance in how to best take the steps forward in ways that would be pleasing unto Him, He sent another angel to share further instructions. On December 14th, I would once again be taken to the heavens where I stood before the great face of an angel. It was facing West. I stood at face level, on the left side of the angel's face. It blinked at me to let me know I had arrived. I was lifted above the oceans as I watched them begin to swirl in a clockwise motion. The angel spoke. "Denying your walk and testament with God is like leaving a bride at the alter." I was returned to Earth to write down the words.

The Proclamation

No sooner had I written the angel's spoken words, than I was taken back to the heavens by that very same angel. The angel spoke. "Go now. Standing before an angel and not acknowledging his wings is like seeing a bird and it choosing not to fly. Go tell everyone the Messiah is coming." Once again I was returned to Earth so I could write down the message. Again I was returned to the heavens. This time I was placed before the great Sphinx, but this one was finished in gold. Rays of light shining outwardly from the head were painted in alternating rows of deep blue. The angel spoke. "Standing before this Sphinx is like standing before God and not taking action. It has the body of the Lord, the face of a man. Run now and tell everyone the Messiah is coming."

Again I was returned to Earth and again I was taken back to the heavens. This time, the angel walked with me down a sidewalk. We walked past two ladies dressed in traditional Jewish attire. The angel spoke. "When you see a Jewish family, do not pass them by for there are milling rights that must be had. Walk carefully and carry them through for those are the ones that helped you in." I was returned once again to Earth to write down the angel's words. And so as it was shared to me, it has come time to share this message with others. This is the reality I have been allowed to see. These are the words that He has asked me to share. Hear His intentions and His phrasings. This is important. These words are as they were when spoken to me.

Supernatural

By this point in the writing it should be evident that there have been countless inexplicable incidents that have occurred in my walk when viewed from an earthly perspective. The way the Spirit moves is quite possibly one of the most difficult concepts to illustrate. In truth, I am not really sure how an outside observer would ever be able to process situations of this inexplicable nature. I have humbly been able to witness angels upon this Earth and angels in the heavens. I have seen the hand of God in action upon the Earth and bowed to the manifestation of God in the heavens. I have seen the works of evil upon the Earth and the manifestation of Lucifer in bodily form. Against my personal opinion, I had to overcome my belief that a soul could never be possessed by a demon. The latter is a point that, in principle, butted up against all I had ever accepted. I wanted to believe that darkness in the world was only the absence of light and not an embodied spiritual form with some darkened version of possession. And while the definition of darkness is truly the absence of light, I really did not want to believe that darkness could exhibit a form of control on another.

The embodiment of Lucifer in a soul upon the Earth and his eventual riddance from that man was a demonstration of

Kingdom

the strength of God as the light that could never be reckoned with. During my daily walk through life, I also bore witness to another man possessed by darkness wherein God showed me how His strength could overpower all of this man's suffering. I witnessed as prayer with another manifested, absent of any explicable earthly justification or answer. I witnessed the spirit pass through my body and heal another. This particular example occurred over and over. The examples continually repeated though out my life, but it would take the last three and a half years to understand how the strength of the Spirit is always there in potential but never to be used in demonstration.

There were times before the darkness when my Genesis began that I witnessed the same supernatural exhibition, the manifestation of good, and the manifestation of evil. Without the understanding that I have gained through the years, the eyes of my spirit were unable to see with definition. If clarity of the earthly human form is the definition of seeing clearly, the eyes of my spirit saw spiritual forms as tree trunks and blobs of nonsense. The supernatural exhibition that was constantly around me in the days that preceded my Genesis could only be classified as an acute sense of foresight and instinct. But as the years bore on, the recognition of foresight and instinct gave way to spiritual recognition and greater meaning.

In the years following my divorce, I spent most of my time in the company of friends. Being in our late twenties meant that we went pedal to the metal overloading the senses with anything and everything that was happening in the city. Every event, football game, and hockey game we attended. A concert or new restaurant opening? We would never miss it. But in the midst of the noise, chaos, and clutter, there were always circumstances that I was fearful to bring up to another. As we went out in large groups of friends, I started to notice that I could always sense how a particular moment was about to play out – like an act of perfect Love or a fight about to breakout. With one friend in particular, I began sharing what I began to witness. He was of similar spirit, pure in his intentions. We never mentioned it in those words, but we each understood the recognition of each other's spirit. His name was Joey, and we always hinted about the recognition of something greater in our lives in passing conversation. To others, I am sure it appeared it was just random things that happened in our lives. But Joey and I began to take notice and discuss the events on occasion. One particular event, and one of the last times I would see him before we parted ways, was an event while we were out with a large group of friends for the evening.

In this situation, we were standing in a circle with friends at a particular location I hated attending. It was a place that I understood was the breeding ground of negative energy. I always told my friends I did not want to go, but I attended nonetheless since they all enjoyed it so. To others, it appeared as a place full of fun and laughter. But every time I stepped foot in the place, my soul was tormented and tortured. As the group I was with stood in a corner talking, there was a moment of recognition that I had to get going. There was not a moment to delay, for I knew something bad was about to occur. I could not put it into words, but I tried to tell Joey. I told him I had to go, that something did not feel right. He told me he felt it too but could not understand what it meant. There was nothing surrounding the situation of laughter and conversation with friends that would have given forewarning to what everyone was about to witness. So, as quickly as I could, I left without even saying goodbye.

Just a few minutes after exiting the building, I received a call. It was Joey. He told me that in the moments after I left, a stranger walked up to the group and a fight ensued with no provocation or warning. It is important to illustrate that no one in that group was a fighter, or would have instigated that kind of commotion. We were always happy and kept the peace with everyone around us. And though the fight ended up not involving any of my friends, the incident began with a stranger walking up to stand where I once was. Whatever the circumstances were that caused the provocation, the only way Joey could explain it was that the fight occurred in a way that defied all logic and odds, and came about with no reason or cause. The brawl cleared the establishment where everyone was standing. It would be the last time I went out with that group of friends, but not for that particular reason.

It was this specific moment when I recognized I was in tune with more than I understood. I understood that if I recognized the difference, then it was equally visible to the spiritual realm… and if that was the case, I did not need to be anywhere darkness could try to prevail. It was a pivotal moment and a decision that I am ultimately proud that I made.

Supernatural

But I cannot say I made the decision alone. For as I prayed to God about the recognition of the warning to danger that night, in the following days I would learn of other circumstances that would lead to my decision. I cannot look back now on the circumstances underlying my decision to break ties with this group of friends as anything other than divine intervention. It was as if God heard my prayer of recognition and said, "Let's step it up once again." He gave me reason to divorce myself from that group of friends, which ultimately occurred at approximately the same time I heard His Voice in the wilderness during my Exodus.

Fast-forward to a point nearly three years later and the same type of experiences are happening, but on another level. In these days, the experiences happen in ways that defy all visual logic and reason. The observers to the situations take witness to what they must only be able to call supernatural occurrences. These are not situations where I have been part of the cause, but rather it is better to see my presence as a reason for the demonstration. For in all things good, the events happen hidden from the sight of another's eyes, or are subtle and understated, though grand in meaning. But when a negative force tries to prevail, it will always try to show out in a grand demonstration.

There is a particular quote shared with my cousin Bryan by an angel. The angel said, "Magic is fuel for the ego, glitter for the ignorant, but unyielding faith and love will take you across the universe and back." This quote holds within it the very essence of supernatural exhibition. For the eyes of man want to see glitter and glamour in the moment. The eyes want proof when controlled by the ego. This is the very emotion that darkness entertains in earthly demonstration of its power. It is this reason that some souls on a seemingly pure spiritual journey derail into a darker practice that gives rise to glitter and glamour for the ego. Being entertained by darkness does not mean a person was not once righteous in faith. It means that at a particular point of the journey – a point when there is a higher set of standards held to those that have been given higher understanding and who have opened the door as a vessel for the spirit – the person chooses glamour over servitude to our Father. In this demonstration, identity of self is placed above the role we are called upon to play, and is a point of no return to darkness and the abyss.

So it can be seen how the role of negative forces would desire to show out around those following His Glory in order to tempt the soul to one side, or to try to slow down the vehicle on the journey. Darkness will never win, for His light can never be extinguished. But during the process of the maturation of a soul through the walk upon this Earth, darkness will try to take reign and dismantle His turf. There could be no greater demonstration by darkness than what happened to me in February of 2015. It was a day following my complete and unbridled acceptance in the role that God had tasked me to play. It was the moment Darkness chose to show out to try to prevent the prophecy from being fulfilled.

It was the first day I had ever witnessed a supernatural action of the devil manifest in such great form on Earth. Yes, I

Supernatural

have met angels and met Lucifer in the flesh. I have witnessed a possession and seen it subsequently be removed. But not once had I ever seen such an event as the one that occurred on that day in February. Early in the morning I had taken my Jeep to the mechanic. It had been exhibiting a component failure that caused a "death wobble" to occur. Maybe the name of the situation my Jeep was going through was coincidence in name, or perhaps it was just another sign of what will happen to the Earth during the End of Days. Regardless of the symbolism, it really did not matter. I dropped off the Jeep and walked over to a nearby shopping center. It was a beautiful day outside, so after breakfast I sat outside on the sidewalk and journaled on my iPad.

Before I had initially chosen a place to sit, I had walked up and down the length of the shopping center. Near the north end there was a bench that seemed like a great place to sit, though when I approached it all I felt was a negative energy surrounding the area. Since I have become more perceptive along the journey I heeded the warning. I returned and sat a good ways away, out of people's way upon the sidewalk. But as I journaled outside with the sun on my skin, a security guard approached me and told me I was not allowed to sit.

As bizarre of a circumstance as seemed to have happened, south Florida has been attempting to crack down on the homeless. Though I am not homeless and I thought I was just innocently writing in my journal away from the crowd, in this moment I understood just how difficult it must be for the homeless. It fires me up inside even as I think about it. I could not even drink my coffee and journal in public. But the greater situation that was unfolding was one of negative control. The security guard was a puppet to the man in rose-colored glasses. He pointed me over to the bench I had walked by earlier but felt the negative energy pervading. He told me that was the only place I could sit without any hassle. So, despite my efforts to steer away from that area, I was pushed right back to that area of negative energy.

What happened next, I can only describe as something from a movie. It did not even seem real, or possible, and left the crowd flabbergasted in amazement. After having been sent to the bench, I drank my coffee and journaled, a wind began to blow, but something was not normal. I watched to my left as the wind began to swirl the leaves and dirt upon the sidewalk like a small tornado. And then out of no where, the wind erupted into a burst stronger than I have ever witnessed.

Behind me, a frail older lady had just exited a store and was only a few feet over my shoulder when the wind began to blow. I watched as she was literally lifted up off of two feet and slung to the ground. If a person could see what I witnessed it would have been a dark form performing a body slam. The wind was so strong that my full cup of coffee was blown several feet away from the bench on which I was sitting. There were several people around that just gasped in amazement.

I turned to discover the lady was conscious but holding her head. I immediately reached down and put my hand behind her head to support her. This lady was also wearing long sleeves at the time, but the motion of the wind had caused her sleeves to be pushed up her arms to her elbows ripping every bit of skin off of her forearms in the process. In earthly terms I do not even see how this could have happened. Even with the strongest grip and a tremendous amount of friction. One arm in particular was worse than the other. Every bit of her skin was ripped off like tissue paper.

The crowd could not believe what they saw. In truth, I understood what happened but was struggling to process all that I had witnessed. The lady was dazed and could not understand what had happened. I immediately took her to get help and bandages. As we walked I made sure to hold her in my arms. It seemed the touch helped her body hold together. We walked nearly a block away to a grocery store that was open. We went up to the counter to get first aid and call for an ambulance. But when we got to the counter the lady decided she would be okay. When I let go of her hands I watched her arm begin to bleed. In the block that we walked, not a drop was shed. It was only when I quit touching her and she waited to have bandages applied that her arms started bleeding like a river around us.

It was clear she was on blood thinner, which made the circumstance even stranger, because her arms should have begun bleeding the moment her flesh was opened. As I bore witness to this situation unraveling, I spoke to the woman about her situation. She laughed and said, "I really think something is trying to kill me." I laughed with her thinking she was joking. But as I shared in response to her words, her face became stern and she said, "No. I'm serious." At this point I was still processing all I had witnessed, but I knew in that moment she recognized the same darkness. If someone were watching a television show or a movie, this situation would have been presented as a demon performing a body slam on this lady. So, as the reality of the moment came into focus, we shared in conversation and she told me, "You must be my angel."

As the conversation progressed, I learned her name was Ruth. I called her two sons until someone answered and could come provide her help. It was at this point that the situation had found resolve, but I knew there was still more to be understood from our conversation. After we parted ways, I began to research the name Ruth. I knew there was a Ruth in the Bible, but did not recall any of the details behind it. And while I cannot say that the next part of my research is completely applicable to the Ruth that I met, it was still a pointer of God's finger to further revelation in all of His messages.

I learned that Ruth had a son named Obed, who was the grandfather of King David. David was the father of Solomon and the father of Daniel. But, this is where it gets really interesting. David had a wife named Uriah – a name that I had never heard until it had been given to me in the heavens. Obed is another name that I had also never heard, but had been previously given. In Book V – Rebirth II, there is a particular experience in the heavens where a female angel told me to speak to "Obeeda" though I could not pronounce the name correctly and was left somewhat stumped at the name I had been given. It was a name that I could not make sense of at the

Supernatural

time. But now looking back, this earthly meeting of Ruth could not have been more divine. To add further significance to this particular experience in the heavens, the day I heard the name "Obeeda" was Christmas Day, 2013. This was extremely early in the journey, but again paints the picture of all that was being shared even in my naiveté to His story.

The name Uriah was one that I was shared in November of 2014. It was shared to me alongside the name Jahiel. It was the latter name that, after great research, caused me to order two specific books. These books were "The Lesser Key of Solomon" and the "Clavis or Key to the Magic of Solomon" – two books which I have still not read. But what is interesting about the subjects of the books, is that they involve Solomon, the son of David. At the time, the only information I could find on Uriah was it was the name of the angel that claimed "Babylon has fallen." So, it is more than coincidence in one earthly experience, all of the lineage to Ruth began to be revealed.

But one last part of the lineage held its own great significance. It was that Daniel's mother was "Abigail" another angel that I have met and documented. Abigail was referred to as Abby in most of my experiences. But early in my Father's communication to me, I was given her name in full though I am not sure it was ever documented. In the days early on names were a swirl of confusion. Names I was given seemed attached to humans only while names withheld seemed to represent the angels. But perhaps the greatest take-away from this interaction was perhaps God was answering the very first question I ever asked Bryan the night of our very first conversation. In that question I asked him, "What is different about our family?" I felt led to follow our lineage, though my grandparents stopped that from happening. Every one of my siblings and relatives that have ever tried to trace back the history of our ancestors has been met with intentional redirections by our grandparents. They hold the keys to understanding our lineage but would rather not allow it. For some reason, this was the mystery that started the first conversation with Bryan.

And here I was standing nearly three and a half years later, with a supernatural experience that backfired into the revelation of a specific lineage. I cannot say for certain that my ancestors fall in the line of Ruth, King David, Solomon, Uriah, Abby, and Daniel, but it would make sense that this is entirely possible. In the context of the Love story that my Father has penned, I cannot help but think it is foreshadowing to the invitation list. It would be like one of those moments when preparing the invitation list to an earthly wedding, that the Groom calls his Father and asks who all should be invited. In that conversation, the Groom learns of family members He has likely never known – perhaps some names are familiar, others stories or legends, maybe a crazy uncle or two, and others known since birth. But if one is to observe this Love story from when it first began, it is clear to see that the interactions from the earliest days involved names that are all descendants of Moses and Aaron.

And just to add one more pillar of support to this thought, one of the most recent experiences I have had in the heavens, involved an emphasis placed on a book with Aaron's name on the cover. Again, this book was another indication of the most divine sequences of interactions I could never have scripted, and the discovery of a lineage that always existed. Written records do not exist from this time no matter how far back I could be successful in going. The only true way of ever knowing is to trust in my Father with this truth as in all other aspects. And whether blood lineage is important for spiritual lineage to remain intact, to me, this list of names was the invitation list to my heavenly family. The experience with Ruth happened just days after the proposal to my Bride-to-be, an experience divine, masquerading in the supernatural for earthly eyes to see.

The Day Of
The Proposal

The idea that the supernatural occurrences read about in the Bible happened in a way similar to how Hollywood portrays a man with inexplicable powers is a fallacy and the primary principle at the heart of spiritual misguidance. For while the way that Hollywood portrays a man with seemingly supra-earthly powers is partly true in execution, the idea that a man has any reigning control of the power is what separates the two. For any soul that appears to wield control of an ability or power has demonstrated the primary divide in an earthly versus heavenly example. For to wield control demonstrates the ego is active in action. This could never be true if it were God's intention. For even if a man were to wield supernatural powers, the force behind this example would be one of darkness and surrender to egoic control.

The demonstration of a heavenly power comes through the submission to God and humbly seeking an answer to a question. In the example of healing, if a man is to heal another soul, the one performing the healing is only a conduit for the spirit to enter and exit another's soul. But if that is the case, why would the healing have to occur? It is because the one in need of healing has either not found or fully opened his door. So the one who can demonstrate the ability to heal, is truly just demonstrating the role of a vessel. For if the spirit is seen as a rolling river around us, the soul is a doorway and a conduit to this spiritual water. To open the door is to ask a question. "Father, if it is Your will and Your will alone, it is my desire that You help heal this man. If it is not Your will, I understand. But in either case I ask that this man feel Your spirit, touch His soul. He is in need of light and instructions on how to open his door. Use me as a vessel to help this man. Take a piece of my spirit, my life-force, and shorten my life. Use it in a way You see fit to help this man take the next step in his life. And whatever the outcome may be, whatever his next step is in Your eyes, I ask humbly for Your help through the demonstration of my sacrifice."

The question asked in demonstration to help another is a question only to be asked in silence between a soul and his Father. For even if those words, or the idea of those words are uttered aloud, it becomes a demonstration of ego and pride. A demonstration aloud negates the idea of servitude and humility in how to open up the spirit. This is why there are no scientifically-proven examples of supernatural demonstration. But the other aspect of the demonstration, is to be given from the one receiving the healing. For if an abundance of the spirit has the potential to be poured out, there must be a humble recipient willing to submit to His will. It can be observed in all examples ever given in the walk of Christ, for a demonstration

The Day Of The Proposal

of God always involves a call and response. Perhaps a person was tasked with fulfilling his half of the instructions. An example would be when a person Jesus sought to heal was subsequently instructed to "Go now, and wash your eyes in the water." These instructions were delivered after Jesus performed the miracle of his Father, but before the miracle manifested due to the demonstration of faith required in another.

Most people reading any verse where Jesus demonstrated the ability to heal will see the Son of Man wielding some sort of supernatural power. But the truth that should be illustrated so there is no further misguidance, is that Jesus was always just an unobstructed vessel for the Spirit. And perhaps that may be the greatest definition of the Son of Man, for it would be "the completely unobstructed vessel to the spirit." This is an accomplishment greater than most will ever achieve, but it is the ideal to strive toward. It is the difference between a man and a King. Take caution to these words, for it is important there is no misinterpretation. The illustration given is not one to lessen Jesus's demonstrations or the role he played that we have celebrated throughout the ages. The words in this illustration are to help bridge the divide, for at the heart of every religious divide is whether Jesus was the Son of God or merely a prophet. But perhaps it is best to see how man's definitions have formed dividing lines skewed in interpretation, for he is neither and both, the division and the bridge that joins the divide. He is the answer to both sides of the definition, but is not limited to one or the other. And this marks the reason why He was so different than any other before Him, for His vessel was completely unobstructed. His relationship with His Father was second to none. He was the first to speak with clarity of the Bride, the Groom, and the Kingdom. He was the purest vessel of any ever known where the voice of God flowed freely through His bodily form. This is the very definition of Christ and the earthly example that occurs when a Groom takes His Bride in the heavenly Kingdom.

But before a Groom takes His Bride, there is a period of engagement. In earthly terms it is the period of separation to the moments a person commits to another and the public fulfillment to the promise. The wedding banquet is the subsequent celebration, the wedding reception. The period of engagement is the promise of Ever-After. It is a test of faith, and a test of commitment. To most, the engagement should be unassuming at best. It should be the next step of the evolution to the destination of marriage. But for some who were unprepared for the commitment, the engagement turns into a last will and testament. It is the time their dedication is tested to the extreme. It is the time that temptation becomes ripe at the seams. It is the period of time that generally makes-or-breaks a divine union to come. It is the period of time when a commitment is more likely to become undone. For the closer a soul approaches the next level of commitment, the soul is defined as worthy of the blessing. And, as a soul approaches the destination, it is also a time for darkness to rear up in agitation. This was the example given in the previous chapter with Ruth.

The Day Of The Proposal

This was darkness's demonstration in the days following the announcement of my formal spiritual engagement.

Just as a period of engagement exists on Earth, a period of engagement also exists in the heavens. As I came to understand how His Love story was being written, I saw the world fall away and the heavens adorn my earthly surroundings. The idea that this journey began with an earthly Love seems like generations of yesteryear in hindsight, for the Love that is before me is the Love of Christ's Bride. She is a beauty that reigns more beautiful than any other. She is the one I want to wake up holding in my arms every morning. And when days are hard and struggles exist, I hope she will say the words with extended arm, "Come here and let me hold you. It will all be okay."

And while some that read these words may think they are full of metaphors and wordplay, the journals included in Books IV – VII will reveal the words are the truth of the world that I see above me. So, it is to be understood with truth that the Love of my life is not of this Earth, but is waiting in the heavens, to be my wife. But before that ceremony can begin, there had to be a commitment. On February 3rd, I asked her the question.

How do you ask a bride to be your wife in the heavens? Perhaps it is better understood as a commitment to God. For on February 3rd, the last three and a half years of His message were as apparent to me as it would ever be. The understanding of the role that was always intended as my purpose, was revealed in December through all of the spiritual experiences in the heavens. And while it took me over a month to digest and accept it, the role was always intended to be one of the two witnesses. When I was able to fully come to terms that this was the role for me to perform, I knelt before my bed and prayed for all with ears in heaven to hear my words.

The proposal to my Bride was performed through the demonstration of acceptance. The day of the proposal was an actionable demonstration of my complete understanding (to this point) of both the journey and the destination. It was a prayer that was akin to an inspirational speech given in times of war. It was a call for all of the angels to hear, and a recognition that I heard their call. It was the moment that I lay down my life upon the Earth. I cast aside earthly commitments in lieu of Heaven in sight. It was a speech addressing the spiritual war that has been raging, and a commitment that I would be a vessel for this special occasion. It was a commitment wherein I promised to fight the good fight. I understood I was to prepare the way for the arrival of the Messiah. And in moments akin to setting the date of the wedding, I made it clear that I understood that we would be wed through a demonstration of Baptism.

If it is to be seen that at eight years old I gave my life to Christ, it should be seen that on the last day of my thirty-third year on Earth, my soul was given in wedlock to Christ's Bride. The wedding day falls on the last day of twelve hundred and sixty and is also the eve of my thirty- fourth birthday (a divine number that sums to seven). Perhaps the greatest twist of the story, is the name of my bride is Eve, otherwise revealed

The Day Of The Proposal

through my journals as Zoey. For my life was given to Christ on the eve we celebrate His birth, my soul was given to Eve – our Father's daughter, Christ's Bride – on my last mortal day on the Earth. Every day after, whether on the Earth or in the Heavens, is the next step of experiencing the days of new marriage.

Washed In Water

During the time of Jesus, and even to this day, to be consecrated as a priest, a person must be washed with water – a baptism. Few think about the concept of baptism at its point of origination. Nearly every religion believes a baptism is required to wash away a person's sins and become a "member" of the faith. Most Christians are taught that a person must be baptized in Christ, just as Jesus demonstrated to the people in his day. To many Christians, the origin of the baptism began with Jesus. It is a definition that has transcended generations, for today, to declare oneself a Christian in the eyes of others, baptism is a requirement.

On an even more acute level, when a Christian changes churches or denominations, many churches require that a person become re-baptized to profess his faith within the body of the new church. In Leviticus 8:6, Exodus 29:4, and Matthew 3:16, baptism is referenced for salvation. But it is most important to note that baptism was required long before Jesus walked upon the Earth. These concepts predate a skewed modern understanding of the origin of these efforts. And while baptism carries many meanings, it is most important to understand why the start of the ministry of Jesus began with a baptism.

Kingdom

In the days of Jesus – and dating back to the origin of the written record of priesthood – baptism was required for "all who enter the service to do the work in the tent of the meeting." This was written about in Numbers 4:3 and discussed in the chapter of this book entitled "Thirty-Three." It was specifically reserved for those who reached the age of thirty and above. But it should also be understood that those who were once baptized before this age were still washed in the water, but in a way that is better understood as a moment of "first touch."

Few think about the early days of Jesus's life. These are the days before he turned thirty and began his public ministry. To think that the Son of Man, for the majority of his life, walked upon the Earth without the public baptism everyone of faith has come to understand is a topic few of religious faiths choose to explore. Unquestionably, Jesus performed miracles before becoming baptized. These are written about in the first books of the New Testament and preached about in a way to support his calling at the earliest stages of his life. But a single philosophical question is always unanswered among those of the strongest faith: If Jesus was to have died before his baptism, would he have gone to Heaven?

Few challenge the question, for there has been little written in the Bible that could give rise to an answer… that is until all that is to be revealed in this chapter. For a baptism in the day of Jesus could not happen until the age of thirty, and all those who came before him had no example to follow. Even in the moments when Jesus walked into the water toward John

Washed In The Water

the Baptist, John initially refused to baptize him. Think about that for just a moment. The way for a person to be saved in that day was to be washed in the water, yet John already saw Jesus as more than the action could offer. But Jesus said one of the most important statements that has ever been said. In Matthew 3:15 "Jesus replied, 'Let it be so now; it is proper for us to do this to fulfill all righteousness.' Then John consented." In this statement, the evidence of all that would be set into motion was fulfilled. The Son of Man who walked upon the Earth, demonstrated that even He had to be washed in the water.

So would that mean that Jesus was not worthy of salvation before the age he could be baptized? Most certainly this question will rock the boat to the teachings of most Christian denominations. While some denominations see the demonstration of baptism as the public testimony of a person's walk in faith, others see it as the only way a person will ever be saved. And in that philosophy, the divide severs the commonality of all religions – not just Christianity, but every other religious division. At first it may seem that these words dismiss the idea of baptism, but it could not be more the opposite. To understand the concept of baptism, a person must first view it in the context of a relationship. At the heart of the question of baptism, the question truly being asked is, "Is there only one way to have a relationship with God?"

To understand the answer to this question, a relationship must first be explored through the eyes of a child. Think about the first time you experienced a first love or a first crush.

Kingdom

Think about the butterflies inside – the feelings, the rush. As a child begins to understand the concept of Love, a parent understands the child must be granted an amount of grace to explore the landscape of all of the emotions – the likes, the dislikes, the differences between lust and a love that will forever go unbroken. There will be mistakes, endless loves, and heartaches experienced along the way. This is how a child first understands the concept of Love and the heart's complexities.

There is also a concept of "you do not know better until you have better" that is introduced in every aspect of life, though it is no more apparent than in the aspect of Love. The rush of the first experiences of Love's emotions sets off a fire inside, an indication of eternal Ever-After wrapped up in the glitter and glamour of the heart's eyes. It takes a great amount of discernment and refining of the senses for a person to understand what the soul is truly seeking. It is a feeling that few are fortunate to find. And it is even rarer in modern times. The idea that love is composed of the glitter and the glamour is the same concept that dismantles religion. Somehow it has become a label and status symbol versus a testimony of action. It is often formed on falsehoods and childish demonstrations of the ego pretending to know it all without truly understanding.

So, in the context of faith, think of Love as learned through a child's eyes. Finding a walk of faith in youth is no different than learning to date. The youthful nature in these new experiences sets off a fire inside, an indication of something greater awaiting. Many misunderstand this foreshadowing as the destination. But again, in thinking in the context of relationships, to dismiss the possibility that a child can find true love in the first experience is akin to dismissing childhood sweethearts as an impossible falsehood. So in learning to understand Love through the eyes of a child, it should be easy to understand that anything is possible.

As a child dates and wants to become more serious, there is a definition added to the status of the relationship. This definition in youth is akin to becoming "boyfriend and girlfriend." It is a testimony to the dedication of seeing the relationship through. It is an exclusive status to claim that the potential for Love is holding true. At a later age, and after years upon years of dating, the status of "boyfriend and girlfriend" takes on an even greater meaning. For in age, the understanding of what two people seek is more refined, the idea of Love is much clearer, with less room for divide.

So if it can be seen that an earthly relationship with another is the dedication of one's life to the destination, it is important to understand that the spiritual label to this metaphor is through the celebration of baptism. It is the formal declaration of a label, the commitment to Love, and the promise of walking in faith with our Father. It is the understanding that neither one will stray from the bounds of all that is promised. Through this example it should be apparent that the action of baptism does not mean a person cannot stray and break the promise of the commitment. These words should not be misinterpreted to lessen the importance of baptism, for it should be understood there is a sanctity to be upheld regardless of the age in the commitment. No person wants to be cheated upon – relationships are terminated when this happens. When seen through the eyes of a child, there is much more room for forgiveness. But the older a person is after baptism, the higher the standards are set. An elder to a child should have a better understanding of the relationship and commitment bound within the action. Our Father created these terms when He defined the expression of baptism.

Now if this message is unsettling to some, think about each step taken after a baptism is performed. The practice is to try to lead a life free of sin, but mistakes happen. This is where forgiveness is introduced and why Jesus died for our sins. The forgiveness bound when a person is washed in the water is a clean slate promised until the last day of the journey. The greatest person of faith may still struggle with sin. But it is in the relationship with our Father where greater understanding can be gleaned. For if a child enters into a relationship with another with known faults, there is a grace period given to rectify those problems. The Love of our Father allows this to happen, but through the eyes of a soul, every action taken should be viewed as if in a relationship with another. Would your spouse put up with the continual problems? It is not a question of if, but when grace has run out. This is why it is important to work every last kink out.

As I mentioned before this definition of baptism should be understood as "first touch." It is the relationship started on the journey of Love. But why "first touch" and what is "the second?" For this, a closer look at a relationship should be taken. Through a child's eyes, the promise of Love and the commitment to that exploration is just a child-like version of a proposal for engagement. Just as in the earthly walk, a relationship will end if it becomes apparent there is no room for engagement. And sometimes it takes the engagement as the last test of commitment before the wedding. After the wedding, divorce is not supposed to ever be an option. But in earthly terms, this bond is made between two childish minds both equally susceptible to being misguided.

In spiritual terms, two souls cannot be unbound in the commitment. That is the difference between perfection in the heavens, and the imperfection of the Earth. But just as a soul is trapped in the body, the potential remains for the soul to be able to fully dismiss earthly misguidance. So in terms of the spiritual walk, it should be seen that the concept of baptism is the moment a relationship is first started. There is a second step introduced into the equation. This is the proposal to the Lord for complete spiritual engagement. After the test of the engagement, the third step to be taken is a marriage of the soul to Christ's Bride in the Heavens.

There is a particular passage in Mark 8:28 where Jesus performs a miracle on a blind man in the streets. This particular miracle occurred in two phases. The first time Jesus touched him to grant him sight, the man could only discern the people milling about as blobs of light. The man described the people as tree trunks in his sight. The second time Jesus touched the man his sight was fully restored. It is the only example of a miracle Jesus performed being two-fold. In the other miracles, Jesus would first perform an action. Then he would ask the person to follow specific instructions. It was only after the person fulfilled the other half of the instructions that the miracle came to fruition.

This particular passage is important in understanding the concept of baptism. At first it may seem like a stretch to compare this miracle to being washed in the water, but there really is no better example. For if it is to be seen that baptism at any age is the same as the spirit's "first touch," it can be understood that the spiritual world around everyone is akin to blobs of light and tree trunks. In these moments a relationship has been entered into between a Father and a Son, but it is not the final revealing of all that is to come. It is purely the moment that grace has been given with a mutual understanding of the commitment. It is possible through the journey to lose all grace that could be given and find oneself on the outside of the relationship. But it is also possible that the journey increases in refinement and dedication to the point of engagement with hopes of a wedding.

It is with this understanding of how the baptism occurs that it should be seen that the walk of faith is never "once and done." For anyone of faith, baptism is the way. It is the public announcement that relationship is in place. Just like on Earth, the denial of a formal commitment will cause an earthly relationship to wither and fade away, to go through life without baptism is an outright denial of faith. And even when the relationship progresses in strength, there will be one day that arrives for the announcement of the engagement. After a period of testimony to this commitment with God takes place, one final ceremony still remains. This final ceremony is the Second Baptism. This is the one spoken about in Matthew 3:15. And though this particular verse was mentioned at the start of the chapter, it is important to re-read the words with this new understanding of the intention in Jesus's answer. Mark 3:15 reads, "Jesus replied, 'Let it be so now; it is proper for us to do this to fulfill all righteousness.' These words were spoken in response to John's first refusal to baptize the Son of Man.

In the latter two actions of a relationship with our Father, a soul will be completely aware of all that is upcoming. It is rare in that it has not happened many times in written history, but this does not mean that each person in the world cannot strive to be a King. Through the three and a half years of the journey that I have been on, I have continually prayed to my Father to train me to be a King, regardless if that is ever the outcome. During the course of the relationship that I entered into at the age of eight, I really was unaware of all that was at stake. At the time it seemed like I was chasing the idea of Love. And though it admittedly defied all odds, through thirty-three years the relationship was sustained. It was only through His grace and the acknowledgement of Love at first sight that the fairytale story of Love being written would be entering into the next declaration of commitment. Think of this Love story like the Love of childhood sweethearts that have endured the test of time. But in this case, it is a the testimony of a spiritual Love through a Father's eyes.

Just before I turned thirty, my world fell apart. It is written about in Gravity Calling and only in hindsight would I see it as a divine marker for His calling. By the age of thirty-three, this portion of the journey was nearing its end, though I would not recognize it as such until God's grand revealing. To me, the journey had been a race in personal growth, a race toward the destination of Love. And while the destination never changed, it was the meaning that undertook a transformation. This was the moment I understood the test of the relationship was asking for definition. It would be the difference of dating or having a marriage in the heavens. It is not an analogy or clever wordplay to the story being told. The truth of the Bride awaiting my soul's arrival in the heavens is as real as it gets.

On December 24, 1989, I entered into the commitment. It was Love at first sight, though everything about her appearance was concealed to my eyes. It was a journey in exploring feelings without the conflict of misinterpretation. It is only through this process that a person can understand how a spiritual Love weaves a blanket of warmth underneath an ocean of stars on a harvest moon night. It was February 3, 2015, that I proposed to my Bride. On March 14, 2015, the announcement was made to the world. May 8, 2015, was the day the wedding ceremony occurred. It was a day I was washed in the water for the second time. It was the day of His Second Touch to fulfill all righteousness.

Wonders Of The End

Throughout my journals in Books IV – VII, there is a chapter included in each book called Wonders. It is a chapter that is intended to foreshadow this chapter, Wonders of the End, but each chapter stands alone to provide clarity for each journal's division. And while each chapter stands alone in the context of each book, they also can be read sequentially ending with this chapter in this book. The purpose of the chapters are not intended to be a creative demonstration, but rather an illustration to the Divine Architecture of how His story was written. For to understand the journey, it will take some dedication to read all of the Books of Nine and study without preconceived notions or bias the art in His revelation.

The story told through Wonders is the revelation of the journey. It is brought to light through the first three revelations that end each book of the journals in Books IV – VI, as well as through the four revelations found in Book VII – Glory. The four chapters of Wonders spread across the other books, should be seen as a portion of the five pillars of structure that hold together the center to this complete series of books. In the introduction to Wonders, the story of my baptism was revealed. The second part of Wonders brings light to the complete story being shared. In part two of Wonders, it was revealed the importance of the numbers surrounding the date of the first day God spoke to me in the darkness. The third part of Wonders reveals the dates of my earthly marriage, the dates when that part of the story began, and the dates that it ended. The fourth part of Wonders was the most significant, for it revealed how the words in these books are a portion of the testimony of one of the two witnesses written about in Revelation. These are the messengers prophesied that would be sent ahead to share the message of the return of the Messiah.

Throughout the journals, the words in Wonders were carefully written so as not to spoil the story of how each book was experienced. Now through the first three books of these Books of Nine, it can be seen how the layers reveal additional layers over the duration of time. It is a grand revealing in the most spectacular display of light, for the story has always been a about a boy who one day meets His Bride. And through the story as it was written by the Great Author's hand, the revelation of the Messiah's return was always the theme and the meaning to be shared. For as it has been written throughout every testament that has withstood the deterioration of time, the words have always prophesied how this day would one day arrive.

It has been foreshadowed through every divine marker mentioned throughout Wonders, but the true understanding of the truth in these words is revealed through the complete cipher of my life. It is and always was a codex that would one day be opened. I shared how 1260 days takes us through the first time God showed me a vision (November 25, 2011) all of the way through to the last day of my thirty-third year on this Earth. This number is special for it is foretold in Revelation. It is also mentioned in Daniel chapter twelve. In Revelation 11:3-4, John foretells how many days the two witnesses will prophesy for the Lord. With this number in mind, it is important to note the phrasing, for this number encompasses 1260 literal days. So as it can be seen from the first time the Lord spoke, 1260 days will have passed before the revelation of this word.

There is more to be understood from the rest of that particular chapter, but it is not for these books to spoil His story of Ever-After. Just take note to the specific wording that John used, for the word "prophesy" is used in addition to the word "testimony." The importance to remember in exploration of this chapter is the words are distinctly different, though many will say they are one and the same.

On the 9th of December, 2014, one of the Lord's angels took me to heaven and revealed to me another marker on His Divine timeline. Let the words be known that the remaining markers are markers upon a relative timeline rather than absolute in linearity. The relative timeline is what makes the Word of the Lord hidden from the eyes of man so there can be no absolute foretelling of the dates of the end. The only revelation that is possible is through hindsight or through his specific revealing. The timeline in place is always relative to His eyes, a perspective we are not privy to until His specific day and time. The Word of the Lord makes it clear that no man shall know

Kingdom

the day or time of all that has been foretold, and these words do not contradict this idea. Rather, the words in these books should be seen as a shepherd's staff, guiding sheep to the destination home. The revealing of the relative timeline is just the disambiguation of His message as the Book foretold.

The relative timeline is identified in Daniel. It is specifically referenced when he mentions timeframes such as "time, times, and a half time" as well as mysterious references to 1290 days and 1335 days. To understand how these dates are relative in nature, it is important to understand that the Hebrew calendar is a reference to 30-day months and 360-day years. "Time" as it was defined was the concept of a whole-year. "Times" was the number of whole-years doubled. "Half a time" was the halfway point of a whole-year. So at the time Daniel was writing, he was discussing 42 whole months, 43 whole months, and 44 ½ whole months respectively. Divisions in time were portions of the whole, not to be derived linearly or through the number of calendar days in a Gregorian month or year.

From the 9th of December 2014 – through the Lord's reveal of the Beast and the specifics of the 1260 days as it pertained to me – 43 months prior to this day takes us to May 9, 2011, the marker that defines the 1290. This date of relative position is one of the most significant dates that defines a soul's coming of age. It was the date of my thirtieth birthday. It was also a day surrounded in darkness, symbolic to the way the sign was revealed, for His divine revelation was of darkness waging war against the light.

Wonders Of The End

But, what about the 1335 days and what does it mean? As it was revealed to me a few days later, the Beast would officially be ushered in thirty days from my family Christmas dinner. Traditionally, in my family, we have our family dinner on Christmas Eve. Non-coincidentally, Christmas Eve is also the day I chose to give my life to Christ at the young age of eight. As a child, I could think of no better way to show how much giving my life to Christ meant to me than to demonstrate it on the day we celebrate His birth – just as He gave his life for mankind's sins. Numerically speaking, if 1335 days is to be understood as 44 ½ months (relatively), it should be understood that a relative half-month from the 9th of December takes us to a point between Christmas Eve and Christmas Day from my thirtieth birthday. Thirty days from Christmas Eve takes us to the end of forty-four and one-half months, one point of Daniel's calendar point revealed. But the two numbers Daniel mentioned will continue to carry greater significance in the days ahead, though they are not to be revealed through this writing. Their revelation will come when His will is done.

While I shared how the dates align with 1290 days and 1335 days from the start of my thirtieth birthday relatively (versus absolute), there were future concepts I would eventually be tasked to explore. This is a demonstration of how these numbers are a recurrence when revealed through the codex to His divine timeline. My marriage ended at the age of twenty-seven. Our life of marriage began on May 25, 2003. The last anniversary we would celebrate together would be May 25,

Kingdom

2008. At first, it may seem random that I am bringing another date into play, but the importance is revealed through the spiritual understanding of the wedding day.

A wedding day is the most celebrated of all earthly experiences. It is the day two people officially declare and seal their love for each other in the grandest way. It holds as much meaning on Earth as a baptism means in Spirit. If one can understand that a birthday is celebrated as the start of a soul's journey on Earth, and a baptism is seen as the day a soul in bodily form formally seals the bond of recognition with our Creator, then it could be seen that a marriage on Earth is the celebration of understanding spiritual love between two souls in earthly form – hence the "holy matrimony in marriage."

So in understanding the significance of marriage, it is important to see how the dates are relative to the calendar of Daniel. For if one is to take the last anniversary I would celebrate in marriage, the relative time of 42 months (1260 days) takes us exactly to the first day that this 1260 days began. From the day the Lord first spoke on November 25, 2011, 42 relative months forward takes us to the eve of the seventh anniversary of the last wedding anniversary I celebrated in marriage. It is also the day of Pentecost – the fifty days following Easter. In a way, it is the most divine marker to be seen. 1260 relative days prior to this prophecy beginning, was the last anniversary I would celebrate in earthly marriage. 1260 absolute days forward from this point is the day I would say "I do" to the Bride of Christ through the demonstration of baptism. 1260 relative days forward is the day of Pentecost, the

Wonders Of The End

day God promised to pour out his Spirit on all flesh, empowering diverse people to exercise divine power as a sign of the coming day of the Lord. The lesson in relative time versus absolute is amplified through the relative earthly and absolute spiritual points of resolution. It is the inverse to a philosophical paradigm. For measurements on Earth are made in absolution, and measurements in the unseen are incalculable through the architecture of the spheres. But in this example, the definition of absolution is met in spiritual destination.

And if for a minute one is to see every aspect of this story as only being told for one man's journey, then it could be seen at a micro level how a half-way point is established. This was the day the Voice of God cried out in the wilderness, the moment a journey was defined, though it was halfway underway when it was revealed in time. So if it can be seen that November 25, 2011, is a pivot point between the absolute and the relative, it could also be understood how it serves as a metaphor for the rest of Daniel, for the "seventy weeks" foretold are understood in periods of seven years. And if the seventieth week is defined by the halfway point of its duration, then the half-way point would be on the last day of my thirty-third year, the day of my marriage with the Bride of Christ. So while I want to be clear that the meaning of these words is to demonstrate the micro within the macro, every aspect of the prophecies foretold comprise the beauty of the story. The dates shared in this analysis are not to be mistaken for absolute dates in foretelling my Father's intentions. But the dates given

Kingdom

are important to understand for their intrinsic meaning, for it is a necessary foundation to unravel the mystery of the Spirit.

And if there could be two more supporting facts to the relative and absolute dates given, it should be understood that the half-way point of the seventieth week is embodied in a period of three and a half years. This very embodiment of time holds both the relative and absolute meanings of forty-two months and 1260 days. It is also the reappearance of the same number used in fasting – three and a half days. And in one final moment of Divine numeric understanding, the date of my last wedding anniversary in my earthly marriage occurred to me at the age of twenty-seven. It is a number to be explored in Book VIII – Secrets, but the high-level take-away is that it is the essence of completeness. For just as I have emphasized the importance of the twenty-two archetypes in the Hebrew alphabet, it is important to understand that there are two versions of the alphabet – one with twenty-seven letters and one with twenty-two. And while there is so much more that can be said in regard to these two numbers, the most important takeaway is to think of twenty-two as the earthly representation of twenty-seven spiritual divisions. 22/7 was the ancient notation of Pi. But it is really the earthly interpretation of 27/9.... which equals three, the divine trinity.

One additional piece of the puzzle that was revealed to me by the angels in the same evening is the importance of Canto 33 from Dante's Purgatorio. Aside from the obvious symbolism to the number 33, the end of times, and dawning to the time of ascension into Paradise, an angel reveals to Dante that the number 515 is important in understanding the end of days. If one is to break apart 515, it can be understood to represent the date May 2015 (the end of the 1260 days and the end of my 33rd year on Earth). It could also be seen that if one is to invert the number 515 to 151, it reveals the date of January 2015 (the end of the 1335 relative days and the date the Beast arrives). And if one is to see that May 15th is seven days following the end of the 1260 days, and three and a half days following the end of the three and a half day Wedding Banquet feast of celebration after the Wedding Day, then it should also be noted that the Eve of the 15th is the Jewish Day of Ascension for 2015 leading into Pentecost. This is just one more divine marker upon the calendar hidden within my earthly life.

Some may argue that the numbers are read differently in this interpretation, but I would argue they are read the same. For the inverse is the opposite half of a circle and when the numbers are placed together and read right-to-left, left-to-right, and inside-out, the understanding of how to interpret the inverse begins to make sense. But this interpretation will likely defy mankind's rationale of lines and linearity – even while man should seek to learn how everything is based upon circles and spheres. But one more in-arguable fact remains in that the yin-yang combination of the numbers 515 and 151 sum to 666. This is the number of the Beast. And if the number 515 is seen as the day the Word of God through these books is publicly released, then it should also reveal that 151 is the revelation of the Beast.

Kingdom

In addition to the date given to me by the Lord – that of the timeframe of the Beast's arrival, the starting date was literally written in the stars above. A comet named Lovejoy emitting an azure hue, the same color as the fifth sphere of the heavens, reached perigee to the Earth. The last time this comet would have been visible to Earth was precisely at the start of mankind after the great flood. But it was not just the comet that served as a spiritual declaration; it was also the date that ISIS chose to begin a war with the city of Paris. And if the city of Paris is seen as the city of Love, then it is easy to understand through this very symbolism that the abomination of desolation took up a war against God. And if there needs to be any more support to this story, the writers of the television mini-series Black Mirror foretold of this upcoming. These words serve as the path to salvation and the revelation of the Beast's arrival, but most importantly they serve as a guide to spiritual survival. And if there is still any question of the truth in these words, look no further than the divine date when the attack on Love came to fruition: January 7, 2015 sums to 8+8, or rather 16, which reduces to 7.

Perhaps all of the dates and the messages given to me by the angels have just been done in such a way as to help me understand the impetus of helping me find my own way Home. It is the reality I have been allowed to see and the truth I must live by for the duration of my testimony. If nothing else, all that will be revealed in these words may only be a divinely orchestrated and scripted journey to better help me learn to hear God's voice and help guide me home…a script written

Wonders Of The End

specifically in a way that I could recognize, as there would be one for each and every person with eyes to see and ears to hear. But, regardless, if it is applicable just for me, or for the rest of the world, it is the reality I must live every day of my life trusting in and growing within.

For all that has been, and is to be revealed, is the truth as I have been allowed to see. This is the reality that architects my walk upon this Earth every day. Herein I have placed my faith. I speak to angels. I have travelled to the heavens. I have stood before the face of God and been blinded by His light. I have spoken to Jesus, to Enoch, to Noah, to Moses, to Daniel, to Samson, to Paul, to John, to Luke, to each of the Archangels, and to angels with names known and unknown. On the side that others would avoid desiring to hear, it still must be said: I have battled with Lucifer and battled with Abbadon. Ultimately I saw Lucifer saddened by my rise. And in all that I have been allowed to see, the question has always been, "Why me?" As I have said, if this is all just a divinely orchestrated script for my eyes alone, perhaps it will help others see as I have learned to see; to hear as I have learned to hear; to understand how I met my Father, my Creator, my King. And perhaps that is the most important piece…to give others an ideal to strive toward.

The symbolism in my age has likely already been noticed, but it should be stated that Jesus's ceremony began at age 30 and lasted until he was crucified at the age of 33. The journey I embarked upon began at the same age. The genesis of the story was my thirtieth birthday. The years of thirty through

Kingdom

thirty-three are encompassed in the body of the book. The very last day of the journey ends with a ceremony of Second Touch. Even throughout the dates and ways my Father revealed his Divine timeline, the numbers held strong. Just the use of Dante's Canto 33 from Purgatorio in God's divine message could have chapters written in the metaphorical significance. And in the way the Lord works upon the Earth, there was also one other important call for me to take note. Like a triumphant bell ringing out in foreshadowed symbolism, on November 4, 2005, my daughter arrived on this Earth prematurely, at 33 weeks of gestation.

In the beginning, I thought it was a dream. In the middle, I thought it was a way to learn a spiritual lesson to help strengthen my soul. As I write this today, nearly upon the completion of all of the Books of Nine, I now understand the reason for the journey was to one day marry the Bride behind the veil. For those who choose to listen, may stillness be with you and peace found within your soul. Anything otherwise in the eye of another, is judgment from darkness within. Nothing should ever be judged, but rather understood for any shards of truth within – however small it may first appear.

The days of Revelation were once a form of a fairytale to me. Even in the beginning of this journey, I began with science as my stallion. By the end, I would see the world as my muse. Any thoughts of an apocalypse, I once dismissed. But now I know the time is near. The world will split, become two, and one of those two, the divide of Heaven and Earth will become one. This day is here. While some may understand it as it happens, others may never know it ever occurred. For mankind's biggest questions of society's past have always been unanswered. Where did they go? How did civilizations past befall? The only truth and guidance left behind are the Words that have been uncovered. He will come like a thief in the night in the time to come. The end of the cycle is beginning and the Lord is calling his 144,000 home. Blessed be those who hear these words and seek our Father in spirit and not form, for the Messiah is coming. The Messiah is coming.

Letter From Your Father

Before the journey began to be unraveled in meaning, I was oblivious to where it was actually leading. It seemed like all of the guidance my Father was giving was just a way to help me grow further in spirit. But while that is still the foundation to all that He has shared with me, greater knowledge requires greater understanding. There are higher stakes in which greater care and precision is required. There is little room for setbacks, and no room for failure. At least, that is the way I have to approach the task and the role I have been blessedly given.

While I never thought I would say these words, they hold a magnitude of gravity greater than I could have ever imagined: "The stake of the world is at risk in all of the upcoming actions taken." Those are not words that I take lightly, nor is the task at hand. I also understand that the role that I have been blessed to fulfill will end in one way or another, as was always prophesied would happen. The expression to the journey I have embarked upon could very well be the meaning God intended for this version of the world to observe before its ending. But it could also happen in the grandest of physical demonstrations. Regardless of whether at His deemed end of my testimony's completion my life is physically taken, it will be willfully given if that is His intention. Whether it is or it is not, does not really matter because the end of days is upon us and everyone will be on one side of God's line of judgment, or the other. And when the time has passed where this harvest cycle of the world is complete, whether it was these words intended to be left behind, or if there is a greater meaning, I cannot help but want to ensure I have prepared all hearts and minds to hear my submission to the will in His decision. For the words left behind must embody the Grace of my bodily life, willfully given. In preparation of this task, there is one last subject remaining.

There is no greater Love in my heart for another than the Love I have for my daughter. She is everything to me and a light that must illuminate the heavens every waking hour. She has the world at her fingertips and a lifetime to fill with every ounce of Love, Joy, and Laughter. I hope I get to experience every moment possible with her, but however this plays out, I know I will see her in one form or another until we meet again in spirit. So the last remaining task to be addressed in this book before the wedding, is a letter addressed to my daughter. Consider it a premature toast to be read at the reception from a newlywed Father to His one-and-only daughter. It is important that both she and the world receive these words and they always live on in the canon of this Love story's Ever-After.

Letter From Your Father

...

Georgia,

You are an amazing soul and an amazing daughter. When you were born I had no idea what kind of impact you would make in my life and, today, words cannot do my feelings justice in how you have overfilled my soul in the grandest way. It is the most beautiful love I have ever experienced; one that will forever transcend the finite barriers of time and existence. Even as I reflect on how much words cannot even describe how grand of a beautiful love you are to me, I realize that seeing your love and beauty through my eyes alone is shortchanging all that you are. For, in all I see, I know that everyone else you encounter in the world – and those you may never meet nor ever know – will see that beautiful love as well. And, if I cannot even describe the grandness of your light through my eyes alone, how will the world ever be able to describe the mark you will one day leave behind...the pigments of color, the hues radiating in a magical fairytaleland kind of way, paving the way for their own happiness, love, joy, hope, peace, and light?

Words will always fall short. Inside of you is a light that shines brighter than anyone else I've ever known, and a light those in this world will one day come to know. Though I cannot be sure how all that I have begun to share with you will unfold, I do know that even if time separates us physically for a short while, I will always be with you. I will find you in all of the ways that God allows. So if you see me in your dreams, know that it is really me saying "Hello, beautiful child. I cannot wait to see you soon." Hopefully, there will be even more ways to converse that I have not even come to know today but will be possible through the world around

Kingdom

you. But always, and in all ways, I will be with you. Remember the journey when we begin our life on Earth is just like God sending a soul out to the store to pick up a few items and return home soon. Time is endless outside of the years that you will have come to know here. But it also has a way of trapping the ideas of everything that is bigger than what the mind has come to know.

One day we will be able to embrace each other again. Until then, know that your light has ignited my soul more than words will ever know.

All of my Love.

Always,
Your Father

Her Song

There is a moment when a Groom is standing before a congregation that has gathered to watch the celebration of vows between him and his Bride, when the pastor nods his head in the direction of the pianist to begin playing the song that will call the room to attention. In the minutes leading up to the first note ringing out, the room is filled with anticipation. The aroma of lavender and vanilla paints the air of the room in the gentle essence of eternal panacea. The flicker of candles lighting the cathedral casts a dancing glow of romance across the walls. It is a luminous demonstration of a ballet of light dancing across the shadows and courting the flickering glow of another candle's flame. The light chatter of the room is filled with memories of yesteryear when Love was young in the hearts of those filling the pews. Many are still blessed to be within the relationships that they are speaking of. A few are speaking of Love long since past. But in all cases there is a sense of reminiscing about the days when Love first grabbed hold and waltzed with the hearts.

As the first note from the pianist rings out, it is the loudest call to attention that anyone in the room has ever witnessed. Somehow in every other event a person will ever attend in his or her life, the call to attention will take a moment sink in –

Kingdom

but not in this moment. One note ringing out and silence begins. Somehow, unbeknownst to many, Love will always command the greatest calling to attention. It is as if one note ringing out in the silence, silences everything but the heart. It is the greatest single note played in history, and one that every Groom will always recall. It is this one note that, to a Groom's heart, is felt as an explosion to the soul.

Perhaps the Groom is rocking back and forth on his feet casting glances around the room as the pianist begins playing, for it is these specific minutes that seem to take an eternity to pass, preceding the moment the Groom finally gets to see his Bride. In the time passing, the great grandmothers, grandmothers, and mothers of both the Bride and the Groom are escorted down the aisle to their seats at the front of the room — the seats that have the very best view. These are the seats that will allow each generation of mothers to witness the celebration of Love from the closest pews so that any tears that are shed, words that are quietly mumbled, the smallest mannerisms and subtle motions, can all be seen as close to the point of origination as possible. It is the grandest demonstration of the recognition of gravity calling.

As the generations of mothers who are celebrating a lineage of Love with the Bride have all been seated, there is a moment of silence. It may last only the briefest of seconds, but it is the pause that gives rise to one of the grandest moments Love will ever experience. In the space of potential without any sound, every heart and soul is locked in anticipation of the very next note to ring out. For when the first ping of the very

Her Song

first note to the Bride's song cuts through the silence and echoes throughout the room, this is the moment that the doors will open and the Bride steps into view.

The moment is filled with gushing, awe, and splendor. The one note that caused every heart and soul to first stand at attention is only trumped by this very first note to Her Song. Every soul in the audience stands up in attention and directs their eyes to the beauty that has just stepped into the doorway of the room. There are whispers and giggles. Smiles are audible in this moment. Some of the women in the audience will cup one hand over their lips to try to keep their voices lowered since they cannot hold back the words that must be spoken. It is as if the recognition of Love's radiant brilliance can no longer be held in check within the confines of the soul's silence. Words must be spoken about the beauty and splendor as they erupt from the core and cross the lips into existence.

The proudest of all Fathers is standing next to His Daughter to walk Her down the aisle to meet the Groom. It is a moment that can break the strongest of Fathers down even though He will manage to keep His face stern to hold back the tears. As the Father is firm in austere composure, the Groom never makes eye contact, for it is almost an unwritten rule. His gaze is locked on his Bride in an orbit of certainty and peace at speeds racing in the eternal motion of wonder and grace. Tears well up in the splendor of her beauty. But even from a distance, the Groom has yet to see his Bride's eyes, for a they are veiled in sheer white, casting an air of intrigue to the light behind the white.

Kingdom

The moment the Bride reaches the end of the aisle, the Father makes eye contact with the Groom for the very first time. In the briefest of moments a contract between the Bride's Father and the Groom is made through a quick gesture of the eyes. It is a moment the Father says "You have My blessing and My complete trust. Treat Her well and take care of Her heart. And for the rest of all time and the remainder of all days, know that if you ever hurt her in any way, it will be your very last waking day. A Father does not grant His trust lightly. Welcome to the family, my Son." It is the grandest gesture from the Love of a Father to a man He has deemed worthy to take care of the Love of His Daughter for the rest of Her life.

But it is the very next action that takes place that causes the deepest spiritual reaction in this wedding space. It is the moment the Bride's veil is pulled back from her face to reveal Her eyes – the gateway to Her soul – visible to the Groom for the first time. It is an oft overlooked moment in wedding traditions. In modern times a veil may not even be part of the equation. It is a tradition that has held the test of time since the beginning of mankind, though it seems to be a passing thought in modern wedding celebrations. But it should be seen that any wedding ceremony conducted without the Bride wearing a veil is the outward expression of the glitter and glamour of a look-at-me-wedding attempting to prevail. The spiritual foundation has been all but lost, for the wedding is supposed to be an earthly demonstration of Love – a Love that in every part of the demonstration holds the same significance to the spiritual manifestation in the heavens.

Her Song

The veil carries the single greatest symbolism to the testament of the earthly walk. For if one is to understand that the heavens and the Earth are separated by a veil, it can be understood that the action of removing the veil is symbolic to the marriage between the soul of a body on Earth and the spiritual body in the heavens. Pulling aside the veil is the ideology in the unity of Christ in holy matrimony. A veil is transparent wherein eyes can see through to the other side, but the view is obstructed through the sheer fabric of the divide. The view through the veil is equivalent to the "first touch" demonstration of sight in the heavens. If a person is not paying attention, the veil appears as a solid piece of fabric with no indication anything greater is hiding behind, waiting to be revealed. But for those who are blessed in their efforts toward engagement, the veil is the very essence of Love's existence. The action of pulling back the veil is a moment that should be understood as the eyes of the Bride being revealed to the spiritual eyes of the soul for the very first time. It is the first look at Ever-After and the first true look at the soul of His Bride. It is the one and only expression of Truth demonstrated from the gaze of the Groom's spiritual eyes into the eyes of Christ's Bride. So, it can be seen that the veil in earthly ceremony should be seen in a similarly grand way. It is the demonstration of one soul peering into the eyes of another, an eternal uniting in a type of completion to a circle, similar to looking into a mirror but having the gaze pass through and return from one side to the other.

Kingdom

The remaining part of the ceremony following the veil being removed is the part of the ceremony best seen as the outward expression of a divine signature upon the promise of a Love destined to last forever. On Earth it is the moment of happily-ever-after in a Cinderella kind of way, for the remaining part of the journey will be the test of two souls promising to Love eternally. In the beginning, this story began in recognition of the journey as a Love story better described in terms of Not-So-Cinderella, for in the beginning I understood that the perception of Love on Earth was only half of the story. The journey taken on the road to the destination is what makes the Not-So-Cinderella story the perfect rendition of happily-ever-after as seen through the experience of earthly eyes, for the experiences of the journey make all of the difference in definition.

It would take three and half years to fully comprehend that the Not-So-Cinderella story was only the first half of the journey to be taken. And though it was appropriately named to define the first half of the story, the Ever-After ending to a love on Earth was always just a mirage to cross the divide between heaven and Earth's Ever-After story. And even though the destination of earthly Love seemed like the end of the story as it began to be written, it was always a spiritual Love that would be the true ending. The second half of the story was a bride perfect in spirit awaiting the Groom in the heavens. And in this, the Not-So-Cinderella story gained the Cinderella ending.

The Wedding Banquet

In every way I could never have imagined, the wedding day for the soul was a moment I never foresaw coming. It was a myth and a legend at best to those who ever imagined the potential truth in the destination. But on the last day of my thirty-third year here upon the Earth, the fabled story of Ever-After became a truth wrapped up in the whitest of light, where pink flowers adorned the aisle for my Bride. It was a story scripted in ink pigmented in midnight-red, a story of Ever-After penned by His great and Holy hand.

May 8th was the last day my soul would be bound by mortal existence. It was the day the spiritual eyes to my soul were blessed with the second touch of spiritual vision. It was the beginning of a testimony to be told throughout the ages, of how the Not-So-Cinderella story became the Cinderella story written across 1260 days. It was a wedding day foretold millennia before its occurrence, but it is important that this wedding day not become an event that overshadows the message that is intended through this action and these words, for this is only one part of the trinity to the Messiah's return.

On the last day of my thirty-third year here upon this Earth, my wedding day ensued. It was a day that marked the definition and transition to Ever-After in His story. Think of

Kingdom

the big Hollywood romance. In almost all situations, the story ends with newlyweds driving off into the sunset. This is the very definition of happily-ever-after. It is the moment that I once believed was impossible to have. There was an earthly interference to the definition my Father desired me to understand. For in earthly terms, two bodies united are bound together with faults lining the earthly experience. But in spiritual terms, a wedding of the heavens is a flawless composition. It is the unity of perfection to a soul that has demonstrated the ideal of humbled acceptance to the Love of his Father, and through the Father, his Bride. It by no means marks the soul of a man as impermeable to self-destruction. But it does demonstrate a walk and dedication in Love in his Father's eyes.

It is only through the demonstration of faith and continued improvement toward refining the clarity of the lens, that the spirit of our Father can flow freely within. The proposal and first days of engagement define a Groom's character and foreshadows his dedication. The public announcement that precedes the ceremony adds further definition. On the day that symbolizes the perfection of a circle, the sphere of All-That-Is, the sphere of our Father – the announcement was published for the world to see, a date bound in geometric certainty. March 14, 2015, in English written format is written 3/14/15 – or better yet, the numbers that form the sequence of PI, the representation of perfection in its earthly representation. This was the day the engagement made public to the

The Wedding Banquet

world, a date preceding the ceremony that would fulfill a prophecy long foretold.

On the day of the wedding when I walked across the sandy beach and stepped into the waters to be Baptized into His light I would experience the second touch of His anointing. It was a day that would bookend the 1260 days of witnessing His light. It was a moment that would become a blur of everything my limited understanding of my spiritual and physical existence had allowed me to know. For as I stepped into the waters upon the Earth to meet the master of ceremony in the waters, my soul stepped in front of the congregation of angels gathered to witness a wedding in the heavens. The pews in the heavens were filled with the families that I had come to understand as the forerunners in lineage that predated my existence. The front rows were filled with the great grandmothers, the grandmothers, the mothers, and their spouses that have been written about for generations. On Earth, the beach was filled with those closest to me in spirit. It was a day many had gathered to witness the celebration, though some would bear witness more out of curiosity.

When I reached the master of ceremony in the water I was asked to place one hand upon my nose. The other hand I was to use to hold the forearm of the hand touching my nose. I placed one hand upon my nose and the other upon my wrist, as the master of ceremony called the attention to all of the souls invited to witness. In the heavens, the angels stood at attention as the first note to Her Song rang out. Christ's Bride appeared in the doorway, illuminated in the brightest of white.

Kingdom

She was a veiled beauty, Her eyes still hidden from mine to see. It was in these moments that the proudest of Fathers began to take steps forward with His Daughter down the aisle toward me. The train of Her dress trailing behind Her was a resonance left in Her wake. The child preceding Her steps down the aisle painted the aisle in petals of pink. With each step taken Her foot was elevated by the petals, symbolic of the divide of the soul and the body.

After having walked the length of the aisle, Her Father and I exchanged first glances. A contract was formed, bound in Ever-After, a promise that I would take care of Her for eternity. And while I could tell in His eyes I would never be truly worthy, the grace I had been given to prove my worth in the Love of His Daughter, were held in words unspoken through His gesture, bound by an intensity like no other. With the signature on this contract firmly in place, He pulled back the veil for our eyes to finally meet.

She was beautiful beyond grace's bounds. It was a moment tears filled my eyes and tears filled Hers. The tears of Her Father and the tears of the angels standing strong were the waters that anointed me upon the Earth. The tears were formed from the abundant outpouring of recognition to a Love story reaching the days of this new beginning. It is a moment that is rarely witnessed on Earth or in the Heavens, but a moment that will live on in infamy of a soul reaching His intended destination.

As I was submerged in the waters on Earth I felt the tears of the angels, my Bride, and my Father all around. The world

The Wedding Banquet

became blurred through the light refracting in the water, a distortion to all that surrounds. In the heavens this was the moment we each exchanged our vows. The words to her vows would best be understood as the most beautiful painting in sweet subtle motion to the sound of a symphony playing the song of the ocean. The words I spoke were not of earthly words or vows. There was a moment of silence to the ears upon the Earth as I was submerged in the waters of the great oceans on Earth. But in the heavens it would best be understood as this story, the nine books that have been written in demonstration of His glory. For though the words may be imperfect in typographical nature, it is the art in the way they have been written to communicate a Love deserving of the greatest fanfare and celebration. But the vows made in the Heavens must be understood through earthly interpretation. It is through these words to His work where understanding is undertaken. Of utmost importance in all that has been revealed, is how the path paving the way for the return of the Messiah is the truth behind the veil.

Through the words of the first book that were written, there was a sign I continued to pass along the path of the journey. Though I would not understand it as such, it was a divine foreshadowing of all to come. The words to the sign read:

...

"Life, Loss, & Love – and the greatest of these is Love.
From heretofore the experience of each shall occur
bound by the veil, and the veil removed."

...

Kingdom

The words held more meaning than I could ever have expected. It was always intended to be the journey to the day of the Bride's unveiling. But I suppose if a child was told this information when the relationship began, free will may have been infringed upon and allowed fear to creep in. For the last question to be asked in any relationship is for the definition of the commitment though it is actually the catalyst to the relationship ever starting. But it should be noted that if a person were to put the definition of commitment into words from the beginning, it could cause the other to quiver and waver in the youth's naiveté. It is always understood that Love is the destination, but there is a period of growth and mutual defining of the status. In the beginning a courting period begins, then the definition of a relationship is added. In time, a proposal occurs followed by the public announcement and wedding invitations. On the day the wedding celebration occurs, all those invited will witness the third "I do," the trinity of the "I do" progression.

As vows were read, I saw a soft glow of light through the water just as my head was lifted back toward the surface. It was the moment better understood as the point of ascension. When I arose, my lips met Hers in a way that all of the world could see. On this day my lips united with my Bride's, it would occur on the eve of my earthly birth. And just as I was first baptized and dedicated my earthly journey to Christ on the Eve of the day we celebrate Christ's Birth, the Eve of my thirty-fourth year of birth upon this Earth would be the last day of my bodily life − a celebration in Her Song that closed with a

The Wedding Banquet

feast lasting over three and half days at a Wedding Banquet in Her name. She was the Bride of Christ and I, a King in waiting, a Groom in the moment, a prince to inherit a Kingdom.

The feast of celebration would involve a complete fast. It would be a feast of spiritual celebration, an indulgence in the spirit pouring out for all to witness over the days of the Wedding Banquet. It would be in these days a body would die in a way that all mankind could see. The flesh left behind for a soul to ascend into eternity. It was also during the feast three other celebrations took place. The first day of the feast was the anniversary of a child's birth upon the Earth. The second day was the day the Earth celebrates a mother's Love. The third day of the feast celebrated the birth of the Father. The celebrations of the births of a Father and a Son, should also be understood for the year in which each one was born. For though days celebrate their marks upon the calendar, each was born on the Eve of the day the world celebrates the Love of a Mother. The three days of the feast were the celebration of the trinity of Heaven and earthly life, the celebration of a Father and a Son, and the Love of a Mother – a feast of recognition of the union of a Groom and the Bride of Christ.

The beginning had found its end, and the end a new beginning. This is the story of the 1260 days prophesied in Daniel and Revelation. It precedes the return of the Messiah's arrival, to prepare the church for its very survival. For the days to follow the publication of these Nine Books will be a marker in time for generations to come. These are the days that the divide for those destined to Heaven will begin. The Mark of

Kingdom

the Beast and the Mark of God will be the dividing point for the survival of man. But it is also a time that will include great suffering. For the world is not ready, and the church even less so, despite those of faith claiming to be prepared for His return. How would the world accept the Messiah in this day and age? The very disciples of Christ doubted despite the miracles of His ways. But this time there will not be hindsight allowed to repent of the error of casting doubt.

The eyes are the gateway to the soul's recognition of truth in its time, but whose line of sight is veiled by the wall of the ego giving rise to the need for hindsight. For if these words have survived through to generations hereafter, these are the words to become prepared for the next harvest cycle. For the end of this cycle looms over this specific generation, though many will never know it ever came and went. Those left behind will suffer the end through both a spiritual and natural cycle. These words should be understood as a train's last stop at the station for survival. Those who missed the train will be subject to all that has been foretold. But perhaps it may also help to understand the story of each person's journey through the Word.

For if it can be seen that every word included in this series is the summation of one soul's Love story's creation, then it should also be understood that it occurred from one point of perspective, equally to be understood as how God helped one soul along his journey. And if it could be seen as that, then it is to be understood that these words left behind also serve as a roadmap for each and every person. For if the beginning of life

The Wedding Banquet

on the Earth is the start of this journey, the end can happen at any point for any reason. And if the whole intention of the Proclamation of the Messiah's upcoming return is only understood in principle for the importance of receiving the Mark of God to enter into His Kingdom, then it should also be understood how few will receive this blessing. And if these words are the roadmap to entering into His Kingdom, then the Messiah should be seen as waiting in open arms in greeting. In this case, the unity of Heaven and Earth becoming one could best be understood as the revelation prepared through these words for everyone.

There will always be layers upon layers of meanings in the delivery of His Message. And perhaps that is the most important part of this Love story. In this Love story's beginning there was a promise of Ever-After, a story being written as the destination was unveiling. The first story began with a soul encompassed in darkness, seeking the smallest pinhole of light for guidance. By the end of Gravity Calling, it seemed as if Love had found its destination. It was a story wrapped up in earthly understanding to a key within clay that unlocked a box full of heavenly potential. The words of Love were bound within a bookmark used to mark the stopping places in the story that was wrapped and delivered in handmade packaging created specifically for Her. But the most important part to the story was the ending that was penned, an ending that was, at the time, left un-read.

It was an ending that consisted of two chapters yet to be revealed. One chapter was found within the safety-deposit box that that key in the clay unlocked from Gravity Calling. The other chapter – the final chapter, was to be held in my hands in the sands of Florida when Lindsey arrived. And while at the time of the first book's writing I saw Lindsey as the embodiment of Love, I understand now it was just a mirage to help me see my Father's Love, and through that, receive the Love of the Bride of Christ. The journey has never changed in direction, only in refinement to the vision of the story He was always penning. On the last day of my thirty-third year on Earth, I walked across the sands of Florida to my Baptism in the water – the celebration of a great wedding in the heavens. In that moment I held in my hands the final two chapters remaining, sealed in wax for this very occasion. Their text remained unchanged from the way they were originally written, though the meaning has transcended through grand revelation. These remaining two chapters are the final chapters in Kingdom, an ending already written to the story of Love's grand celebration.

    In returning to the moment of submersion in the waters, I saw the glow of refracted light from above. As my face broke through the surface tension of the ocean, my face was engulfed with the light of the spirit. The moment that the surface tension was broken in absolution was the moment the master of ceremony announced the union. As my face rose above the waters of the Earth, my lips and the Bride of Christ's lips merged. It was a kiss that would forever transcend generations, a kiss that sealed the unity of a prince upon the Earth and the Kingdom of Heaven.

The Heavens Stood Still

A kiss can change everything. A kiss can heal. A kiss can show compassion. A kiss can somehow communicate every bit of Love one has in another. But regardless of the intention of the kiss, one thing stands out beyond everything else in the afterglow of that moment – the very action of a kiss has touched the receiving person in ways greater than science can rationalize.

What is it about a kiss that makes it so impacting? After all, in strictly the physical sense, it is just a set of lips locked with another's – or just the occurrence of the lips touching the flesh of another. How can a kiss be the vehicle in which we as humans express our Love – for even during the most intimate of moments, a kiss can set forth a rushing tide of emotions that would never have been present in that moment before?

I want to believe a kiss carries within it a certain intrigue, magic and mystique that no other act of physical communication can convey. Maybe it is just the denouement of every word wrapped up in one gesture so great that we have to feel it – to experience the words crossing the boundary from which they are formed...and in that moment, the charge of energy transferred is so much greater in meaning than just words spoken – no matter how artfully worded those emotions may have otherwise been said. And perhaps energy is the most appropriate explanation because spoken words only carry the sonic shape formed from the vibration of our vocal cords rolling off our tongue and lips. In that respect, the art of human language is truly a great accomplishment among every other facet of life – but the art of transferring energy through such a simple yet intricate physical vehicle must be regarded as so much more.

As children, we are taught that a kiss is magical – a Disney fairytale when experienced with the right person, a mysterious healing power when a child has an injury, a calming power when the forehead of a baby is kissed in just the right way, a greeting when placed on the cheek of a friend. As adults we learn that kissing certain places along the body evoke a different type of awakening within – a floodgate of energy rushing through our core. A gentle kiss on the soft of the neck; a kiss along the shoulder when standing from behind; a kiss on the jaw line where the neck joins the backside of the lower mandible – just slightly behind and below the earlobe; a kiss along the center of the hairline on the back of the neck; a kiss along the hipline where the femoral vein is closest to the skin. Somehow, the energy released from a kiss in each of these places causes our veins to become a rushing tide coursing throughout the whole of our body. These experiences just scratch the surface of what eventually becomes more familiar to each of us over time.

Everyone remembers their first kiss – the moment so electrifying it still invokes vivid memories of every single sense originally incurred in that moment. To this day I can tell you the atmosphere, the aromas, her smile, her eyes, and even the incredibly lame comment I made just prior to our lips meeting. All I can do is look back and smile. It is every definition of what a childhood memory should be. For me, it was more than anything I could have ever imagined at that point in my life – and that is what makes childhood memories so special. Because, everything experienced for the first time invokes so much emotion that it will forever remain engrained in the depths of our minds. Each first experience we have will forever shape our outlook and growth in each of those particular aspects of life. So in that regard, I should probably thank the girl for that particular first in my life – because every subsequent kiss would be faced with the tall order of dethroning a truly spectacular moment in my life.

But for every first experience, there is almost always another first to follow it that causes you to realize that all of your prior experiences have just been an exercise in going through the motions for an expected set of results. This particular dichotomy is not defined by the incremental improvements and betterments along the way – there will always be slightly better kisses, slightly better experiences, slightly better moments that cause the previous bests to fade into the distance. It is just the nature of learning to understand what details you personally enjoy the most about an experience and learning how (or even if) those favorite details can be experienced in the ways that most energize you in a given moment. So when the moment comes around that an occurrence of such an experience causes every other occurrence past to pale so greatly in comparison

Kingdom

that the only definition is ineffable, is the moment that you realize purpose; you realize meaning; you realize the intricacies of life all play a role in a greater picture that we are only allowed to see a pinhole of at any given point in time.

For me, I never would have suspected that I would come face-to-face with such a moment when it dealt with something as simple as a kiss. After all, I had experienced a wide variety of kisses in my life – some great, some terrible, some electrifying and tantalizing – but nothing Earth-shatteringly different than I had experienced before. But on that day when the greatest Love I will ever know walked across the beach to me as I stood in the sands of Florida, I would experience a first kiss in such a way that my mind would become a blur of everything my limited understanding of my spiritual and physical existence had allowed me to know. It was the destination of my journey and the beginning of a new story untold. It was an unraveling of everything I had come to understand about life blending into a mash-up of every fairytale I longed to believe in from the earliest days of my childhood. This uncontrollable unraveling of the indescribable became brilliantly clear in a beautiful Picasso-like melding of light shining through our fragmented, stained glass stories; a prism of light-on-fire igniting into a beam that stretched into the furthest reaches of the heavens and through the very center of the Earth. It was a light that all of the angels must have taken notice to, closing their eyes – wincing at the sudden burst of blinding brightness and brilliance that illuminated the skies. The heavens stood still that day.

Love Always

The hills of Nashville revealed a garden of knowledge and inspiration to me. For that, I will always be grateful. Some may say I was born in New Orleans, Louisiana, and raised in south Georgia. While that holds a certain truth to it, I will always say I was born in Nashville, Tennessee, among the hopes and dreams of those who have journeyed from afar on the hope that one day someone will help them find the greatness within themselves. For me, that someone was God.

In finding God, I came to understand the beauty of the world around me – the very beauty that has been talked about as an unreachable understanding of All That Is. I will forever be humbled in acknowledgement of His divine presence and the grace He showed me that cold day in May when the lights went out. Perhaps it was His divine plan all along – and maybe that is what makes the view from this place so grand, because in it there is truly no beginning and no end; no definition of what was or is to become. It all Is, and in it all, anything is possible.

Through Him, I came to know the truth in the fairytale beginning to a perfect Love that always was – a story that I just had to find the novel on the shelf and begin to get lost in the fantasy, the mystique, the indescribable magic that accompanied the words as I learned to read through the eyes He intended me to use. And once I learned to see, He allowed Her to fall into view. Gravity is a funny thing. Some objects hurtle toward Earth only to bounce off of its atmosphere. Others may burn up and fizzle into ashes before impact. But the rare collide in a moment of sheer brilliance – igniting the very surroundings in a stunning radiance; illuminating everything in a blanket of light. The rare are those collisions held in His hands – collisions that would not be possible without first finding our light within and asking Him to help us see; to help us hear; to help us know Love in a way that defies the greatest fairytales we have come to know as children on Earth – and through that, learn what it is that makes the concept of time truly special.

It is not about today alone, but about today with the potential of tomorrow. We live in a world held between two extremes – an earthly body and a heavenly body. We find emotion within the space between two notes, the words unsaid in conversation. Most people think the Cinderella story begins when the knight in shining armor meets the princess, rarely realizing that someone had to write the story leading up to that moment and had to conceive a storyline following. Most fairytale stories end before the real journey begins. That is what makes the potential of tomorrow the most important thing we can do today. For all we have is today and the potential of what could be in the days to follow. The world is what you make it and that is the reason why the Not-So-Cinderella story is so beautiful. We each have the potential to pen the greatest

Love Always

Love story ever told – a story unique to each, stretching into the days of Ever-After. Everything on Earth will eventually find its ending, but a perfect Love will transcend the finite endings of earthly beginnings and venture onward into eternity. You will find my story written in shades of midnight red on pages of the whitest of light – pages binding my soul to hers; a Love wrapped up in only the warmest blanket of certainty and peace, stitched to the outermost edges of eternity.

Love Always,
Jonathan

...

Forever and ever. Amen.

...

www.ingramcontent.com/pod-product-compliance
Lightning Source LLC
Chambersburg PA
CBHW021137080526
44588CB00008B/95